Queer cinema in contemporary France

Manchester University Press

DIANA HOLMES AND ROBERT INGRAM *series editors*
DUDLEY ANDREW *series consultant*

FRENCH FILM DIRECTORS

Chantal Akerman MARION SCHMID
Jacques Audiard GEMMA KING
Auterism from Assayas to Ozon: five directors KATE INCE
Jean-Jacques Beineix PHIL POWRIE
Luc Besson SUSAN HAYWARD
Bertrand Blier SUE HARRIS
Catherine Breillat DOUGLAS KEESEY
Robert Bresson KEITH READER
Laurent Cantet MARTIN O'SHAUGHNESSY
Leos Carax GARIN DOWD AND FERGUS DALY
Marcel Carné JONATHAN DRISKELL
Claude Chabrol GUY AUSTIN
Henri-Georges Clouzot CHRISTOPHER LLOYD
Jean Cocteau JAMES S. WILLIAMS
Jacques Demy DARREN WALDRON
Claire Denis MARTINE BEUGNET
Marguerite Duras RENATE GÜNTHER
Julien Duvivier BEN MCCANN
Jean Epstein CHRISTOPHE WALL-ROMANA
Georges Franju KATE INCE
Philippe Garrel MICHAEL LEONARD
Jean-Luc Godard DOUGLAS MORREY
Robert Guédiguian JOSEPH MAI
Mathieu Kassovitz WILL HIGBEE
Diane Kurys CARRIE TARR
Patrice Leconte LISA DOWNING
Louis Malle HUGO FREY
Chris Marker SARAH COOPER
Georges Méliès ELIZABETH EZRA
Negotiating the auteur JULIA DOBSON
François Ozon ANDREW ASIBONG
Marcel Pagnol BRETT BOWLES
Maurice Pialat MARJA WAREHIME
Jean Renoir MARTIN O'SHAUGHNESSY
Alain Resnais EMMA WILSON
Jacques Rivette DOUGLAS MORREY AND ALISON SMITH
Alain Robbe-Grillet JOHN PHILLIPS
Eric Rohmer DEREK SCHILLING
Coline Serreau BRIGITTE ROLLET
Bertrand Tavernier LYNN ANTHONY HIGGINS
André Téchiné BILL MARSHALL
François Truffaut DIANA HOLMES AND ROBERT INGRAM
Agnès Varda ALISON SMITH
Jean Vigo MICHAEL TEMPLE

Queer cinema in contemporary France

Five directors

Todd W. Reeser

MANCHESTER UNIVERSITY PRESS

Copyright © Todd W. Reeser 2022

The right of Todd W. Reeser to be identified as the author of this work has been asserted by them in accordance with the Copyright, Designs and Patents Act 1988.

Published by Manchester University Press
Oxford Road, Manchester M13 9PL

www.manchesteruniversitypress.co.uk

British Library Cataloguing-in-Publication Data
A catalogue record for this book is available from the British Library

ISBN 978 1 5261 4106 4 hardback
ISBN 978 1 5261 8238 8 paperback

First published 2022

The publisher has no responsibility for the persistence or accuracy of URLs for any external or third-party internet websites referred to in this book, and does not guarantee that any content on such websites is, or will remain, accurate or appropriate.

Typeset by Newgen Publishing UK

Contents

List of plates	*page* vi
Series editors' foreword	vii
Acknowledgements	viii
Introduction: queer productions	1
1 Olivier Ducastel and Jacques Martineau: moving normative structures	39
2 Alain Guiraudie: queering space, age, relationality	114
3 Sébastien Lifshitz: documenting movements in time and space	174
4 Céline Sciamma: the look of queer representation	249
Filmographies	314
Index	323

Plates

1	Ducastel and Martineau, *Drôle de Félix*, Fox Lorber Films, 2000	*page* 166
2	Ducastel and Martineau, *Ma vraie vie à Rouen*, Wellspring Media, 2002	166
3	Ducastel and Martineau, *Théo et Hugo dans le même bateau*, Epicentre Films Editions, 2016	167
4	Ducastel and Martineau, *Haut perchés*, Epicentre Films Editions, 2019	167
5	Guiraudie, *L'Inconnu du lac*, Strand Releasing Home Video, 2012	168
6	Guiraudie, *Du soleil pour les gueux*, Shellac, 2000	168
7	Guiraudie, *Le Roi de l'évasion*, Peccadillo Pictures, 2009	169
8	Lifshitz, *Les Corps ouverts*, France Télévisions Editions, Silver Way, 1997	169
9	Lifshitz, *Presque rien*, Picture This! Home Video, 2000	170
10	Lifshitz, *Wild Side*, Wellspring Media, 2004	170
11	Lifshitz, *La Traversée*, Lancelot Films, France Télévisions Editions, Silver Way, 2001	171
12	Sciamma, *Naissance des pieuvres*, Slingshot, 2007	171
13	Sciamma, *Tomboy*, Pyramide Video, Hold-Up Films, and Productions, 2011	172
14	Sciamma, *Bande de filles*, Strand Releasing Home Video, 2014	172
15	Sciamma, *Portrait de la jeune fille en feu*, Pyramide Video, 2019	173

Series editors' foreword

The aim of this series is to provide original, theoretically informed, properly analytical studies of the work of French film directors ranging from the already canonical to the lesser known and critically marginalized, and to do so in a style that is accessible for a wide readership ranging from students and film enthusiasts to specialist scholars. The first volumes were published in 1998. More than two decades later, only one of the three words of the series title remains uncontroversial: 'film', though even here the material form that this signifies has altered during the life of the series. 'French' raises complex questions about the meanings and boundaries of national identity, and about the relationship between national, transnational and 'world' cinema (*cinéma-monde*). 'Directors' evokes debates about auteurism, and the danger of reducing a thoroughly collective, team-based medium to the product of solitary inspiration. Throughout its many volumes, the series explores and challenges each of these underpinning concepts, reflecting on the nature of the medium itself, interrogating the meanings of 'French', seeing in the director one highly significant element in the multifaceted process of film production and reception.

The series' essential aim, and its achievement so far, is to host studies of many of the most exciting and significant bodies of film produced in France since the origins of cinema. We intend these volumes to contribute to the promotion of the formal and informal study of French films, and to the pleasure of those who watch them.

Diana Holmes
Robert Ingram

Acknowledgements

I now know that the originary moment of this book was one Saturday evening in Pittsburgh as I sat mesmerized by Sébastien Lifshitz's masterful *Wild Side*, about fifteen years ago. It was a film that I could not stop thinking about and one that led me to many other queer cinematic places. Largely written during the Covid lockdown, this book might be my only silver lining of the global pandemic. During the decade and a half from origin to finish, I talked to a number of friends, colleagues, and students about these films. For help with this queer production, then, I thank those who read parts of the book or otherwise helped me with the writing process, including especially Thérèse De Raedt, David Pettersen, Florian Fricard, and Jonathan Devine. Some of these ideas were tested with PhD students at the University of Pittsburgh, including Cole Cridlin, Yacine Chemssi, and Brooke Wyatt. The first part of the Sciamma chapter on *Water Lilies* was presented at a colloquium on Sciamma at the Sussex Contemporary Directors Symposium. Thank you to the organizers of that event. Two anonymous readers helped me consider new ideas productively. I also appreciate the support from series editors Diana Holmes and Robert Ingram and from Manchester's commissioning editor Matthew Frost. *Comme toujours*, my partner Tom McWhorter helped develop many of the ideas presented between these two covers, frequently during the *apéritif* hour. Thanks to him for taking yet another academic ride with me on this LGBTQ+ road trip through time.

Previously published work is contained here in revised form. A portion of chapter 1 was published as 'The Anti-Orpheus: Queering Myth in Ducastel et Martineau's *Théo et Hugo dans le même bateau* (2016)', *Studies in 20th and 21st Century Literature*, 42, 2, 2018, 1–19. A portion of chapter 3 was published as 'Transsexuality and the Disruption of Time in Sébastien Lifshitz' *Wild Side*', *Studies in French Cinema*, 7, 2, 2007, 157–68. A small section of chapter 3 was originally published as part of 'Representing Gay Male Domesticity in French Film of the Late 1990s', in *Queer Cinema in Europe*, ed. Robin Griffiths, Bristol, Intellect, 2008, 35–47.

I acknowledge the following funding sources at the University of Pittsburgh that supported this project: the European Studies Center, Pitt Momentum Funds, the Hewlett Fund, and the Dietrich School of Arts and Sciences. This project was launched at the Collegium de Lyon during a fellowship year, with funding from a senior EURIAS Fellowship. Unless otherwise indicated, English translations are mine.

This book is dedicated to beloved academic, family member, and feminist Sonja Boos, whose loss haunts my family.

Introduction: queer productions

I begin with two films that conclude in the light of queerness. In the final shot of Sébastien Lifshitz's *Wild Side* (2004), the three queer characters Djamel, Stéphanie, and Mikhail, asleep in a train compartment, are heading back to Paris from the north of France (plate 10). The sun coming through the window slowly moves across their intertwined bodies as the train moves along the tracks through the countryside. The movement of light over the trio emblematizes transformations in and by the cinematic narrative, all three now open to whatever may happen after the narrative ends. Olivier Ducastel and Jacques Martineau's *Théo et Hugo dans le même bateau* (literally, 'Théo and Hugo in the Same Boat', translated as *Paris 05:59*) (2016) ends as the two titular young lovers head out together into the dawn just before 6 a.m., with a horizon of relationship possibilities before them. They have just met earlier that night in an underground gay sex club, but when Théo looks out of the window at the Parisian dawn (plate 3), it becomes clear that they will have a future of some kind beyond this one night.

In both of these cases, the queer characters do not triumph over homophobia, transphobia, or heteronormativity, nor do they 'come out of the closet' or become the gender that they always knew they were inside. Rather, they incarnate open-ended moments of potentiality. The emphasis is on futurity, represented by an affective relation between characters that is optimistic and forward-facing. Something undetermined is on the horizon for these characters as they move ahead towards ways of being, acting, and loving that did not exist for them before the narrative. Queerness – that which could disrupt heteronormativity (the assumption that all characters desire those of the 'opposite sex') and cisnormativity (the assumption that gender assigned at birth aligns with the experience of gender) – looks forward to the future. The viewer cannot know what the future holds for these characters, and that inability to know is precisely the point. Futurity is not determined in advance: these characters' stories are not familiar, solidified stories about lesbian, gay, bisexual, and transgender (LGBT) characters, but stories that conclude by opening up. Characters opened up, sexuality and gender opened up, and narrative opened up. The light moving across their bodies and the morning sun coming up illuminate a future yet to be, a present in movement. That future in both cases is a co-future, constituted by togetherness: the characters are 'in the same boat', but not due to community-based identity politics. The light in the final scenes of *Wild Side* and *Théo et Hugo* stands in for the horizon of cinema as well, the inscription of new, queer ways to construct narrative. To talk in discourse about a new horizon or the dawn of a new life might well be banal, but in these cases light embodies the very move away from the linguistic signifier, from discourse-centred ways to describe identity, towards non-linguistic representation of affective togetherness. Part of the becoming of the characters is the potential of the visual to represent queerness anew.

These two examples are not unique, but indicative of a wing of queer French cinema. This book takes the idea of queer futurity or becoming as its focus, aiming to offer one answer to the question: What is French queer cinema in the twenty-first century? I respond to that question from the vantage point of a corpus of five living directors working entirely or mostly in the twenty-first century: the directorial duo Olivier Ducastel and

Jacques Martineau, Alain Guiraudie, Sébastien Lifshitz, and Céline Sciamma. Each of these directors has made a corpus of films that could, largely or entirely, be labelled 'queer'. Though organized by director, this book does not assume strict coherence over time in any director's corpus, nor does it assume full incoherence either. Rather, each directorial corpus of films is taken as a kind of intratextual web of disjunctions, connections, and references between one film and another. My aim is not at all to create a canon of queer directors or of queer films, but I have chosen these five filmmakers because of their high profile culturally and their innovative approaches to queerness and because all of them have a substantial enough cinematic corpus for a chapter on their films to date. It is ironic that on the one hand queer for me denotes new and open-ended forms of subjectivity and desire while on the other hand my directorial corpus remains limited to these five directors. This book takes into account the critical apparatus around these five directors, highlighting critical trends or debates relating to queerness, when relevant. Following the book series, this study combines close-readings of specific films with broader considerations of the corpus of each director and their place in film history, and it is directed especially at scholars in French or film studies who may not know queer French film and at those in gender/sexuality studies who may not have experience with French film. It builds on a growing body of academic work on these directors and on queer film, including above all Nick Rees-Roberts's ground-breaking *French Queer Cinema*. As the monograph was published in 2008, there are many important films by these directors that have come out since that time. Sciamma, in particular, has come to prominence as a director since then. Organizing his chapters by topic rather than director, Rees-Roberts treats topics such as *beur* representation, immigrant poverty, AIDS, and pornography, and unlike this monograph, his book is not meant to be a comprehensive study of directors per se, nor does it have the theoretical orientation of my book.

The horizons of queerness

By definition, it is difficult to pin down or define what queer film means, and to do so fully would likely detract from the very concept of queer as unstable and ultimately undefinable. From one perspective, queer refers to that which is anti-normative with respect to gender and sexuality, or that which breaks with commonly held, supposedly 'common-sensical' understandings or perceptions of what gender and sexuality are or should be. *Théo et Hugo* begins in a Parisian underground gay sex club and turns into a romantic love story, disrupting normative narratives about 'boy meets girl' and about meeting and falling in love. Opening on shots of body parts not composing a cisgender body, *Wild Side* includes explicit sex between three non-normative characters: Stéphanie, a transgender woman who supports herself as a sex worker; Djamel, a *beur* (French of North-African origin) male sex worker; and Mikhail, a muscular male undocumented immigrant from Eastern Europe. In an erotic moment, Mikhail asks Stéphanie to speak in her 'male voice', leaving open the question of his sexual orientation. The three main characters have sex as a *ménage à trois*, seemingly without orientation. Ubiquitous are the cinematic moments in the work of all five of these directors that refuse normative actions, identifications, discourses, and narrations. In a queer context, the categories of heterosexuality or cisgender are not assumed to be the natural origin or the point of departure for narrative, but to be produced by the repetition and solidification over time of gendered acts and performances. Or, heterosexuality's construction as normative or oppressive might be revealed through a queer character or a queer cinematic moment. Both *Théo et Hugo* and *Wild Side* invent sex and gender from the start as non-normative, turning a blind eye to heteronormativity and cisnormativity. It is not the case that normativity is absent from queer film, of course, but it is often explicitly disbanded as norm. It may make an entrance after queerness is established as a central narrative element. Queerness, too, may enter into the world of gender or sexual normativity and dialogue with it in unique ways. Queer may or may not pertain to people that identify as, or could be labelled as, lesbian, gay, bisexual, transgender, transsexual, queer, non-binary, genderqueer, or gender non-conforming (among other terms). In some cases, the seemingly heterosexual orientation of characters may be located as queer, to the point that they look to be the origin of queerness or to contribute to its manifestation.

From a similar perspective, it could be said that queer reveals a 'mismatch' between widely assumed definitions of sex and gender. As Annamarie Jagose puts it in a well-known phrasing in reference to the stability of a stable sex/gender system in which maleness necessarily equates to heterosexual masculinity and femaleness to heterosexual femininity: 'Resisting that model of stability – which claims heterosexuality as its origin, when it is more properly its effect – queer focuses on mismatches between sex, gender and desire' (1997: 3). The concept of stability is key for thinking about queer, for while queer tends to be connected to the unstable (e.g., unstable or fluid heterosexuality), not all instability is queer. Instability can be a momentary way to reestablish normative gender orders as a cross-dressed man, for instance, may aim to reassert – not destabilize – cisgender heterosexual masculinity.[1] On the other hand, a gay person may be taken as not queer, but as 'homonormative', a term used in queer studies to refer to a gay person who desires a life very much like an imagined normative heterosexual person (including marriage between two cisgender people of the same sex, penetrative sex, monogamy, children, a 9-to-5 work week, a well-paying respectable job, etc.).[2]

---

1 As an example of this model for masculinity, see for instance chap. 5 in Reeser (2010).
2 Early, key discussions of 'homonormativity' include Duggan (2002) and Stryker (2008).

The five directors discussed here do, of course, not take heterosexuality as a predetermined given, they do reveal innumerable mismatches of the gendered kind, and they do disrupt heterosexuality, heteronormativity, homonormativity, and cisnormativity, often in highly innovative or aestheticized ways, and those mismatches or disruptions will form a key element of my discussions of the directors. Still, this book especially interrogates how queerness serves as a mechanism for producing new gender performances or new forms of human relations that move beyond rigid, stable, or traditional definitions of gender or sexuality. Or, as Robin Griffiths articulates the work of some of the directors studied here, they 'project ... a way of life and a personal politics that renders "unfamiliar" the representational traditions and heteronormativities of French cinema' (2008: 17). Those 'mismatches' may be precisely what lead characters to realize that they can 'do' gender or sexuality in ways that are non-normative and unfamiliar. Queerness may disrupt, but in the process of disruption transform what is destabilized or taken apart into a new viable way to be or to perform gender since transformation is by definition unfamiliar. As my opening examples suggested, queerness looks forward more than backward as it takes as its object of interest what a person can or does become instead of what they are not, what they reject, or what they once were. Théo and Hugo's horizon is not in front of them because they have come out of the closet and overcome internalized homophobia, but because their relation – defined on its own complicated terms in narrative – is in itself represented as potential, as future-facing. Stéphanie's relation to her transphobic childhood and her transphobic mother constitutes part of the narrative of *Wild Side*, but the final scene resides in an altogether different vantage point beyond the transphobia in her past.

The films in my corpus are queer not so much because they put into practice queer theory's 'anti-social thesis', based on the assumption that 'queer' denotes a disruption of the normative fabric of culture or of traditional forms of kinship or relationality more broadly. One of the first proponents of the anti-social thesis, Leo Bersani writes in *Homos*: 'homo-ness itself necessitates a massive redefining of relationality. More fundamental than a resistance to the normalizing meth-odologies is a potentially revolutionary inaptitude – perhaps inherent in gay desire – for sociality as it is known' (1995: 76). Referring especially to Bersani, Jack Halberstam describes this thesis as 'a counterintuitive but crucial shift in thinking away from projects of redemption, reconstruction, restora-tion, and reclamation and toward what can only be called an antisocial, negative, and anti-relational theory of sexuality' (Caserio *et al.*, 2006: 823).[3] An influential, early queer French film such as Patrice Chéreau's *L'Homme blessé* (*The Wounded Man*) (1983) ends with the main character Henri murdering his object of desire, an act that could be taken as the destruc-tion of gay relationality itself since, as Ruti notes about the anti-social thesis, 'the gay antihero attains a paradoxical free-dom from social constraint' (2017: 4). In *Sapphism on Screen* (2006), Lucille Cairns studies films of lesbian criminality (from 1936 to 2002) that could be considered in anti-social terms as well. While the anti-social queer recurs in the history of French cinema and could be developed at length, it is not the focus of my project here.

3 Bersani is considered a key figure in the anti-social thesis, in particular because of his book *Homos* as well as *The Freudian Body: Psychoanalysis and Art* (1986) and his canonical essay 'Is the Rectum a Grave?' (1987). For a sustained consideration of this body of thought (also referred to as 'antirelational'), see Ruti (2017). Ruti includes David Halperin's *What Do Gay Men Want?* (2007) in this 'school'. As Ruti points out, the 'antirelational strand of queer theory has been promoted mostly by white gay men interested in the subversive potential of radical negativ-ity' (2017: 6) and 'a politics of negativity ... wants to destroy what exists without giving us much of a sense of what *should* exist' (38, ital-ics in original). Halberstam is also considered in this category as well, especially because of *The Queer Art of Failure* (2011).

Queerness in the cases studied in this book does not so much correspond to theorist Lee Edelman's well-known statement that 'queerness can never define an identity; it can only ever disturb one' (2004: 17). Rather, cinematic queerness here corresponds to the wing of queer theory that takes queerness as a 'becoming' that might be productive or transformational, and that might move towards a utopia beyond the constraints of heteronormativity or gender binarism. Work in gender and queer studies taking this perspective is often influenced by the thought of French philosophers Gilles Deleuze and Félix Guattari whose philosophical model is predicated on subjectivity composed of productive becomings.[4] The notion of becoming may necessarily dismantle normative or hegemonic subject positions, but it also looks forward, towards new ways to be or to become a gendered subject. Those becomings are 'molecular' or micro-subjective elements that are not widely understood or recognized in a single manner. They are not about 'heterosexuality' or 'homosexuality' or other commonly used tags. They are individual and particular. The three characters at the end of *Wild Side* have their own specific ways to be gendered subjects that distances them from tags like 'heterosexual', 'homosexual', or 'bisexual'. They have become 'molecular' as 'becomings are not phenomena of imitation or assimilation', but 'of non-parallel evolution' (Deleuze and Parnet, 1987: 2).[5] Queer characters do not develop in 'parallel' with heterosexuality but in their own manner. As Paul Preciado sums up the concept: 'Molecularity … develops transitory in-progress segmentations that endlessly open processes of becoming' (2018: 142). The story told is not of a stable, static way to be a subject – what Deleuze and Guattari refer to as 'molar' in

---

4 On the queernesss of becoming, see for instance Conley (2009).
5 For a sophisticated discussion of Deleuzian becoming, see Bankston (2017).

A Thousand Plateaus. The molar may be 'binary organizations' or an 'overcoding machine' (1987: 216) invested in highly legible categories (e.g., 'homosexual', 'heterosexual'), very much unlike 'something that flows or flees, that escapes the binary organizations' (216).[6] For Preciado, 'molarity [is] characterized by rigid segmentarity [and] produces fixed political identities without becomings' (2018: 142). Peter Merriman describes 'molar masses or bodies' as 'highly organised, easily represented and expressed' and 'perceived as clearly demarcated and bounded assemblages or aggregates that are frequently aligned with state and non-state actors' (2019: 67). One might associate 'homosexuality' with the organization of sexuality provided by juridical or national definitions or by medical or religious ones. A gay or lesbian-identified person who is fully circumscribed by identity politics (e.g., LGBT rights) would be molar. The category might be 'bounded' by the static idea that one man loves another and wants to be married just like a male–female couple. Or, it might be bound by the homophobic idea that two people of the same gender should not be married and should remain hidden and out of sight.

Although distinct, the molecular and the molar are, however, often in dialogue. Deleuzian becomings 'may be aligned with minor or molecular political actions that traverse, cross-cut and continually undermine molar imaginations' (Merriman, 2019: 67). A cinematic character who comes out as 'lesbian' does not necessarily 'become' simply because she leaves behind the stabilized, molar identity of 'straight' or 'heterosexual' for another identity based on a recognized or easily expressed organization of sexuality. She is not queer if her becoming lesbian 'parallels' becoming heterosexual. She would need to 'flow' from or to 'flee' the molar by rejecting the solidity

6 Deleuze and Guattari take 'bisexuality' too as molar: 'It is as deplorable to miniaturize, internalize the binary machine as it is to exacerbate it' (1987: 276).

and the stasis of both heterosexuality and lesbianism, through a process of becoming that is very much her own and does not have recourse to typical organizational modes of sexuality thoroughly defined by external modes. A heterosexual or cisgender character, too, can produce anti-molar utterances – in the same way that Deleuze and Guattari consider themselves as 'personally homosexual' or molecularly homosexual while being 'statistically or molarly heterosexual' (1996: 70). Preciado calls this concept 'refined conceptual homosexuality' (2018: 147). While molecular homosexuality without queer experience can be politically problematic and threaten to co-opt queer experiences, for the purposes of representational questions, any character – whatever their life experience – has the potential to be a molecular homosexual.

As read through Rosi Braidotti, this approach to queerness as becoming does not have to be unrelated to the anti-social thesis in queer theory. Braidotti describes this process of becoming in two ways: 'These patterns of becoming can be visualized ... as sequential modes of affirmative deconstruction of the dominant subject-position (masculine/white/heterosexual/speaking a standard language/property-owning/urbanized), or else, as steppingstones to a complex and open-ended process of de-personalization of the subject' (2002: 119). Although the anti-social refuses to allow the queer to take part in the normative, a step defined by open-endedness may well follow this refusal. Tim Dean articulates this second step in slightly different terms from Braidotti: 'The second, correlative step is to trace new forms of sociality, new ways of being together, that are not grounded in imaginary identity or the struggle for intersubjective recognition' (Caserio *et al.*, 2006: 827). To become unsocial is to subsequently become 'profoundly connective' (827). The final shot of *Wild Side* conveys precisely what Dean articulates, a connection in light of the three main characters in movement together, defined not by a stable or 'imaginary identity' or an attempt to be seen as stably 'LGBT'. Their relation cannot be labelled in easily recognizable 'molar' terms. Connection between disparate bodies incarnates a momentary or 'molecular' way of existing and of transformation, not identitarian labels or essences assumed not to change over time. In this case, connection follows on a queer narrative that highlights Stéphanie's breaking through her mother's transphobia while locating the queer becoming that was always there, even when she was known as the boy named 'Pierre' and given masculine pronouns. Connection in the final scene doubles back to the opening shots of trans body parts in the first scene, the contrast transforming Braidotti's 'affirmative deconstruction of the dominant [cisgender] subject-position' towards 'a complex and open-ended process of de-personalization of the subject'. Those processes recounted over the course of the film lead to, and culminate in, a connective train ride towards a queer future – in Deleuzian terms an 'assemblage' (*agencement*) of a variety of elements related to desire, gender, corporality, affect, race, space, time, and memory. The movement of the train is also what Deleuze and Guattari call a 'line of flight' (*ligne de fuite*), away from molar structures or recognized, ordered ways in which to exist. As Mat Fournier describes lines of flight in a transgender context, it is a moment 'when the socially determined coordinates of familiarity-identity-gender no longer add up to a legible (legitimate) pattern, when materiality itself escapes the frame of representation, because this frame is built on gender binarism' (2014: 121). Such a flight might (as per the *Wild Side* example) be the culmination of the story, or it may be a recurring element within narrative, part of a series of flights.

Queer becoming can open up cultural narratives frequently employed around LGBT subjectivities, meaning that the 'dominant subject-position' left behind might not be the normative or dominant manner in which LGBT is narrated in written texts, in oral discourse, or in film. Stéphanie's story in *Wild Side* is not a normative transsexual narrative about a 'man' who becomes a 'woman' and about the growing tolerance of the cisgender characters around her. It is not a simplified, linear trans story as might be presented on a talk show or a made-for-TV movie, for very broad consumption, or one that reifies stable notions of what a 'man' and 'woman' are. It is her own individual story, about her mother's death and her affective and sexual relations with Djamel and Mikhail, and it is recounted in a highly complicated and aesthetic manner that resists a linear storyline. It is her own assemblage.

Along with the story of transitioning from one discrete gender to the other, 'coming out of the closet' may be the most common example of a normative narrative that queer film turns and twists into new formats or narrative trajectories or, in Deleuzian terms, into new 'enunciations'. Ducastel and Martineau, Sciamma, and Lifshitz – each in their own way – tell stories that might on one level look to be about men and women 'coming out', but they do so in radically new ways that question traditional narrative conventions around telling or 'confessing' homosexuality. Some of their films resist the establishment of stable or molar heterosexuality, disbanding the cultural assumption that narrative closure equals happy heterosexuality. The films in my corpus tend not to focus on a queer person coming of age sexually, assuming a 'gay' or 'lesbian' identity, or struggling against heterosexism, homophobia, or transphobia, though they are in dialogue with these narrative molarities. Films treating HIV-AIDS avoid narratives of gay men as doomed to nothing but a sad and lonely death caused by sexual promiscuity, rejected by normative culture and without hope.

Some films appropriate and transform normative narratives not about homosexuality per se, queering them in the interest of inventing new ways to narrate recurring myths of Western culture and making them more available to audiences not traditionally included in those normative narratives. They correspond to

Deleuze's interest in – as Preciado puts it – 'creating a set of conditions to produce new utterances' rather than 'determining who can think or talk about what' (2018: 147). A character's own subjectivity obviously cannot be put aside, but the text itself (the utterance) is the locus of production of becoming. In some cases, normative-seeming characters have queer elements to them, suggesting that queer film can open up a broader social field to new ways for any character to act and desire and can allow for movement-based desires or gender presentations on everyone's part. What 'becomes', then, might be characters' subjectivity, but it might also be cultural presuppositions about how characters' stories have been, or could be, told.

On the one hand, this approach to film is not specific to the French context and could be taken in other cinematic traditions since these theoretical elements pertain to being human, not to being from a given cultural context. On the other hand, the approach lends itself especially to French film by virtue of French cultural presuppositions that allowed for Deleuzian thought to arise in the first place. In other words, French film and Deleuze have resonance because they are both produced in the same intellectual context. I take Deleuzian thought as a culmination of a long tradition in French thought, with the most visible starting point Michel de Montaigne's *Essays* (1580).[7] Queer French film can be seen as following in the queer footsteps of writer Jean Genet (who himself made a very early queer short, *Un chant d'amour* (*Song of Love*) (1950)).[8] Or, more directly, it resonates loudly with queer becoming in the work of French theorist Guy Hocquenghem.

---

7 For connections between Montaigne and Deleuze, see Melehy (2020).
8 At the same time, Genet's fiction is read as emblematic of the antisocial. Bersani's *Homos*, for instance, relies on a reading of Genet's play *The Maids*. Todd Haynes's influential queer film *Poison* (1991) also has close connections to Genet, and there are close connections between Genet and Chéreau's *L'Homme blessé*. See Godier (2012).

His landmark *Le Désir homosexuel* (*Homosexual Desire*) (1972) brings male homosexuality and Deleuzian thought together (through Deleuze and Guattari's *Anti-Oedipus*) well before the anti-social thesis was articulated in American queer theory. For him, same-sex male sexual desire – not 'homosexual' identity per se – embodies a series of possibilities. In his language, 'what we may call homosexual "scattering"' (*la dispersion homosexuelle*) or 'the scattering of love-energy' is 'a system in action, the system in which polyvocal desire is plugged in (*en acte de branchement*) on a non-exclusive basis' (1993: 131; 2000: 151, 152). In 'homosexual love', 'everything is possible at any moment: organs look for each other and plug in' (1993: 131). Though Hocquenghem's interest is male–male sexuality, erotic 'scattering' can be extended nonetheless to potentially opening up a cultural space for a whole panoply of sexual desires and acts to be embodied by other forms of queerness. Or, the very idea of non-normative queerness, not simply gay male cruising, might reconfigure molar entities and allow for new molecular or mini-subjectivities. Such a queer becoming is embodied in *Homosexual Desire* by the idea of being 'transexual', a direction towards which homosexual desire leads as 'objects and subjects' disappear. Hocquenghem cites Deleuze and Guattari in his final paragraph: 'We are ... transexual in an elementary or molecular sense' (1993: 150).[9] I take this statement to mean not that someone has to change sex or gender in order to 'become', but that they become when they resist molar identity, represented here by cisgender gender stability, and that becoming is – or is imagined as – changing sex or gender. This striking phrasing by Deleuze and Guattari is preceded in *Anti-Oedipus* by a passage about relationality and gender outside of the molar

---

9 Deleuze and Guattari's quote in *Anti-Oedipus* is actually: 'we are transsexual in an elemental, molecular sense' (1996: 70).

Oedipus complex: 'the male part of a man can communicate with the female part of a woman, but also with the male part of a woman, or with the female part of another man, or yet again with the male part of the other man, etc.' (Deleuze and Guattari, 1996: 69). Communication, or what I might call 'relationality', can itself be 'molecular', breaking down the ways in which one stable gender relates to the other, supposedly opposite sex. One element of a cinematic character's gender might relate to one element of another character's gender in very individualized ways. Mikhail's relation to Stéphanie combined with both of their erotic relations with Djamel, is molecular because it is not an easily recognizable relation and because it is not clear what it can be called or what defines it. Queer film allows for molecules of one character to relate to those of another character, with gender still at play in new ways beyond normativity.

This book extends the approach to queer cinema taken by Nick Davis in his excellent book *The Desiring-Image: Gilles Deleuze and Contemporary Queer Cinema*. In theoretical terms, my book resembles Davis's in that both take a Deleuzian approach to queerness, not a Derridean or Foucauldian one, and both conflate Deleuzian becomings with queerness or with being 'transsexual'. With the exception of Claire Denis's *Beau travail*, Davis does not discuss French film, but his idea that 'desire and cinema follow the same process of production' (2013: 17) corresponds to many of the films in my corpus. They do what Davis describes as 'yield[ing] an *any-desire-whatever*', and in so doing they 'refus[e] to organize [themselves] within an untenable hetero/homo binary or at equidistant, Kinseyan intervals between those poles' (2013: 19, italics in original). Such a refusal, for Davis and for me, is part of a Deleuzian process of becoming. *The Desiring-Image* brings Deleuze's two influential books on cinema (*Cinema 1* and *Cinema 2*) to bear on queer cinema even though they do not treat gender or desire in any direct sense. Extending and transforming the space and time images in these two cinema books into the late twentieth and early twenty-first century, Davis studies what he calls 'the *desiring-image*' as 'a constitutive dimension of *all* cinematic images' that 'take open-ended variation as their guiding premise' and 'work against normative models of sexuality and their social, political, and epistemic buttresses' (8, italics in original). For Davis, playing on Deleuze and Guattari's *Kafka: Toward a Minor Literature* ([1975] 1986), queer cinema is a 'minor art' by virtue of 'deterritorializing … desire into new relations and definitions [and] renouncing structures of heteronormativity [and] "homonormativity"' (2013: 5). While my goal in this book is not to conduct a Deleuzian reading of French queer cinema per se and while I will only rarely read films alongside Deleuze in the chapters, the presence of the theorist's philosophical thought is palpable, whether direct or indirect, whether intentional or unintentional, in a number of the films that I study. Three of the directors are academics in the French university system (Martineau in the University of Paris system (Nanterre) and Lifshitz and Ducastel, at the prestigious national film school La Fémis in Paris), and all of them were trained in film or other disciplines to varying extents in the French university system, meaning that French theoretical concepts likely play some role in the way in which they conceived of their films.

Another slightly different way to consider my approach to queer film comes via the work of Cuban American queer theorist José Muñoz, especially his book *Cruising Utopia: The Then and There of Queer Futurity*. Queerness here is a form of utopia, embodying that which is not yet available but can be imagined in the future. As Muñoz puts it in a discussion of his work, 'queerness is primarily about futurity. Queerness is always on the horizon' (Caserio *et al.*, 2006: 825). One can never really arrive at such a queer utopia and 'we may never touch queerness' (Muñoz, 2009: 1), but the directional pull of utopia is manifested by queerness and the affective pull of hope. It is not an idea or image that repulses or causes fear, but one that attracts and moves bodies forward in a new direction. It is more an optimistic direction towards than a destination where one arrives. For Muñoz, queerness is an aesthetic, and as such, 'can potentially function like a great refusal because art manifest[s] itself in such a way that the political imagination can spark new ways of perceiving and acting on a reality that is itself potentially changeable' (Muñoz, 2009: 135). Queerness in this sense is an optimistic gender formulation that allows one to imagine other ways in which to be or to become, on the horizon as a form of potentiality or as something yet-to-be, by definition. As a result, Muñoz notes, future-oriented queerness is critical of 'the ontological certitude [that] accompan[ies] the politics of presentist and pragmatic contemporary gay identity' (Caserio *et al.*, 2006: 825). The focus is thus not on marriage equality, LGBT workplace discrimination, or transgender health care, but on constructing an aesthetics of queerness.

It is no accident that actual or symbolic horizons or moving light occurs with some frequency in French queer films, as they embody a queer aesthetic of futurity well exemplified through the moving image. In a sense, Muñoz's ideas on utopia put into words what is being 'said' via image in films like the two with which this introduction began. The actual Parisian horizon in *Théo et Hugo* aestheticizes the futurity of the two characters as dawn over Paris, and the light in the train compartment in *Wild Side* shows, instead of tells, that the three characters are riding towards a utopian future back home. They are asleep because they cannot speak this futurity, they can only be made part of its representation and its aesthetics. The light moves across their bodies much as cinematic light moves across the screen. Because quotidian language has a tendency to render identity molar, not molecular, the moving image (not necessarily only film) offers an avenue that can better represent the movement of becoming. It is important to note that Muñoz's approach does not ignore the past, quite the contrary in fact as queerness might be 'distilled from the past and used to imagine a future' (Muñoz, 2009: 1). Stéphanie locates trans becoming in her childhood and, by locating a version of the past, she can then – and only then – participate in that final scene that I have described. In other cases in this book, films appropriate and transform normative cinematic pasts as well as characters' pasts in favour of an open future. While obviously not all the films considered end on light, many do conclude with visual representations that can be read as horizon-like, open-ended and directed towards the future. Queer cinema does not, of course, have a monopoly on this kind of ending (nor do the French), but what interests me here is what specific connections these films make between queerness and this kind of horizon. Whether queerness represents horizon in broader cultural configurations beyond my corpus will remain an open question.[10]

Taken as an ensemble, the films of these five French directors constitute a corpus not part of B. Ruby Rich's 'new queer cinema' that famously defined a 'common style' in the early 1990s (2013: 16–32).[11] Such films contain 'traces of appropriation, pastiche, and irony, as well as a reworking of history with social constructionism very much in mind' (18). In a chapter on

10 Another largely open question is to what extent queer futurity is co-opted by capitalism or neoliberalism for its own desire to make the accrual of capital look like optimism and encourage subjects to become or continue to become capitalist subjects. Guiraudie's corpus engages with this question.

11 The article was published earlier in *Village Voice* in March 1992 under the title 'A Queer Sensation' and also in 1992 in *Sight and Sound*. On new queer cinema and France, see Waldron (2009: 6–10). Stuart Richards argues for a 'renaissance of New Queer Cinema', with examples of films from about 2010 to 2014, including Guiraudie's *Stranger by the Lake* (Richards, 2016: 215–29).

'*nouveau* queer cinema', Rich focuses on François Ozon and André Téchiné, in part because of their broad distribution outside France and their presence in the 1990s as queer film came into its own. Rich describes the French version of new queer cinema as a 'fluid queer world of postmillennial, postidentificatory sexual styles' (215). While it does not include Ozon and Téchiné, my corpus here does often highlight or assume non-normative categories and labels well beyond 'gay' or 'lesbian', at the same time as it codes new sexual or gendered styles as sites of potentiality in which humans can relate to themselves, to their cultural context, and to others in new ways. These are new 'styles', or in Deleuzian terms, I might say that they are new 'enunciations', or new ways of expressing that are produced. As Verena Conley writes about this aspect of Deleuzian queerness: 'It is a matter of undermining the order-word (that is, an utterance that bears an effect of authority or law) of a hegemony in an ongoing movement of becoming' (2009: 26). One might not say that homosexuality should be equal to heterosexuality, for instance, since that statement reiterates 'an effect of authority or law', but queerness instead must produce new expressions outside solidified registers such as legal or medical discourse. The message of the final scene of *Théo et Hugo* is not that same-sex love is 'equal to' heterosexual love or that same-sex marriage is as valid as heterosexual marriage, but rather that it moves somewhere new, into the horizon. Identifactory labels like 'gay' are beside the point, and when images like the horizon arise, they are explicitly not allowing the enunciative norms of language or discourse to tell the story. This avoidance is especially important in narratives about discovering same-sex desire that risk becoming predictable coming-out narratives. Still, despite the omnipresence of queerness, it would be difficult to say that these five directors here have a 'common style', a result in part of the cinematic vistas that new queer cinema, in France and elsewhere, opened up for these filmmakers whose work is necessarily indebted to Ozon and Téchiné, as well as to queer anglophone filmmakers such as Todd Haynes, Gregg Araki, or Derek Jarman.

Seeing queerly

So far, I have focused on queer characters in film. What though of the viewer of queer cinema? Does a viewer become? While cinematic characters undergo transformations related to gender, queerness can also reference the makeup of the image or what a spectator is invited to experience on screen beyond the storyline. These enunciations might pertain to the way in which a scene is shot, or the way a character is framed or positioned on screen. Or, they may pertain to the use of music or light, or to editorial practices such as cutting. Narrative non-normativity could mean that male bodies are rendered objects of desire to be seen and enjoyed, that female bodies are not objects of a male, heterosexual gaze, that the implied viewer of a scene or shot is not hetero- or gender-normative, or that other images common in traditional, heteronormative film are recast. The use of genres (e.g., westerns, road movies, musicals) and the narrative structure may be non-normative, and 'queer film' can suggest not just that there are queer characters, but that stories are told in a queer way. *Wild Side*, to take one example, is told in what I will discuss as transgender time, one type of queer narrative structure. Muñoz's view of queer as 'new ways of perceiving and acting on a reality that is itself potentially changeable' points to moments in which the viewer is invited to see molar narratives anew. The storyline, of course, might invite a new way to perceive, as a given character may perceive situations in new ways that invite the viewer to do so alongside them. Or, the camerawork might invite the viewer to perceive queerly. Lesbian desire is represented on screen queerly in Sciamma, inviting a viewer to perceive same-sex eros in a way that does not assume the norms of a heterosexual male gaze. Ducastel and Martineau portray the emergence and articulation of same-sex desire as a visual phenomenon, not as a linguistic one that labels humans in molar ways. Guiraudie puts viewers in the observational position of one of his gay main characters, such that they are invited to begin to experience the form of becoming taking place within him. These innovative interpellations to perceive queerly form part of the fabric of queer utopian representation as queer film moves towards constructing new relations between viewers and the screen. This visual relation constructs the 'unfamiliar' referenced above, corresponding to what Davis describes as the political need 'to foster the conditions for perceiving and producing escapes from habits of recognition' (2013: 24). A normative visual habitus is queered in a host of ways in this corpus.

Reframing does not necessarily mean that a given viewer will see queerly, just as there is no guarantee that a queer spectator 'sees' the same as a queer character does. A viewer may of course be repulsed or disgusted by a queer image or viewpoint on screen. And a queer viewer does not necessarily see from a queer character's perspective. Spectators leave their gendered subject positions regularly: as Evans and Gamman put it, 'we enter some sort of "drag" when viewing' (1995: 47) since viewer identifications are 'multiple, contradictory, shifting, oscillating, inconsistent, and fluid' (45). The queerness of the films in my corpus does not result from an assumption that any viewer will view in a non-normative way but rather that the films have the potential to uproot normative ways to see gender/sexuality, at times questioning what normative looking is and suggesting new optics in its place. In fact, a spectator may not take on the viewpoint of the camera at all: a film might play with the very idea of perception and viewpoint, or open up a liminal space that does not invite direct spectator–character identification.[12] There may or may not be a direct relation between spectator on the one hand, and character or the eye of the camera on the other. Laura Marks takes up the erotics of 'haptic visuality', which for her means that the spectator may lose control over the object(s) seen on film, not dominating the image but opened up by it: 'I come to the surface of my self ... losing myself in the intensified relation with an other that cannot be possessed' (2000: 184). This spectator–film relation operates as a kind of touch and not an entry into narrative: 'the object's touch back may be like a caress' (184). Queer images might well caress a spectator of any orientation or sexual proclivity as film's touch may not be gendered in the first place. A cisgender heterosexual male viewer might be touched by queer male representation, but not necessarily put into the body of a queer character on screen. Or, he may be caressed affectively and not erotically. Jennifer Barker studies how the camera itself has a kind of body that provokes corporeal reactions in viewers, on their skin, in their muscles, or in their viscera. It is not just the gaze that must be considered in thinking about spectators and film, for touch with the camera is instrumental in audience response: 'It is not a matter simply of identifying with the characters on screen, or with the body of the director or camera operator, for example. Rather, we are in a relationship of intimate, tactile, reversible contact with the film's body' (2009: 19). The body of the film might touch in an erotic way, or it might push a spectator

---

12 Morgan argues that the viewer–film relation should be considered around what he calls 'epistemological fantasies' (2016). Morgan's thesis does not fully reject the possibility of the camera as a subjective eye (of character or viewer), but reframes it in broader terms. Queer, too, may well be an epistemological fantasy and not defined through the viewpoint of a spectator or of a character, but a projection of a non-normative viewpoint more broadly that does not belong to a queer character.

away, in my case away from queer cinematic corporality. A viewer oscillates in their dialectic reaction: 'This dialectic includes moments where we and the film are in perfect harmony ... Other times, there is resistance. The film might drag us along while we try to pull away during scenes that are "too much"' (91). A viewer moves in and out with respect to queer film's body and a stable response of any kind cannot be assumed. Queer sex acts or desire – if too much – might provoke a move away from the screen, just as they might create a rapprochement as well. If the body of the camera and the cinematic construction of an ideal or implied viewer are part of my analysis, how viewers actually respond to queer film is not. Unlike Darren Waldron's *Queering Contemporary French Popular Cinema: Images and their Reception* (2009), this book does not take broad audience reaction into account (with the exception of select film reviews), even as there is much work still to be done on the relation between screen queerness and audience response.

Queer contexts

My focus in this book is a cinema of productive becomings falling within the broad temporal frame of the first two decades of the twenty-first century. While the current century did not at all invent the idea of becoming, the representation of queer becoming on film might be more possible or more widespread in this century than it was in the previous one. It may be only now in certain parts of the West that queerness does not so routinely have to map onto negative depictions or have to be stamped out in favour of heteronormativity. The era of cinematic clichés or stereotypes of LGBTQ people may be largely over in France, and even the need or market for films about invisibility/visibility or coming 'out of the closet' may be located in the past. Coming-out films are an established narrative since at least Téchiné's important and César-winning *Les Roseaux sauvages* (*Wild Reeds*) (1994). While such films do not necessarily end unhappily or in tragedy and while they may be affirmative stories for gay characters, their narratives have often been largely predictable, centring on communal homophobia, tolerance for homosexuality, and self-acceptance. To take just a few examples, Christian Faure's *Juste une question d'amour* (*Just a Question of Love*) (2000), Sylvie Verheyde's *Un amour de femme* (*A Woman's Love*) (2001), Fabrice Cazzeneuve's *A cause d'un garçon* (*You'll Get over it*) (2002), Patrick Grandperret's *Clara cet été là* (*Clara's Summer*) (2004), or Didier Bivel's *Baisers volés* (*Hidden Kisses*) (2016), despite their variations on the theme, all recount a familiar narrative that differs markedly from the queer films by the five directors in this book. While there are films in my corpus that could be considered coming-out films, they do not follow a linear trajectory from hidden or trapped 'in the closet' to being 'out' after a verbal declaration of homosexuality, as they reposition the very narrative used to tell such stories in the first instance.

The futurity of queer cinema is rendered possible by specific twenty-first-century cultural conditions in France. After 1999, the French had a legally recognized form of domestic partnership, *le PACS*, which allowed two people of any gender to share in most of the rights granted to heterosexual couples. Visible debates and protests over marriage equality ('*le mariage pour tous*') and the subsequent passage of full marriage rights in 2013 for all couples meant that domesticity and relationality were recurring themes in LGBTQ film.[13] With these legally recognized domestic relationships seen as relatively new phenomena in 1999 and 2013, queer cinematic

---

13 On debates on marriage and questions of teaching gender theory in French schools, see for instance chap. 1 in Perreau (2016). On *PACS*, see McCaffrey (2005, 2006); Fassin (2014).

characters may want to live in ways not previously recognized or possible, either as married couples or as married-like couples, or they may want to imagine new ways to be in a couple in the face of such legal arrangements. Or, on the other hand, the very idea of gay domesticity (or 'homonormativity') may be critiqued while other non-government-sanctioned ways to relate may be taken as more desirable than legal ones focused on the domestic sphere. Queerness might be intended to dismantle legal normativity (whether hetero- or homo-) in order to build something else that does not require sanctioning by the nation-state or defining a relationship in stable terms. As legal discrimination became less of an issue culturally, queer film was in a sense able to take on other topics and not be concerned as much with cultural homophobia or LGBTQ rights.[14] Gaining this right meant that new representational possibilities were opened and that LGBTQ characters or concepts of queerness could opt out of dialogue with legality or domesticity. The highly visible legal progress made available to LGBTQ folks meant that queer could signify progressive movement itself in broader and more abstract terms. To return to my opening examples, the forward-looking final scenes of *Théo et Hugo* and *Wild Side* might have been made possible by the forward-looking pro-marriage side in the debates around *le mariage pour tous*, even if these characters may or may not get married to each other later on. Other important cultural factors that help make sense of my corpus are the growing visibility of *beur* homosexuality in French media, the increasing acceptance of transgender people in law, medicine, and culture broadly, and changing perceptions of the connections between male homosexuality and HIV-AIDS in an era in which the disease was no longer seen as a tragic death sentence.

---

14 On ways in which French films in the 1990s were focused on implicit arguments in favour of gay (male) domesticity, see Reeser (2008).

The omnipresent principle of French universalism – by which one is defined as a citizen first and LGBTQ second – risks relegating gender and sexuality to the back burner of discussions of French identity, particularly in the political realm.[15] But it also offers opportunities for cinematic characters to not be molar and fixed in a stabilized identitarian category. The queerness of film may, in part, be enabled by a political philosophy and cultural context that does not necessarily highlight minoritizing labels like 'gay', 'lesbian', or 'transgender'. If a character is not singled out as 'gay' but simply as a member of the body politic, queerness is not necessarily linked to that character and has greater potential to circulate among all members of the body politic. The trope of coming out might be appropriated and transferred to non-LGBTQ characters, rendering it a broader or universalized phenomenon that does not ghettoize LGBTQ people and force them to confess their sexuality to the norm. Or, a heterosexual character might be analogically queer because some non-sexual element of their subjectivity (ethnicity, race, economic marginalization, etc.) is taken as in parallel with desiring people of the same gender. A cisgender character may have transgender elements or be transed over the course of a film.[16] Taken in this way, queer French universalism might also suggest that Anglo-American identitarian claims are not necessary – or even desirable – for the construction of queer in a French context. My corpus of films in fact is largely devoid of direct dialogues with Anglo-American culture, since French cinematic queerness in these cases operates on another model that balances same-sex sexuality or transgender with universalizing tendencies that go beyond a political or identitarian focus on gender and sexuality.

15 On this large topic, see for instance McCaffrey (2005); Provencher (2007). A good introduction to the broad concepts is Schor (2001).
16 On transing in French culture and film, see Reeser (2013a, 2013b, 2017a, 2021).

Other cultural elements influencing how queer is represented in my corpus relate to the playing field on which film is made and distributed in France. The renowned French national film school in Paris, La Fémis, plays a key role in the careers of these directors: Sciamma studied scriptwriting and wrote the script for her first film there, Lifshitz and Ducastel both teach there currently, and the latter is the head of the directorial track (with Christine Carrière). How queerness is taught, received, or learned there is difficult to determine, but what is clear is that the school is deeply influential in the ways in which films are made in France today.[17] One key element of the school's pedagogical approach is a mastery of the history of cinema, which would explain why directors who have worked there are in such close dialogue with French and non-French cinematic traditions, while other directors (most notably, Guiraudie) who do not have a connection to the school or to cinema studies more broadly, are seemingly less influenced by French traditions and might be less subject to them. Claire Simon's revealing documentary about the school, *Le Concours* (*The Competition*) (2016), includes a scene in which Ducastel clearly has sway over who is admitted. On the other hand, Simon notes in an interview about the film: 'it's the most important film school in France and one of the most important in the world, which sometimes leads to them having a bit of a traditional way of thinking about cinema' (Killian, 2019). The role of French television and, in particular, the pay channel Canal+

---

17 On the school, see Palmer (2011). François Ozon also studied at La Fémis. Palmer includes La Fémis's list of '156 films that you must have seen' from 2004, which includes Téchiné's *Wild Reeds* and Wyler's lesbian film *The Children's Hour*. A more recent list of 208 films (La Fémis, 2008) includes these along with Ang Lee's *Brokeback Mountain*, Gus Van Sant's *Elephant*, and Chantal Akerman's *La Captive*. Work on finance structures in France and Europe and their relation to queerness would help complete this picture.

and the Franco-German station Arte cannot be underestimated as telefilms have increasingly treated queer themes. Some of the films in my corpus were funded by and made for television, or they were given wide release on French television. In some cases, as Roth-Bettoni puts it, queer telefilms are 'almost more bold than wide-release cinema' (2007: 603). The growth of LGBTQ film festivals in France has brought queer film – and attention to queer film – to a broader public as well, most notably via the festivals Chéries-Chéris in Paris and Ecrans Mixtes in Lyon. The Queer Palm, awarded at the Cannes Film Festival in late spring each year since 2010, brings international visibility to queer film, even as it is not officially part of the film festival. All of the five directors studied here have had some relation to the award, and their inclusion in this book is in part a result of this success at Cannes or in other festivals. Ducastel and Martineau participated in creating the Palm and in 2016 were the presidents of the selection jury. Sébastien Lifshitz won that year (for the documentary *The Lives of Thérèse*), and he was also in competition in 2012, with his documentary *Les Invisibles*. Guiraudie won the Queer Palm in 2013, along with the *Un Certain Regard* Prize in Direction, for *Stranger by the Lake*, and he was again in competition in 2016 with *Staying Vertical* (losing to Lifshitz). Sciamma competed with *Girlhood* in 2014, but won the Queer Palm in 2019 for *Portrait of a Lady on Fire*. *Théo et Hugo* did not compete in 2016, but the film won the prestigious Teddy Audience Award for an LGBT film at the Berlin International Film Festival that same year.[18] Lifshitz won the Teddy Award for Best Feature Film for *Wild Side* in 2004, and won again for best documentary film in 2013 for *Bambi*. Also in Berlin, Ducastel and Martineau won the Jury Award and the Reader Award for *The Adventures of*

---

18 A third key prize in Europe is the Queer Lion in Venice, awarded since 2007, but none of these directors has won that award.

Félix in 2000, and Sciamma's *Tomboy* won the Jury Award in 2011. Needless to say, as Antoine Damiens notes about these 'A-List festivals', 'awards carry with them a certain amount of symbolic capital, in effect legitimizing the winning films *as art* while making them more viable on the market' (2015: 93, italics in original),[19] and almost paradoxically these awards also 'validate [a film's] queerness' (95). The Jean Vigo Prize, awarded for an independent spirit film and for a short film, has been awarded to three of these directors (Lifshitz in 1998, Guiraudie in 2001, Ducastel/Martineau in 2009). Guiraudie, Sciamma, and Ducastel/Martineau have all been nominated for César awards as well for best director, best first film, or best film, and Lifshitz won the best documentary César for *Les Invisibles* in 2013.

Scoping the queer

The constraints of a director-based monograph series mean that this book cannot come close to treating all directors or all films that could be labelled queer, and selections had to be made. A key factor in director selection was that the directorial

---

19 Damiens also notes that to qualify for the Queer Palm, a film does not have to present LGBTQ characters per se, but 'anything falling outside of traditional representations of gender and sexuality' (2015: 98). Still, the list of winners suggests a different judgement. In so doing, the competition 'attempts to address both queer circles and more traditional circuits' (98). For queer film festivals, see Damiens (2018). Taking a Bourdieuian approach, Damiens discusses here the symbolic capital of queerness and the role of distribution of queer films. That queerness is culturally coded in distribution is an important factor in the reception of queer films. Sciamma's *Tomboy*, which was coded in the UK and US as an LGBT film, was not coded as such in France (2018: 36). See also chap. 2 in Perriam and Waldron (2016).

corpus be located largely – though not necessarily entirely – in the twenty-first century. It goes without saying that the work of a number of directors beyond the scope of this book has contributed in important ways to the history of cinematic queerness. Given their importance in the history of queer cinema and their large corpus of films, both Patrice Chéreau and André Téchiné would make sense to incorporate, but born in 1944 and 1943 respectively, they are of a distinctly different generation than the five directors selected here. In addition, a monograph on the latter director has been published in the same book series as this one, Bill Marshall's *André Téchiné* (2007). Chéreau's *L'Homme blessé* and Téchiné's *Les Roseaux sauvages* are ground-breaking films in terms of gay male representation, and the directors in my corpus build on or respond to them as they are part of a twentieth-century canon of queer film. *Roseaux sauvages* in particular brought male homosexuality and coming out onto the screen in visible ways: Roth-Bettoni calls the film 'the beginning of a brand new presence of homosexuality in French cinema' (2007: 601). But in both of these cases, gay relationality does not work out well: the films do not firmly gesture towards queer futurity. That said, Téchiné and Chéreau can nonetheless be taken as the queer 'cinematic fathers' of the directors treated here.[20] This is not to say, however, that these two directors' more recent films could not be included in the context of the intellectual approach taken here. To take two examples, Téchiné's *Quand on a 17 ans* (*Being 17*) (2016) was co-written with Céline Sciamma

---

20 For Gerstner and Nahmias, Chéreau and Téchiné, along with Jacques Nolot, are Ozon's and Christophe Honoré's 'cinematic fathers', as gay/bisexual followers of French New Wave cinema (2015: 6). More prolific as an actor than director, Nolot has three films to his credit, including the 2007 *Avant que j'oublie* (*Before I Forget*). Belgian director Chantal Akerman could also be considered a queer mother of Sciamma, if not of the male directors studied here.

and ends in a way that opens out toward an undefined future, and his film *Nos années folles* (*Golden Years*) (2017) highlights innovative ways to think about early twentieth-century transvestism and spectatorship. Chéreau's *Son frère* (*His Brother*) (2003) queers the relation between a gay and straight brother. Winner of the Queer Palm in 2021 for *La Fracture* (*The Divide*), Catherine Corsini has a substantial lesbian/gay corpus as well, including *Les Amoureux* (*Lovers*) (1994), *La Répétition* (2001), and the feminist-lesbian love story *La Belle Saison* (*Summertime*) (2015). But born in 1956 with a first film in 1987, she too does not fit the time frame of this book.[21]

Mega-director François Ozon, probably the most prominent director of queer film in France alive today, and perhaps of all time, is a notable absence here. Ince refers to Ozon as 'France's first mainstream queer *auteur*' (2008: 113). Short and feature-length films by Ozon such as *Une robe d'été* (*A Summer Dress*) (1999) and *Une nouvelle amie* (*The New Girlfriend*) (2014), to take a few examples from his extensive corpus, can be called postidentificatory. Schilt notes that Ozon problematizes 'the fixity of things and people' (2011: 38), and Asibong describes Ozon's 'ongoing experimentation with the dynamics of ... metamorphosis' (2008: 7). To take just a single example, in *Une nouvelle amie*, the gender of cisgender heterosexual character Claire is transformed by virtue of her relation with transgender character Virginia (formerly David), leaving her not really cisgender and not really heterosexual but in a new relational mode fully in line with this book's approach.[22] In the final scene, too, the two main characters literally head off into the horizon. Two excellent monographs have been

---

21 It would also be difficult to fit some of her films into the approach of my book. *Summertime* for instance could be called a lesbian film and *Lovers* a gay male coming-out film, but neither are really 'queer' in the sense used here.
22 For this reading of the film, see Reeser (2021).

published on Ozon: Andrew Asibong's *François Ozon* in this same book series (2008) and Thibaut Schilt's *François Ozon* (2011). An edited volume on the director was published in the 'ReFocus' series at Edinburgh University Press edited by Loïc Bourdeau (2021), and there is a relatively large critical apparatus on Ozon in English. My reasons, then, for not including Ozon here are more pragmatic than intellectual.

Born in 1970 and part of the generation of directors treated here, Christophe Honoré, too, would be a logical director to include. I agree with Gerstner and Nahmias that Honoré is a 'queer auteur' (2015: 3) who 'challenges the contemporary cinematic form and a reliance on a cinema of narration' and 'troubles the very definitions of "queer" in French culture'.[23] The only reason that he is not part of my corpus is that these two scholars have already published a monograph devoted to Honoré: David A. Gerstner and Julien Nahmias's *Christophe Honoré: A Critical Introduction* (2015). A number of this director's films could be considered here: *Chambre 212* (*On a Magical Night*) (2019), *Chansons d'amour* (*Love Songs*) (2007), and *Dans Paris* (2006), for instance, all invent queer ways to be a subject.[24]

Other, lesser-known directors without a substantial critical apparatus in English could have been part of this corpus, and are not included because of space constraints. Robin Campillo's *Eastern Boys* (2013) and *120 Battements par minute* (*BPM, Beats per Minute*) (2017) both articulate queer transformations. Deeply queer, Rémi Lange's oeuvre opens up

---

23 They contrast Honoré with Ducastel and Martineau as the latter 'neatly and linearly organize sexual and political identity through fait accompli cause-and-effect narrative structure' (Gerstner and Nahmias, 2015: 4). I do not disagree with them, but I would note that the two directors' films transform normative narrations precisely via this 'cause-and-effect structure'.

24 On *Dans Paris* and potentiality, see Reeser (2017b).

new gendered possibilities in films such as *Omelette* (1994), *The Sex of Madame H* (2005), and *Partir* (*The Tunisian*) (2009). Director Yann Gonzalez has made films and shorts very well suited to a Deleuzian-style reading, including *Un couteau dans le coeur* (*Knife and Heart*) (2018), *Les Rencontres d'après minuit* (*You and the Night*) (2013), and the Cannes Queer Palm short winner *Les Iles* (*Islands*) (2017). Directors with relatively small corpuses who fall entirely or partially in the intellectual direction of this book include Sylvie Ballyot, Philippe Barassat, Anna Cazenave-Cambet, Dominique Choisy, Michaël Dacheux, Virginie Despentes, Nathan Nicholovitch, Jérôme Reybaud, and Camille Vidal-Naquet.

Each of the five directors that I do treat has a full chapter devoted to their corpus, with Ducastel and Martineau together in one chapter because their feature films are all co-directed. Given the limitations of a director-centred volume, I offer an overview of key elements of each director's corpus while nonetheless considering each major film. I balance broad links and recurring elements within each director's corpus with the specifics of each film. Needless to say, all of these directors change over time. In almost all cases, I treat their full corpus of feature-length films or major shorts, but certain of their films lend themselves better to my overall approach than others. Some of the films are analysed in detail precisely because they harmonize so well with my overall optic and a sustained close-reading offers major insights into queerness. When possible, I establish resonances between the directors. The five directors are presented in order of age, which also means that they are presented loosely in order of the date when they began making films. Ducastel and Martineau are first because they are older in years than the other three directors and might be considered the most established, with Guiraudie and Lifshitz following. The last chapter treats Sciamma, the youngest of the directors studied here. Her first film came out in 2007, significantly later than the four other directors.

References

Asibong, Andrew (2008), *François Ozon*, Manchester, Manchester University Press.

Bankston, Samantha (2017), *Deleuze and Becoming*, London and New York, Bloomsbury Academic.

Barker, Jennifer M. (2009), *The Tactile Eye: Touch and the Cinematic Experience*, Berkeley, University of California Press.

Bersani, Leo (1986), *The Freudian Body: Psychoanalysis and Art*, New York, Columbia University Press.

Bersani, Leo (1987), 'Is the Rectum a Grave?', *October*, 43, 197–222.

Bersani, Leo (1995), *Homos*, Cambridge, MA, Harvard University Press.

Bourdeau, Loïc, ed. (2021), *The Films of François Ozon*, Edinburgh, Edinburgh University Press.

Braidotti, Rosi (2002), *Metamorphoses: Towards a Materialist Theory of Becoming*, Cambridge, Polity.

Cairns, Lucille (2006), *Sapphism on Screen: Lesbian Desire in French and Francophone Cinema*, Edinburgh, Edinburgh University Press.

Caserio, Robert, Lee Edelman, Judith Halberstam, José Esteban Muñoz, and Timothy James Dean (2006), 'The Antisocial Thesis in Queer Theory', *PMLA*, 121, 3, 819–28.

Conley, Verena (2009), 'Thirty-sex Thousand Forms of Love: The Queering of Deleuze and Guattari', in Chrysanthi Nigianni and Merl Storr, eds, *Deleuze and Queer Theory*, Edinburgh, Edinburgh University Press, pp. 24–36.

Damiens, Antoine (2015), 'Queer Cannes: On the Development of LGBTQ Awards at A-list Festivals', *Synoptique*, 3, 2, 93–100.

Damiens, Antoine (2018), 'The Queer Film Ecosystem: Symbolic Economy, Festivals, and Queer Cinema's Legs', *Studies in European Cinema*, 15, 1, 25–40.

Davis, Nick (2013), *The Desiring-Image: Gilles Deleuze and Contemporary Queer Cinema*, Oxford, Oxford University Press.

Deleuze, Gilles and Félix Guattari ([1975] 1986), *Kafka: Toward a Minor Literature*, trans. Dana Polan, Minneapolis, University of Minnesota Press.

Deleuze, Gilles and Félix Guattari (1987), *A Thousand Plateaus: Capitalism and Schizophrenia*, trans. Brian Massumi, Minneapolis, University of Minnesota Press.

Deleuze, Gilles and Félix Guattari (1996), *Anti-Oedipus: Capitalism and Schizophrenia*, trans. Robert Hurley, Mark Seem, and Helen R. Lane, Minneapolis, University of Minnesota Press.

Deleuze, Gilles and Claire Parnet (1987), *Dialogues*, trans. Hugh Tomlinson, London, Athlone.

Duggan, Lisa (2002), 'The New Homonormativity: The Sexual Politics of Neoliberalism', in Russ Castronovo and Dana D. Nelson, eds, *Materializing Democracy: Towards a Revitalized Cultural Politics*, Durham, NC, Duke University Press, pp. 175–94.

Edelman, Lee (2004), *No Future: Queer Theory and the Death Drive*, Durham, NC, Duke University Press.

Evans, Caroline and Lorraine Gamman (1995), 'The Gaze Revisited, or Reviewing Queer Viewing', in Paul Burston and Colin Richardson, eds, *A Queer Romance: Lesbians, Gay Men and Popular Culture*, New York and London, Routledge, pp. 13–56.

Fassin, Eric (2014), 'Same-sex Marriage, Nation, and Race: French Political Logics and Rhetorics', *Contemporary French Civilization*, 39, 3, 281–301.

Fournier, Mat (2014), 'Lines of Flight', *Transgender Studies Quarterly*, 1, 1–2, 121–2.

Gerstner, David A. and Julien Nahmias (2015), *Christophe Honoré: A Critical Introduction*, Detroit, Wayne State University Press.

Godier, Rose-Marie (2012), 'Sous la surface des rêves: *L'Homme blessé*, 1983', *Double jeu. Théâtre/Cinéma*, 9, 125–35.

Griffiths, Robin (2008), 'Introduction', in Robin Griffiths, ed., *Queer Cinema in Europe*, Bristol and Chicago, Intellect, pp. 14–19.

Halberstam, Jack (2011), *The Queer Art of Failure*, Durham, NC, Duke University Press.

Halperin, David (2007), *What Do Gay Men Want? An Essay on Sex, Risk, and Subjectivity*, Ann Arbor, University of Michigan Press.

Hocquenghem, Guy (1993), *Homosexual Desire*, trans. Daniella Dangoor, Durham, NC, Duke University Press.

Hocquenghem, Guy (2000), *Le Désir homosexuel*, Paris, Fayard.

Ince, Kate (2008), 'François Ozon's Cinema of Desire', in Kate Ince, ed., *Five Directors: Auteurism From Assayas to Ozon*, Manchester, Manchester University Press, pp. 112–34.

Jagose, Annamarie (1997), *Queer Theory: An Introduction*, New York: New York University Press.

Killian, Nellie (2019), 'Inside La Fémis: Claire Simon Uncovers the Politics of Film School', *Criterion*, www.criterion.com/current/posts/6222-inside-la-f-mis-claire-simon-uncovers-the-politics-of-film-school (accessed 19 August 2021).

La Fémis (2008), 'Les 208 films qu'il faut avoir vus', www.femis.fr/IMG/pdf/liste_des_208_films_e_dition_de_2008_.pdf (accessed 31 August 2021).

Marks, Laura U. (2000), *The Skin of the Film: Intercultural Cinema, Embodiment, and the Senses*, Durham, NC, Duke University Press.

Marshall, Bill (2007), *André Téchiné*, Manchester, Manchester University Press.

McCaffrey, Enda (2005), *The Gay Republic: Citizenship, Sexuality and Subversion in France*, Ashgate, Aldershot.

McCaffrey, Enda (2006), 'From Universalism to Post-universalism: The PaCS and Beyond', *Modern and Contemporary France*, 14, 3, 291–304.

Melehy, Hassan (2020), 'Off the Human Track: Montaigne, Deleuze, and the Materialization of Philosophy', in Pauline Goul and Phillip John Usher, eds, *Early Modern Écologies: Beyond English Ecocriticism*, Amsterdam, Amsterdam University Press, pp. 23–47.

Merriman, Peter (2019), 'Molar and Molecular Mobilities: The Politics of Perceptible and Imperceptible Movements', *Environment and Planning D: Society and Space*, 37, 1, 65–82.

Morgan, Daniel (2016), 'Where are we?: Camera Movements and the Problem of Point of View', *New Review of Film and Television Studies*, 14, 2, 222–48.

Muñoz, José Esteban (2009), *Cruising Utopia: The Then and There of Queer Futurity*, New York, New York University Press.

Palmer, Tim (2011), *Brutal Intimacy: Analyzing Contemporary French Cinema*, Middletown, Wesleyan University Press.

Perreau, Bruni (2016), *Queer Theory: The French Response*, Stanford, Stanford University Press.

Perriam, Chris and Darren Waldron (2016), *French and Spanish Queer Film: Audiences, Communities and Cultural Exchange*, Edinburgh, Edinburgh University Press.

Preciado, Paul B. (2018), *Countersexual Manifesto*, trans. Kevin Gerry Dunn, New York, Columbia University Press.

Provencher, Denis M. (2007), *Queer French: Globalization, Language, and Sexual Citizenship in France*, Burlington, Ashgate.

Reeser, Todd W. (2008), 'Representing Gay Male Domesticity in French Film of the Late 1990s', in Robin Griffiths, ed., *Queer Cinema in Europe*, Bristol and Chicago, Intellect, pp. 35–48.

Reeser, Todd W. (2010), *Masculinities in Theory*, Malden, Wiley-Blackwell.

Reeser, Todd W. (2013a), '*Trans*France', *Esprit créateur*, 53, 1, 4–15.

Reeser, Todd W. (2013b), 'Universalising Transgender Representation: Emmanuelle Pagano's *Les Adolescents troglodytes*', *Modern and Contemporary France*, 21, 3, 265–79.

Reeser, Todd W. (2017a), 'Transsexuality and the Production of French Universalism: René Gaveau's *Adam est ... Eve* (1954)', *French Review*, 91, 2, 126–39.

Reeser, Todd W. (2017b), 'Theorizing the Masculinity of Affect', in Josep M. Armengol, Marta Bosch-Vilarrubias, Àngels Carabí, and Teresa Requena-Pelegrí, eds, *Masculinities and Literary Studies: Intersections and New Directions*, New York, Routledge, pp. 109–20.

Reeser, Todd W. (2021), 'Transing Dynamics: Ozon's *Une nouvelle amie* (2014)', in Loïc Bourdeau, ed., *ReFocus: The Films of François Ozon*, Edinburgh, Edinburgh University Press, pp. 143–61.

Rich, B. Ruby (2013), *New Queer Cinema: The Director's Cut*, Durham, NC, Duke University Press.

Richards, Stuart (2016), 'A New Queer Cinema Renaissance', *Queer Studies in Media and Popular Culture*, 1, 2, 215–29.

Roth-Bettoni, Didier (2007), *L'Homosexualité au cinéma*, Paris, Musardine.

Ruti, Mari (2017), *The Ethics of Opting Out: Queer Theory's Defiant Subjects*, New York, Columbia University Press.

Schilt, Thibaut (2011), *François Ozon*, Urbana, University of Illinois Press.

Schor, Naomi (2001), 'The Crisis of French Universalism', *Yale French Studies*, 100, 43–64.

Stryker, Susan (2008), 'Transgender History, Homonormativity, and Disciplinarity', *Radical History Review*, 100, 145–57.

Waldron, Darren (2009), *Queering Contemporary French Popular Cinema: Images and Their Reception*, New York, Peter Lang.

1

Olivier Ducastel and Jacques Martineau: moving normative structures

A crowd-pleasing directorial team, Olivier Ducastel and Jacques Martineau have to date made nine full-length films. To be discussed first because it is their first film, *Jeanne et le garçon formidable* (*Jeanne and the Perfect Guy*) (1998) sets the scene for their later films with its musical numbers and its narrative about a victim of HIV-AIDS. *Drôle de Félix* (*The Adventures of Felix*) (2000), *Ma vraie vie à Rouen* (*My Life on Ice*) (2002), *Crustacés et coquillages* (*Muscles and Cockles*) (2005), *Nés en 68* (*Born in 68*) (2008), and *Juste la fin du monde* (*Just the End of the World*) (2010), each in their own way, produce non-normative familial constructs or forms of kinship. The reconfiguration of family is closely connected to male homosexuality, which serves as conduit for new relations between humans, effectively queering heteronormativity. Those new relations often pertain to the way in which the closet is constructed in a familial context, transforming the confessional structure with respect to a gay character who 'comes out'. The unstudied film *L'Arbre et la forêt* (*Family Tree*) (2010) treats the coming out of an elderly patriarch in a family mourning the death of one of its members and the ways in which the process leads to new ways of being *en famille*, in parallel with the transformations that the death of a loved one can produce. This film pairs well with *Ma vraie vie à Rouen* though the main characters are of two very different generations, because they both redefine the coming-out process. The penultimate section of this chapter will be devoted to an in-depth reading of Ducastel and Martineau's *Théo et Hugo dans le même bateau* (*Paris 05:59: Théo & Hugo*) (2016), which radically queers a foundational myth of heterosexual love in Western culture (Orpheus and Eurydice) while recasting the tragedy of AIDS found in *Jeanne et le garçon formidable*. The chapter concludes with a consideration of queer relationality in *Haut perchés* (*Don't Look Down*) (2019).[1]

Re-representing HIV-AIDS: *Jeanne et le garçon formidable*

The duo's first full-length film, *Jeanne et le garçon formidable* ushers in a new form of AIDS cinema. In the opening image, which functions as a cinematic cipher, the main character Jeanne, played by Virginie Ledoyen (who will later become very well known), works as a receptionist at a large vacation company, and her desk is located in the main lobby next to a large revolving door. The shot of the revolving door, which serves as the point of entry for various characters, as if in a play, emblematizes the contribution of the film itself. It will be

[1] Ducastel, without Martineau, made a nine-minute short *Le Goût de plaire* (*The Desire to Please*) (1987), a Demy-inspired musical using the music of Charlie Parker. Two self-described '*séductrices*' flirt with a man in a park in Paris, resulting in a musical threesome by the end. The film does not treat homosexuality, but might be taken as queer in the sense that it destabilizes two-person heterosexuality and renders gay cruising a female and a heterosexual possibility. On the other hand, the short also shows that gay cruising and female heterosexuality fit together awkwardly. The short pairs a brunette and a blonde, likely referring to Jacques Demy's *Les Demoiselles de Rochefort* (1967). The choreography and lyrics resemble those of the 'Chanson des Jumelles' in the film.

a film about coming and going, about the old leaving and the new coming in, about circling back around but with new representational elements entering the scene. One of the characters who repeatedly enters via the revolving door is the handsome delivery boy at whom Jeanne makes eyes during their brief encounters. He comes and goes, as do other men with whom she flirts. Her love life is in fact a revolving door. Most visibly, Jean-Baptiste (Frédéric Gorny), a co-worker from a wealthier class background than Jeanne, is a lover set up to fail because of class difference. The two are dating and though he likes her, Jeanne tells him that she cannot see him any longer, to his great dismay. And then the titular man appears.

What then of Jeanne and the 'perfect' guy named Olivier (Mathieu Demy) whom she meets on the Paris metro? Is she going in circles with him? Is there a revolving door with him? Or does she come out the door different than she went in? Is Olivier yet another man in her life? This heterosexual AIDS victim does not actually break up with Jeanne because his illness gets worse and he leaves to go live with his parents, such that Jeanne cannot find him. The break-up is not decided by her, as is the case with other men, but by him. Jeanne does promise, in a musical number in his hospital room, to be faithful to him from now on and to love 'only' him. But it is not clear whether she sings this song only because she feels bad in the moment as he is dying. When he leaves the hospital for his parents' house and does not tell Jeanne where they live, she tries to track him down. By chance, she meets his friend on the metro and learns the details of his funeral. Yet, in the final shot of the film, Jeanne – who is perpetually late in general – arrives late to the funeral. She trips on the way to the service and screams 'to hell with it' ('merde'). This final scene is ambiguous: is she expunging him from her psyche, sending him out the revolving door, as it were? Or has he become part of her in such a way that she does not need an event like a funeral to pay tribute to him? Does she want to remember him as her 'perfect guy' and not as a man who has died? The revolving door cipher recurs earlier in the film as Jeanne goes to visit Olivier at the hospital and jumps quickly into the revolving door of the hospital. She is going in to see him, despite his illness, but we do not see her come out. Has she, in a sense, gone in to stay with him?

Jeanne is standing in, I would suggest, for broader cultural relations to HIV-AIDS victims in the 1990s. The film likely takes place before *trithérapies* become available in France, and the question of the French nation-state's broader relation to AIDS remains an important question in the film. A secondary character named François (Jacques Bonnaffé), a friend of Jeanne and Olivier (though they do not know that they have the same friend), works with ACT-UP Paris, and participates in marches and protests. Although heterosexual, Olivier attends a demonstration with François, but in the middle of the march he leaves to go meet Jeanne for a date. Later, when François comes to visit Olivier, he tells his sick friend about his PhD dissertation on AIDS activism that he is writing. The heterosexual love story takes place in parallel with political activism, but the two storylines do not directly converge. François operates as a hinge for the two narratives (love and politics). He tries to convince Jeanne to come to a march, but she politely refuses. She ends up in the protest completely by accident, asking 'what's all this?'. Later, she comes to the ACT-UP office, but only because she is attempting to locate the address of Olivier's family so that she can see him, not at all for political reasons. Although she falls in love with an AIDS victim, politics are not involved, though they are constantly present just off to the side of their relationship. The key question, then, is whether her relation to politics changes at the end of the film. When she says 'to hell with it' in the final scene, is it because she is rejecting depoliticization? Is she coming out of the film different than when she went in? Is she opened up to a new political way of being? These questions are raised but never fully answered.

The question of Jeanne's possible transformation is closely linked to the construction of the narrative. In many ways, a more important question is not whether Jeanne becomes more political as a character, but whether the way of telling a cinematic story about HIV-AIDS is transformed. One of the musical numbers without Jeanne takes place in a bookstore when Olivier goes to buy her a novel for her birthday. He asks the bookseller for suggestions for a 'histoire sentimentale' (a romance novel). Eventually, after some discussion in song, they settle on a book about the beach called *Un weekend à Saint-Sébastien*. The song and dance number with the flirty bookstore clerk and Olivier is awkward and musical at the same time, calling attention to the difficulty of finding the right novel. Olivier is seeking a new sentimental narrative for Jeanne, one that will take her in a new direction. The bookstore clerk points to a book and notes that it is a best-seller but that 'it is not good'. Dominant or popular narratives about AIDS are not good ones and are not good for Jeanne: another narrative is needed. The book that the two settle on, however, is a beach novel: it is pleasant and not heavy, but still sentimental. French writer Marguerite Duras is rejected by name as her novels are too 'intellectual' and Olivier needs something 'more modest'. The narrative that they are referencing, of course, is the very narrative that we are watching: pleasant and modest, not intellectual per se, not a crowd-pleasing bestseller that might stigmatize a character with HIV-AIDS. The old should be moved out through the revolving door and the new should be allowed to enter.

The bookstore scene refers to AIDS narratives, such as Cyril Collard's *Les Nuits fauves* (*Savage Nights*) (1989) or Hervé Guibert's *À l'ami qui ne m'a pas sauvé la vie* (*To the Friend Who Did Not Save My Life*) (1990). It also implicitly references AIDS films of the time that are not modest and not musical, but tragic and artistic at the same time. Olivier wants Jeanne to read a narrative that falls in another category, one that is like a beach novel. Films implicitly referenced as intellectual might include the quintessential French AIDS film, Collard's 1992 *Les Nuits fauves* (*Savage Nights*), which is based on the director's own written account and ends in the main character Jean's symbolic death, or Guibert's 1992 AIDS home-made documentary *La Pudeur ou l'impudeur* (*Modesty and Shame*), which has the potential at one point to become a filmed death by suicide. Other major AIDS films from the late 1980s and early 1990s end tragically or are tragic in nature. Paul Vecchiali's *Encore* (*Once More*) (1988), one of the very first AIDS films in French, narrates a story over time of a man who leaves his wife, contracts HIV-AIDS, and dies in the final scene.[2] Jonathan Demme's American film *Philadelphia* (1993) – the most visible American film from the 1990s about AIDS – depicts the descent into illness of the gay main character played by Tom Hanks, ending tragically with his death and funeral. Xavier Beauvois's 1995 *N'oublie pas que tu vas mourir* (*Do Not Forget That You Are Going to Die*) is likewise heavy-handed as the HIV+ main character Benoît (played by the director) launches into a life of drugs and sex work before becoming a mercenary and getting shot violently at the end of the film. A heterosexual romance in Italy constitutes one section of the narrative, but Benoît leaves Claudia (Chiara Mastroianni), afraid of a sexual relationship while HIV+. The film is not a musical, but has an artistic element: Benoît is an art history student, and European art implicitly comments on HIV and on the film. A series of ten shorts about same-sex love during the AIDS crisis came out under the title *L'Amour est à réinventer* (*Love Reinvented*) in 1997, helping to establish the idea

---

2 François Margolin's 1993 *Mensonge* (*The Lie*) tells the story of a woman who discovers that she is HIV+ and learns that her husband contracted the virus through sex with men (and is gay). Neither main character dies, but the final diagnosis is not good.

that the AIDS narrative can be reinvented, like love itself.[3] The idea of reinventing both love and narrative is one that *Jeanne* takes up also, albeit differently, by reconstructing the narrative as less heavy, more modest, and more 'pleasant' than most of its cinematic predecessors. Like Jeanne who enters the hospital and does not come back out the revolving door, Ducastel and Martineau's new coding of AIDS victims should stay and replace its heavy-handed predecessors.

That the AIDS victim is a heterosexual male – not a gay or bisexual man or a woman who contracts the disease from a man who has sex with men – is one of the film's contributions to cinematic history. But it is above all the musical nature of the film that allows for a new, more 'modest' way to narrate AIDS. The opening shot of the film, before the image of the revolving door discussed above, hovers over the skyline of Paris while the opening credits roll. The camera moves downward, and we see that the camera is not shooting the skyline directly, but a glass building (the one where Jeanne works) and that we are seeing Paris's reflection in the building. What we see will be mediated and the camera and the film will not look directly on the object of the film. AIDS will not be directly gazed upon, as it were, but approached through the prism of the musical genre in the tradition of director Jacques Demy. That Demy himself died from AIDS and that his son Mathieu plays the lead male role implies that *Jeanne* pays tribute to Demy and his oeuvre, as well as reconfiguring the French musical genre so that AIDS can be a bona fide topic, one that Demy was not able to take on.[4] His son's cinematic

---

3 Didier Roth-Bettoni offers a full history of AIDS films in France (2007: 591–9).
4 The directors characterize *Jeanne* as 'an homage and as a proposal to continue the kind of musical film that Demy initiated' (cited in Oyallon-Koloski, 2014: 96). For Demy–Ducastel/Martineau connections, see Waldron (2015: 164–7). Demy's wife and Mathieu Demy's

death at the end of this film in a sense reinscribes the director on screen, bringing his death back to life and making part of his life story more available, but it also reorders French AIDS narratives by mixing Demy and the director's musical style with such narratives.[5]

Music was, however, not totally absent from earlier French AIDS films. Vecchiali's *Encore* (*Once More*), despite its seriousness and tragic ending, contains a campy, musical number sung by the main character Louis and a large chorus of characters. Not a musical per se, Roth-Bettoni terms the film a 'comédie musicale en pointillés', or an 'impressionistic musical' (2007: 591). The new narrative presented by Ducastel and Martineau's film is a partially political musical comedy with some of the tragic elements of earlier AIDS films still maintained. During an evening out with Jean-Baptiste and his friends, Jeanne hears well-off men at her table talking about finding jobs and how difficult it is to find a well-paying position. 'We're not in the 80s now', one of the young men notes. He is ostensibly talking about the economy of the 1990s, but he is also talking about narrative. The relative lack of AIDS narrative in the 1980s and the focus on tragedy (e.g., Vecchiali) no longer pertain in the 1990s. Now, in the last decade of the twentieth century, a new narrative situation exists.

One element of this new narrative approach is that classical texts are incorporated and transformed. In their duet titled 'A Sunday in Bed' ('Un dimanche au lit'), Olivier and Jeanne begin their morning in bed having breakfast. Olivier tells his lover that he wants to: 't'embrasser mille fois / Et mille encore, à l'infini'

---

mother, Agnès Varda, made a film *Kung-fu Master* (1987) co-starring her son who falls in love with a much older woman, in a context that highlights the threat and spectre of AIDS.

5 Similarly, director Christophe Honoré's play about men who died of HIV-AIDS, *Les Idoles* (2019), brings Demy back to life as a character on stage so that his life and death can be reimagined.

('kiss you a thousand times / And then a thousand more'), and the two sing together: 'Donnons-nous cent mille baisers / Cent mille encore, tant de milliers / Que le plus aigri de jaloux ne pourra / Ne pourra jamais les compter' ('We'll share a thousand kisses / [Thousands and thousands again, so many thousands] / Even the bitterest man on earth / Could never count them'). They repeat this call for kisses again later. This song recasts one of the most famous Roman poems in Latin, Catullus #5, which begins: 'Vivamus, mea Lesbia, atque amemus' ('Let us live, my Lesbia, and [let us] love') (Catullus, 1921: 6, 7). The male poet calls for his love Lesbia to give him 'a thousand kisses' ('basia mille'), and 'then a hundred' ('deinde centum'), then a thousand again, and then another hundred, etc. until they and any 'malicious' person ('malus') lose count of how many kisses have been given or received. The two lovers should live and love and not accord any value to the 'talk of crabbed old men' ('rumores ... senum severiorum'). Life is short, Catullus tells Lesbia in poetic form, and so the time for endless kisses is now. The call to love in the face of death and in the face of those 'malicious' men who think that Jeanne should not love an AIDS victim fits the storyline of the film. The use of a classical poem known by many schoolkids who study Latin suggests that classical or well-known narratives are being adapted for new ends in a broader sense. Appropriating Catullus in the era of AIDS gestures towards a new form of narration that transforms old texts, of course, as it allows for the call to love light-heartedly as if there were no tomorrow in the context of AIDS films. The musical will continue despite the outside world's attitude towards the love plot.

In this sense, this film is opening up classical narratives. The opening musical number takes place in the lobby of the building where Jeanne works at 6 p.m. as the office workers are leaving the building. Out of the back appear people of colour who clean the building in the evening and at night. They sing about the nation-state's refusal to let them or their children become French, to keep them as contingent labour without the rights of citizenship. Nonetheless, one singer notes, they have no 'hate' despite all this. They sing, too, about the act of cleaning up, and how specifically they do the manual labour for the building. The song serves as a kind of musical prologue suggesting that the film is cleaning up as well: the heavy-handedness and the realism of previous films will be cleaned up in this more modest film. A second song later in the film is performed by a plumber who comes to the building to check on the toilet and sings about 'unclogging' ('déboucher') the toilet. His musical performance mirrors Hollywood song and dance swimming numbers from the 1930s (Oyallon-Koloski, 2014: 94–5), suggesting a mixture of campy Hollywood numbers and this film's more quotidian elements. The cinematic toilet is clogged up, the generic conventions of AIDS films are stuck in a sense, and this film – like the plumber – will open them up to new configurations. Oyallon-Koloski (2014) examines the specific ways in which the film mixes together established musical cycles with modern dance, mixing forms influenced by Demy and by Hollywood to create new configurations. Lagabrielle suggests in a reading of the film that there is a '*potentiel politique*' (2016: 161) as the voices of those marginalized with respect to HIV-AIDS are integrated into the musical genre. In this case, the working-class singers and dancers demarcate the concept of marginalization to open up political potential around the character of the AIDS victim via the musical genre.

Queer kinship: *Drôle de Félix*

The investment of political potential in the AIDS victim pertains as well to Ducastel and Martineau's next film, *Drôle de Félix*, which highlights the episodic road movie aspect of the film over the happy-go-lucky or 'drôle' element of the French title. Meaning 'happy' in Latin, the main character's name Félix suggests that this HIV-film differs from more pessimistic ones that end in death, including *Jeanne*. As Rees-Roberts rightly notes, the film 'situate[s] AIDS as a commonplace feature of gay male interpersonal relations rather than as a drama in itself' (2008: 105) and 'the historical shift between [*Jeanne* and *Félix*] is from AIDS to seropositivity' (105). Olivier's song and dance is fleeting while Félix's adventures will continue after the narrative. Played by the handsome Sami Bouajila, Félix had a white French mother and a father of Maghrebi origin whom he does not know and plans to go find after his mother dies. Félix also happens to be HIV+ and gay, with a stable partner named Daniel (Pierre-Loup Rajot), but these ethnic, sexual, and embodied elements of his subjectivity do not in general cause problems for him, remaining incidental in many ways to the narrative (with the notable exception of a racist incident early on in the film). Almost always happy, Félix charms many people that he encounters, and as he travels through France, he brings happiness to those that he meets. Félix has, as a contemporary reviewer put it, 'the expectation of a future' (Arroyo, 2001: 47). What he lays out for French queer cinema is a form of representational futurity itself, not just his own character's future, through the medium of innovative relationalities. As a signifier of happiness, Félix helps create emotionally positive relations that are familial-like, but not limited to biology. An assumption of happiness defined through a biological, nuclear family is displaced onto Félix and the family that he creates wherever he travels.

At the opening of the film, Félix lays out what could be taken as the movie's agenda, announcing that he is going to 'mettre de l'ordre dans mes affaires' ('to put some order in my life'). He is recently unemployed from his job at a ferry company in Dieppe on the English Channel. He has time on his hands, he needs to sell his mother's apartment and, most importantly, he discovers the address of his biological father on a letter left by his mother in her apartment. The address is in Marseilles, a city at the other end of France, meaning that he will have to cross France from north to south, from the English Channel to the Mediterranean, to meet him in person. He has verified with the help of the Minitel that his father still lives in Marseilles and has not moved from the address that he has. His 'adventures', recounted in episodic form in a variety of locales, however, denote anything but 'order'; they are composed of a series of random encounters that are disorderly for a variety of reasons. Above all, the order of white heteronormative kinship (a white mom and a white dad who have white biological children from the same parents) is disordered by transitory relations that are defined as familial relations. Each episode begins with a name of a family member type flashed on the screen (e.g., 'my brother', 'my sister', 'my cousin', 'my grandmother', 'my father'), presenting each segment as a form of relationality that one might have in one's biological family. As the encounter continues, each relation becomes more and more similar to the one shown on the screen at the start of the episode. In the final encounter, Félix meets an unnamed man fishing near Marseilles who functions as a momentary father figure and who unambiguously advises him to leave his birth father alone since he clearly wants nothing to do with his son. This scene replaces what should, in theory, be the endpoint of the road movie where Félix finds what he is seeking in his quest. Pratt reads this empty telos as destabilizing patriarchal order based on the law of the father: '*Drôle de Félix* ... can be thought of as reinventing the possibilities of kinship beyond the decrees of the authoritarian paradigm' and 'proactively addresses the centrality of the law of the father – and then ... rejects its contingency in favour of more democratic conceptions of psychic wholeness' (2004: 97, 99). As the father is not the end all and be all of the search for the self, the notion of the father itself, or the law of the father, is not the endpoint of the quest. The topos of locating the absent or lost father in order to feel complete is rejected as a narrative necessity. The fisher is himself wounded in a sense, aware of his own absenteeism and of his own need to leave the house and go fishing to avoid the parts of himself of which he is not proud. By virtue of fishing, he is seeking something that he does not possess, removing himself as a paternal endpoint that will complete Félix.

The fishing father character, played by well-known Algerian-born actor Maurice Bénichou, is modelled on a recurring medieval character, the Fisher King, who plays a key role in Chrétien de Troyes' *Perceval*, a medieval Arthurian romance about a quest for the Holy Grail by a young man with an absent father (McGonagle, 2007: 28–9). In a key scene in the romance, Perceval is received in a hall by the King, and a bleeding lance and a grail pass before him. Perceval 'saw them pass, but didn't dare ask who was served from the grail' (Chrétien de Troyes, 2015: 29). Not asking the right question becomes a major impediment for Perceval's quest for the Grail. In the film's adaptation of the character of the Fisher King, the point is that Félix does not ultimately seek some ultimate knowledge from the fisher father figure, but rather leaves knowledge about his father unknown. Is this his father? Is this a substitute father? His own projection of his father or of a father, like the flashbacks of himself as a boy that he has imagined earlier? Who exactly is his father? And does it really matter anyway? Instead of obtaining answers to questions, Félix flies his kite with the fisherman, sharing a moment of youthful connection not based on knowing who is who or what is what. The fisherman confesses his own faults to Félix, meaning that, according to Pratt, 'if Félix finds a father, then it is a father who is inherently fallible rather than the font of all self-knowledge' (2004: 100). Like the Fisher King in the medieval tradition, the fisherman is castrated, not a source of phallic knowledge and the resolution for Félix's sense of paternal absence. When he proclaims that he is leaving Dieppe to find his father, his partner Daniel expresses his concern that this father might not be 'stable' and that he should not go. He is right: the father is not a stable signifier of paternity or patriarchal order, like a kite blowing in the wind.

If the father proves not to be the order that he seeks, Félix's overall physical movement in this road/quest movie is defined by disorder as well. He does not drive through France, as might generally happen in a road movie, nor does he take the train. Instead, he hitchhikes, walks, and in one segment, steals a car with his 'brother' Jules (Charly Sergue). Later, after having sex with a man who works for the railroad who picks him up in his car and then continues on his way, Félix starts walking across a bridge to keep heading south towards Marseilles. The camera takes the position of a car driving by, behind Félix at first and then in front of him looking back on him. This shot invites the viewer to ask whether they would pick him up on the road based on what they see. Earlier, a man who picked him up as a hitchhiker asked him to get out of his car because an attractive woman hitchhiker appeared at the side of the road and he preferred to be alone with her instead of a man. In both of these scenes, the film raises the question of who picks up whom based on what forms of identity are visible to the driver of the car. Would the viewer not pick up Félix because he is not white? And because his encounters have all been defined through family constructs, the viewer driving by – were they to pick him up and have an encounter with him – would also have some kind of defined relation with the main character. What kind of familial relation would the viewer have with Félix? Cousin? Sister? Brother? Would the white viewer be able to have a familial relation with Félix at all? The bridge shot opens up the film beyond the actual encounters that take place into the realm of hypothetical encounters with viewers, asking implicit questions about the role of ethnicity and biology as organizing principles for what family means.

The concept of lack of stable order is represented by movement itself as the opening and closing scenes introduce and then leave the main character in physical motion. The film begins with a long travelling shot as Félix rides his bike down a promenade on the Norman coast in Dieppe, and the film closes with Félix on board a ferry heading off from Marseilles with Daniel to an undisclosed vacation location that may well be Corsica (plate 1). The road movie contained between these two scenes is only one element of the movement of the film which neither begins nor ends in stasis. Félix embodies movement because his subjectivity is non-normative three times over: he is gay, he is mixed-race *beur*, and he is HIV+. With a new way to hold these three subject positions on screen, he queers relationality itself by virtue of his three-part subjectivity. For Pratt, Félix 'reconstruct[s] a sense of identity coloured differently from the subjugated and shamed positions that routinely disempower homosexuals, racial minorities, people living with HIV and AIDS' (2004: 101). I would say that 'sense of identity coloured differently' puts relations into movement more broadly in a way that a mixed-race *beur* or a gay man might not do alone. The force behind that reconstruction is predicated on the force of multiple non-normative identities that intersect to produce a radically new way of being. The viewer learns in a clinic waiting room scene in Dieppe that Félix is undergoing a successful tri-therapy while others in the waiting room have different numerical therapies (one a bi-therapy, another a penta-therapy). This idea of threeness is no accident: the character *is* a tri-therapy for normativity. His ethnicity, his sexuality, and his HIV status together cure a representational lack in French film by bringing these three elements together in a single body, depicting an intersectional subjectivity and its relations with others.

Though he is a character in perpetual motion who puts representational norms into movement, Félix is also on the other hand very orderly. He tells the unnamed man with whom he has sex that he would like to bring his partner to this part of France for a vacation, reasserting homonormativity in the face of a one-time sex act. Earlier, in front of Chartres cathedral he meets his seventeen-year-old 'brother' Jules (Charly Sergue), who has trouble drawing the sculpture of Aristotle on the medieval façade. Félix takes over, drawing the Greek philosopher who represents dialectic, or the art of disagreement and lack of synthesis (see Franklin, 2015: 121). That disagreement, we learn as the two characters continue to interact, pertains to gay male sexuality as Jules wants to have sex with older men including Félix, who avoids sex with an underage person and a 'brother', seemingly committed to his age-appropriate partner. He spends the night in the same bed as Jules, sneaking in through the window with him to avoid his parents, but when morning comes Félix will not touch his 'brother'. He may queer and reconstruct familial relations, but he does not seem able to have his own 'child'. When Jules and Félix steal a car, it turns out there is a baby in the back seat and though they are committing a criminal act, they find a way to return the baby to its mother since they 'are not going to adopt it'. The possibility of becoming a gay or *beur* 'father' is rejected, the scene revealing that paternity is not possible on his part.

Orderliness is political as much as sexual. Félix will end his road trip on vacation in Corsica, a classic French tourist destination, not a representation of identities in movement at all but a signifier of mainland domination over the island and the incorporation of Corsicans into the French Republican nation-state. Indeed, in a broad sense, Félix does not destabilize racial uniformity via his new familial constructs, as all the characters he encounters are white (except possibly his 'father' whose ethnicity is not clear). It may not be that the character queers familial relations then, but that he embodies the integration of a non-white body into the normative body politic. Swamy notes that the film affirms 'the myth of the Republican idea of a seamless integration into a "French" melting pot'

(2006: 62), and Tarr suggests that the main character is 'a model of successful assimilation, whilst demonstrating the limits of Ducastel and Martineau's vision of a multicultural France' (2005: 150). Félix may well be what Provencher terms a '"good" French sexual citizen' (2008: 52), proving French universalism's orderly merits instead of queering them.

As such, Félix is a character caught between order and disorder, between normativity and anti-normativity, between his marginal identities and French universalism. It is in fact hard to know who Félix is by sight, and the inability to know who someone is based on their '*gueule*', or the way they look, is a recurring topos of the film. 'Do I have the face of a Norman?' he asks his 'sister' Isabelle (Ariane Ascaride) after she asks him if she has the face of a cop. The answer to both questions is no. Félix may or may not be read as gay: his 'grandmother' Mathilde (Patachou) whose house he visits does not suspect that he is gay, and, when he tells her that he is, she says that she believes him because he tells her so, not because she figured it out or sensed it on her own. We never really know whether his looks factor into the reaction of those he encounters or not, and we do not know how HIV-status affects his actions, and we do not always know who reads him as gay. He embodies oscillation, as a character hard to read. Schilt (2007), Archer (2013), and McGonagle (2007) all read the character along these lines, as in movement with respect to identity. McGonagle sums up this approach to the film: 'Félix is a complex, subtle character whose contradictions keep the play of identity open and prevent his from being pinned down' (2007: 31). The fisherman tells Félix that the quest to find his father whom he never knew is not 'very original'. The quest for the absent father is an old, tired narrative, but what is original in this particular quest is the opening-up of identities into constant flux and the production of an unending series of ways of relating to others that may or may not be related to those identities and whose relation may or may not be discernible or knowable in the first place. It is not the case that Félix is simply fluid, nor that he becomes a universalist citizen beyond subjectivity. He has moments of identity stasis, moments of universalist identity, and movements where it is not quite clear whether his identity is orderly or disorderly, static or in movement.

While passing through central France, Félix visits a temple to Hermes with Jules, who notes that Hermes is the god of thieves and of merchants, protecting contrary interests. Félix, too, guards two contrary interests: normativity and anti-normativity. On the day of the visit to the temple, it is foggy and it is not possible to actually see the statue of Hermes. This stop in the road movie emblematizes its approach to subjectivity and to queerness: it is not the temple of Hermes that is foggy, it is how to read subjectivity – or hermeneutics, the word itself coming from the god Hermes. It is unclear how the other characters can and do read Félix. Do his homosexuality and his ethnicity dismantle or destabilize universalism? Reaffirm and construct it through erasure? Both? Does the relation to universalism change from one episode or moment to the next? The critical approaches to this film that I have cited do not agree over the extent to which Félix is a 'good citizen' or another type of citizen. These approaches, I would suggest, are all correct and, taken together, constitute the queerness of the film – in the end an oscillating relation to citizenship and universalism. If as Arroyo noted in a review of the film, Félix 'is offered the expectation of a future', it is not only because he is an HIV+ character not doomed to die, it is also because he has a whole series of future encounters and ways of being that have yet to be determined. The movement of the ferry in the final scene allegorizes the movement of relationalities and identities that will produce new ways of being, not yet fixed or determined in the present, with new people, not yet in the cast of familial characters, and new relations to French universalism, not yet determined.

Revisualizing the closet: *Ma vraie vie à Rouen*

On one level, Ducastel and Martineau's *Ma vraie vie à Rouen* – literally 'My True Life in Rouen' but translated as *My Life on Ice* – could be taken as a coming-out film. The handsome teenage main character Etienne (Jimmy Tavares) does not articulate his 'true' sexuality or his 'homosexuality' nor does he 'come out of the closet' via words however.[6] Instead, Etienne receives a video camera from his grandmother at the very start of the film and begins to film himself, his surroundings, and people around him. The relation between same-sex desire and the main character develops as the visual autobiography progresses, opening up new ways to become a sexual subject. As Pullen describes the process: 'The camera ... enables possibility for him [and] becomes an active agent, stimulating potential' (2008: 58). While Etienne films his mother (Ariane Ascaride) at a bookstore where she works, a random customer buying books asks if the camera is digital ('numérique'). This moment emphasizes that the coming narrative about sexuality will not be told with words – in the way that the narratives in the books sold at the bookstore would be – but via the moving image and that it will narrate a coming to homosexuality – not a coming out in a traditional sense – at the beginning of the digital age in the twenty-first century. The film asks the implicit question: What might it mean to come out in the digital age in a French context? How can becoming gay be narrated in the twenty-first century outside the realm of discourse and language? What new ways of narrating can be articulated in the digital medium? Grandena (2009: 78) offers

---

6 Grandena describes this aspect of the film as 'how to say the unsayable' (2009: 80), and takes Etienne as having to 'deal with precise inadequacies specific to French language and culture – that is linguistic and cultural shortcomings related to the difficulty or even the impossibility of expressing same-sex desires verbally and positively' (81).

a discussion of what the digital medium in the film means about sexuality: the technology permits 'an utterly subjective and fragmented realism' that leaves queer subjectivity 'subordinated to specific camera movements' and 'the camera ... in charge of the narrative' (79). 'The insertion of "imperfect" or "accidental" shots ... seemingly filmed by chance or by mere clumsiness' (78) allows for Etienne to be seen gazing upon male bodies without meaning to and for his queer desire to be registered in visual, non-discursive terms beyond his control.

When the bookstore customer says that it is good that Etienne has a 'passion', his mother responds that for her it is a problem that he always does solitary activities, namely ice-skating and filming with his camera, and that she would prefer that he do 'collective things' like team sports such as hockey. Filming his gay 'passion' (in both senses of the word, suffering but also erotic experiences) will be individual, despite his mother's wishes, and will not be a communal expression of sexuality as often done by gay people. He will express his passion in a new way. 'I don't like teams', Etienne responds to his mother. He will not participate in a collective manner of coming out or of becoming a sexual subject. His mother's use of 'collective' reflects an important concept: Etienne will not accept the French universalizing imperative that places the citizen first and homosexuality second. He will search for a third way, neither an Anglo-American identitarian, discursive approach to coming out nor a French approach that takes coming out as anti-universalist. Not discursive but also not gay avoidant, visuality, or the act of filming, constitutes another technique by which to become a gay subject.

Discourse is juxtaposed with visuality on a number of occasions to establish and re-establish that the two forms of expression are opposed. In a scene early on, Etienne is helping his best friend Ludovic (Lucas Bonnifait) rehearse a speech from the play *Suréna* by the classical playwright Pierre

Corneille. Out of context, the lines are confusing and do not convey much meaning. But when Etienne helps by reading the lines of the person to whom Ludovic's character is speaking and films his friend, the focus of the film transfers from text to image. Laurent (Jonathan Zaccaï), Etienne's handsome history-geography teacher, happens to walk by the steps of the church where they are rehearsing, and Etienne moves the camera away from Ludovic to film his teacher. The scene ends as Etienne zooms in on Ludovic who no longer speaks and captures his face for an extended period. Etienne's scopophilia, the pleasure he takes in looking at his friend, is put on full display. The scene charts the move from a scopophiliac accidental distraction or errancy towards a more sustained focus on the male body as object of desire, developing the freedom to look queerly. What is emerging is a gay gaze that looks on attractive male bodies along with a consideration of what that visual orientation means – a move from classical textual expression in the guise of a Cornellian tragedy to visuality as locus of expression. Later on, as the two adolescents walk together to a party and Etienne films him, Ludovic asks if he can 'say something', to which his friend responds in the negative because his developing gay gaze expels language and relies on visuality. Etienne's discovery of his body as locus of eroticism is coded visually: he films himself undressing with shots of parts of his body, and later he films himself fully naked. The visual undressing of the self replaces revelation in words.

Central to the displacement of discourse is the explicit rejection of the confession of homosexuality, the announcement that 'I am gay'. Two key scenes reveal that this film will not be about confession. In the opening scene, as Etienne films his mother and grandmother for the first time, he states enigmatically what they will have to do in front of the camera: 'Il faut tout avouer' ('we will have to confess everything'). His grandmother looks at him as if he is about to confess something to her, but then the question turns to how his grandmother was able to afford the camera. She reveals that she won some money in the lottery and bought the camera. The possibility of a familial confession on Etienne's part is transferred into a harmless confession about buying lottery tickets. Confession is relegated to the status of non-confession, mocked as a technique for revelation in the first place. This will not be a film about sexual confession, this prologue to the film tells the viewer up front, but about visuality.

In the middle of the film, another possible confessional moment appears one evening. Now Etienne's mother's boyfriend, Laurent takes his shirt off as Etienne is filming him. Though still his teacher, the drunk Laurent starts to pose for him, provoking him, but then realizes that Etienne does in fact find him attractive. Etienne has in a sense come out here although it is unclear if the latter will remember the moment in his drunken state. Laurent wants to know why he has nothing to say and toasts 'to silence'. Etienne notes that he has nothing to say either. Despite being in an erotic situation, he will not confess his homosexuality. Laurent continues and asks Etienne: 'You think I'm hot?' ('Je te plais, c'est ça?'). Etienne is still filming, and Laurent tells him to give him the camera. Homosexual desire has been conveyed visually to us and Laurent, but not spoken. The moment of unidirectional eros opens up the possibility of reciprocated eros with a gay man later on, with this moment a step in a process as Laurent plays the role of desirable but inaccessible erotic male body.

A scene near the end of the film reveals that *Ma vraie vie* will not culminate in Etienne's announcement of his homosexuality. Etienne and Ludo spend time together on the coast during the summer, sunning themselves shirtless next to each other in a shot with unavoidable homoeroticism, and it may seem like the moment for Etienne to come out to Ludo has finally arrived. He asks his best friend: 'Do you think it's possible to love a boy?' Ludo does not respond well to the question, referring to a boy who loves a boy as a 'faggot' (*pédé*). He follows up by asking: 'What are you trying to say?' Etienne answers: 'Nothing ... I mean ... I don't know. It's hard to say'. He does not say that he is gay, but Ludo understands, telling him that he does not want to hear what he has to say and quickly leaves. Coming out will not happen in words in this film, we now know for sure, but will take another route. In a sense, it is this film – not Ludovic – that does not want to hear what Etienne has to say. It wants us to see what he sees. The film cuts to a shot of Etienne sitting alone down on the beach, with the cliffs behind him, where, we had learned from his grandmother, no one was allowed to go because of fallen rocks. No one, indeed, goes there except for Etienne. No one goes there because he is going rogue not in terms of space, but in terms of representation. The twenty-five-second still shot of Etienne sitting alone emphasizes again that coming out will be defined visually, not discursively, and that he has entered a representational space off limits. He will do something on his own that is not 'allowed' – like climbing down to the beach – and define his sexuality in visual terms. It is his own approach, not French culture's. Breaking the rules here paves the way for the final scene: as Etienne seems to be contemplating suicide and to jump off the cliffs, a young man comes along and, we assume, saves him from suicide by asking if it is his camera.

Etienne finally 'becomes' gay by moving fully beyond the confessional mode. The cliff scene with the young man who happens to come by then transitions to a bed where, it is clear, the two of them have had sex. The nameless young man has the camera and is filming Etienne who is in bed, naked. Etienne tries to take the camera, since he has never been in a situation with another gay person filming him and is uncomfortable in this role. He is not used to being the object of the gay gaze itself, so out of habit he wants to be the one filming. But this time is different. The young man tells him not to touch, but to be seen on camera. 'Look', he says. Something has changed, but it is not defined as a tag like 'gay' that can be attached to him in language. What is changed is that he is being seen in a new way. His new friend says: 'We look so different after making love' (literally, 'we really have a different head after love'). Etienne is out because he is filmed as having had sex with another young man. He 'looks different' here, but not because he has tagged himself in language as different. He does not need to express his erotic desire visually with his heterosexual best friend nor with his mother's boyfriend, but with an age-appropriate, gay male who reciprocates.

But he 'looks different' in a second sense, a literal one. He is gazed upon differently than he was before. Coming out in this film cannot uniquely be a question of how a gay man looks at male bodies but must include how he is looked at as erotic object himself. To be a fully formed sexual subject, it is not enough to look or to see as a gay subject since that visual relation is unidirectional, predicated on a distance between self and other via the lens of the camera. 'T'es joli' ('You're cute'), he is told as he is being filmed. He can be seen as someone who has had sex with another man, and he can now be seen as an object of beauty to be admired queerly. What can now happen is not so much that he can live his life as 'gay' but as someone who can be seen as cute by another gay male. He can be looked at and desired with a gay gaze. The lover turns on the camera to film them together. 'Is it really the moment?', Etienne asks, receiving the response that it is. Once the camera is on, Etienne gives the impression that he wants to take the camera away, but his friend will not let him be the gazer. He must be gazed upon, both as a gay man and as part of a gay pair. This had been the missing piece of the gay puzzle with respect to visuality all along. Etienne had been able to see increasingly as a desiring gay subject, albeit with inappropriate objects of desire, and he had even been able to be seen as non-heterosexual by heterosexual male subjects, albeit awkwardly. The look of the other is no longer one of judgement but of desire and beauty. The aborted 'avowal' of the opening scene has now happened in the final scene, but in visual terms. The accidental lottery win has become an accidental visual encounter. The image goes fluid as the two touch each other, and the camera is no longer necessary. Visuality has become touch, the camera has led to touch (plate 2). The eye of the camera has been extended out of the realm of the lens into the realm of skin. The camera becomes haptic, transformed into an erotic and affectionate gay corporality. If confessional discourse becomes inscribed on the body (e.g., the 'gay man' becomes a gay body by virtue of naming), here gay visuality turns into the body itself, meaning that visuality does not surveil the gay body but is transformed into an affective relation with it. The body is not watched over, kept in the closet, or forced to be sexually normative under threat of insult, violence, or harassment, but rather is watched with affect and desire. The haptic image signals the end of the separation between viewer and viewed which has so far characterized the film. Etienne might be seeing more and more queerly, but that queerness had been predicated on a gap between the eye of the viewing subject and that on which he gazed. The caress or the touch of the lover closes the gap, giving up the mastery of the watching subject in favour of a relational mode that is more slippery. As Marks explains this concept, 'The ideal relationship between viewer and image in haptic visuality is one of mutuality, in which the viewer is more likely to lose herself in the image' (2000: 184). Etienne's visual process expands out now from looking erotically into the possibility of a mutual erotic loss. The lover's caress in the scene is key since 'when vision is like touch, the object's touch back may be like a caress' (184). Etienne is now 'vulnerable to the image, reversing the relation of mastery that characterizes optical viewing' (185).

This 'form of visuality', according to Marks, 'is itself erotic' (185). Etienne does not end the film so much as 'gay', as a subject that can desire and have sex with other males, as much as he enters into the realm of queer eroticism, where he can (and will) maintain a homoerotic manner of looking coupled now with a reversal in the queer gaze, resulting in melting into the other's gaze. He becomes someone who can now experience 'loss of self in the presence of the other' (Marks, 1998: 347) in 'an elastic, dynamic movement'. In a sense, it is Etienne's ability to melt dynamically into the erotic realm with another male, to disappear in part as a queer looking subject, that is his final destination. It is no accident that the other male has no name: he embodies not so much a character but the concept of a similarly aged, gay other that facilitates Etienne's loss of self. This is not a love story, but a story of queer 'dynamic movement'.

This moment of loss of self builds on earlier moments in which Etienne is seen by presumably heterosexual men who take his camera and gaze upon him through the lens. Laurent holds the camera in the living room and films Etienne going through his ice-skating moves. As he does so, he gets hotter and removes more and more clothing, revealing his body. The eye of the camera is queered by virtue of the presence of a male gaze on a male body. Later, in a key scene at the local swimming pool, Laurent steals the camera, unwilling to return it, and films Etienne while asking him questions about desire. In an erotic pose captured on some versions of the cover of the DVD, Etienne sits in his swimming trunks with his toned skater's body in full view for Laurent's filming eye. He later films the young man alone in the showers as he undresses, mirroring an earlier scene in which Etienne films a friend of his undressing in the locker room. In these cases, even as the gaze is not gay per se, there is nonetheless something queer about Laurent's eye, as the camera permits him to manifest a bit of queer desire inside the safe realm of his presumed heterosexuality. Boyle takes this element of Laurent's scopophilia as indicative of a broader visual ethics in the film in which the viewer is put in a gay viewing position: 'Laurent ... demonstrates that he – like the spectator – is able to see, even if only momentarily, with a gay gaze' (2012: 62). For Boyle, the film asks the viewer (presumably the non-gay viewer) 'to look on *with* a gay protagonist, not to look on *at* him' (66, italics in original). All viewers are invited to see that a young gay man is not just gay by virtue of definition and desire, but that he also sees as a gay man, noticing handsome men and taking pleasure in looking at them. In the same way in which Etienne learns to see queerly, the non-gay viewer has the chance to do the same via Laurent.

It is no accident that the scene with Laurent filming takes place at the pool, as he is a bit fluid in terms of desire. Before meeting Laurent, Etienne's mother needs a word for a crossword puzzle, the cue being 'Flowing African'. Etienne cannot help her, but suggests that he ask his geography teacher and then asks his mother if she liked him when she met him briefly. Laurent is linked to water, to fluidity, but fluidity that – like the crossword puzzle answer – fits into clearly delimited squares and does not pour over into the realm of other sexualities. His contained queerness might be taken as intergenerational or incestuous in some sense, but Laurent's objectification is one step removed from heteronormative watching, in the direction of a more fluid gay visuality that will help affirm Etienne's sexuality.

The film's affirmation of homosexuality does not in the end really result in a state of queerness – unlike the end of *Drôle de Félix* – but the process to arrive there can be taken as queer. This unique narrative corresponds to Michel Foucault's desire for sexuality to not be the revelation of 'a secret side of our desire' but a process of definition (1997: 163). Foucault takes sexuality as 'something that we ourselves create – it is our own creation, and much more than the discovery of a secret side of our desire' (163).

With desire established, he adds, 'sex is not a fatality: it's a possibility for creative life' and it is 'to *become*' (163, italics in original). The film puts into practice Foucault's idea, focusing on the creativity with which Etienne articulates his sexuality. While sex offers the possibility of creativity here, the creativity of expression in turn offers the possibility a fully realized sexuality.

By contrast, the structure of the closet, a culturally sanctioned process, is anything but creative. The closet is, theoretically speaking, oppressive: only some people are required to come out, and heterosexual people do not have to do so. In Foucauldian terms from *The History of Sexuality*, modern societies encourage, do not repress, talking about sex, provided that it is discussed as a secret. The necessity of making sex a secret that gets revealed, with coming out one way to do so, suggests the subjection of a person to regimes of power that control how a subject expresses themselves and functions as a sexual subject. Foucault famously described sex as a secret to reveal and as a problem, by noting that 'Western man has become a confessing animal' (1978: 59). With its visual focus and its rejection of discourse as the confessional mode, the film keeps Etienne – to a certain extent at least – from acting as a 'confessing animal' subject to power. In inventing his own way to come to terms with sexuality, he skirts the problem of French universalism, which does not in theory recognize a citizen as a gay subject. The visuality of same-sex desire avoids the discursive definition of citizenship or official state-sanctioned ideas on what homosexuality is in the first place.

The film invents a way to come to subjectivity in the realm of film history in which coming out or 'becoming oneself' (Roth-Bettoni, 2007: 608) begins to be shown more and more frequently on screen in the 1990s.[7] *Ma vraie vie à Rouen* is

---

[7] Roth-Bettoni documents a series of French films about adolescents and what he calls 'l'affirmation de soi' (2007: 608–10), affirming one's identity as a sexual subject. Along with André Téchiné, he lists

necessarily in dialogue with such films, including previous films that could be labelled as coming-out films. Most famously, André Téchiné's *Les Roseaux sauvages* (*Wild Reeds*) (1994) employs a visual metaphor for self-reflection as well, but as a way to make a confessional enunciation ('Je suis pédé, je suis pédé' ('I am a faggot, I am a faggot')) sink in better as François talks to himself in the mirror, not as a way to question or to avoid the discursive act itself. Ducastel and Martineau's film in some ways extends Rémi Lange's 1994 experimental film *Omelette*, in which the director comes out to family members but turns his camera on them, such that the centre of attention is not his own sexuality but their reactions to him during this process.[8] *Ma vraie vie* is not so much a film about heteronormality's relation to coming out, but like Lange's film it does create visual agency for the queer subject insofar as he can come out in a non-discursive way.

Reconfiguring family life, reconfiguring sexuality: *Crustacés et coquillages*

A central element of the comedy in *Crustacés et coquillages*, translated as *Côte d'Azur* (in the US) and as *Muscles and Cockles* (in the UK), is that married couple Béatrix (Valeria Bruni-Tedeschi) and Marc (Gilbert Melki) believe that their teenage son Charly (Romain Torres) is gay while in fact Marc is in the closet and comes out as gay at the end of the film.

---

directors Gaël Morel and Lifshitz. Lifshitz's *Presque rien* certainly falls in this category, though there is no act of sexual enunciation per se.

8 Ducastel and Martineau's interest in this film is manifested by writing a forward ('avant-propos') to Lange's book *Journal d'Omelette* (Ducastel and Martineau, 2011: 5–8). Their text is very engaged in the topic of the family's response to outing.

The juxtaposition of father and son embodies the film's approach to the closet as a flawed structure. What one thinks about the closet is wrong. When Charly's friend Martin (Edouard Collin), who is out as gay, talks to Charly about when he came out to his parents, he notes that his mother cried but that it was 'pour la forme' ('because she thought that's what she was supposed to do'). His father, on the other hand, ignored the whole process entirely. *Crustacés et coquillages* treats coming out and the closet in another way entirely, not as a structure that requires predetermined actions 'pour la forme', nor as something to be ignored as if it did not exist. Rather, the film offers a non-normative way to represent the transition to homosexuality.

Not gay, Charly has to come out to his parents as 'not homosexual', putting the adolescent in the shoes of a homosexual assumed to be straight and thereby turning the closet inside out. Charly stands for the morphology of a sexuality not typically imagined as an orientation – the masturbator. A running joke revolves around the fact that he repeatedly takes showers, using all the hot water, and that his father does not know the reason why. There is no girlfriend or even expression of heterosexual desire on his part (until the very final moment of the film, but even then, there is no young woman physically present). The category of the masturbator allegorizes a larger idea, namely that orientations other than heterosexuality, bisexuality, and homosexuality exist and that they are connected to an epistemology of the closet. Eve Sedgwick in her influential *Epistemology of the Closet* asks but does not answer the question 'why the category of "the masturbator"' did not come to 'specify ... a particular kind of person, an identity' (2005: 9) in the same way that in the mid-nineteenth century, as Foucault famously proclaimed in volume one of *The History of Sexuality*, 'the homosexual was now a species' (1978: 43). Pre-modern masturbation remained in the category of act where it remains even today, not coming to constitute a 'species' defined through discursive conventions in medicine, psychoanalysis, law, etc. In Ducastel and Martineau's film, the masturbator is the one in the closet, not the actual homosexual. The physical see-through shower in the family's bathroom has the metaphorical form of a closet in which the masturbatory act takes place over and over, replacing the closet that the actual gay character (Marc) is in. That metaphorical space does not actually hide Charly however, for it is a glass closet that allows knowledge of his quasi-orientation to become known by others in the house. As such, then, it functions as the closet might for gay folks, as a structure that does not so much hide sexuality or keep it hidden, but that contains discourse about sexuality. Sexuality is an open secret, but still isolated and not operative outside the delineated space. The film refuses to allow the closet to function as a simple confessional structure for gay/lesbian people, expanding it in another direction to challenge its perceived necessity for gay subjectivity in the first place.

Other non-gay characters relate to this epistemology as well. Béatrix has a secret, we learn, as she goes to the train station to pick up her lover Mathieu (Jacques Bonnaffé). Her hidden lover, who will be revealed to her family over the course of the film, signifies a queer secret within a heterosexual relationship. When he emerges from secrecy and Charly meets him for the first time, he has just come out of the glass shower, the closet stand-in. He wants to be out in the open with Béatrix and her family, and part of the narrative trajectory is his transition from secret to acknowledged lover. Heterosexual infidelity is trapped in the closet and then outed, following a 'gay' process.

Béatrix's coming out to Marc is structured in direct parallel with his coming out to her as gay. Charly proclaims 'Mon père est pédé' ('My father is a homo') at the very same moment as Mathieu emerges from the bathroom. With the two outings – one gay and the other heterosexual – structurally identical, homosexuality is revealed as just one way in which a secret has to be revealed. This structural parallel continues in the film. A shot/countershot of Béatrix and Marc, who are not together but are on the same road walking in opposite directions towards each other, reveals their direct juxtaposition. They both plan to confess to their spouse, Marc about his homosexuality and Béatrix about her lover. They reach each other from opposite directions and can each announce their secret to the other. Their simultaneous coming out solves both of their problems: Béatrix can be with Mathieu while Marc can be with his old flame Didier (Jean-Marc Barr). Marc's coming out, while it might seem to be a classic case of a married man realizing at last that he is gay and announcing the news to his family, is complicated: he had loved Didier in his youth, before meeting his wife, and his coming out is not a new state of being, but a return to a sexuality before heterosexual marriage. Didier is a local plumber whom Charly calls to come fix what he believes is a hot water heater malfunction in the house. Like the plumber in *Jeanne et le garçon formidable*, he cracks open a sexual narrative. Marc is, in a sense, curtailed by marriage and heterosexuality and needs to be 'unclogged' or opened back up to homosexuality. But the plumber is not technically needed: Marc had taken out the electrical plug so that the hot water heater would not work and Charly would not spend so much time in the shower wasting energy. Didier is called to the house, but he is not necessary for the coming out process, which presumably would have happened without him. Marc's homosexuality is not something new that he realizes in middle age: it has always been there, and he returns to a time before marriage blocked it.

The film opens and closes with an image about visibility that allegorizes the idea that there are alternatives to the normative closet. Marc is sure that there is a castle that he can see from their house in the distance. Béatrix notes that it was visible when he was a boy, but that the trees have grown and hidden it. At the tail end of the film, the castle is revealed as visible; it has always been there, even if it has been hidden somehow. Homosexuality – the blatant metaphor suggests – is not a secret but something always present that was hidden or forgotten over time. Marc was not 'in the closet' and then 'out' of it, but rather he was not able to see what he knew was there. Béatrix 'chose' Marc, she mentions twice, suggesting that the closeting mechanism was not so much created by Marc's fear of homosexuality or of contracting AIDS, but an aggressive heterosexuality that convinced him to be and to remain a heterosexual married man.

One could say that *Crustacés et coquillages* renders the closet structure majoritizing instead of minoritizing. It makes visible the heterosexism of the closet, forcing queer people to act to make themselves known as what they already are, whereas heterosexuals can be taken for granted as heterosexual. Here, the closet structure proliferates, takes multiple forms, and can relate to most everyone, whatever their orientation. The final dance number (to the titular song) mixes together sexualities into a choreography at once unified and discrete as everyone ends up in the same place.

The epistemology of the secret is coded as Franco-American, or at least in part an American imposition of stable identity onto the complication of sexuality or French universalist conceptions of sexuality. Didier is half American, he shouts a few phrases in perfect American English, and we learn that he had gone to live in California with his father (presumably American) when he was younger. Unclogging Marc's pipes, as it were, represents an American identity-driven model of coming out that is not fully disbanded in the film. As Marc prepares to talk to Béatrix and rehearses what he will say to her, he yells to himself in English 'I'm gay'. However, when he actually speaks to her, he tells her that he 'loves the plumber', not that he 'is gay'. His coming out, or rather his return to homosexuality, may be coded as American structurally and linguistically (he has to tell his wife and he thinks he has to label his sexuality ('gay')). But on the other hand, it is not American because it reconfigures a binary transition (from 'heterosexuality' to 'homosexuality') as a ternary (from homosexuality to heterosexuality back to homosexuality). The plumber, after all, is not really needed to unclog sexuality and though an American identitarian model may be evoked, it does not need to be part of this reconfigured model of the closet coded as ultimately French.

Outing familial structures

Questions around the secret and the closet are central to the narratives of *Ma vraie vie à Rouen*, *Crustacés et coquillages*, *L'Arbre et la forêt*, and *Juste la fin du monde*. In none of these cases, however, does a closeted homosexual simply reveal his secret to family and friends, and the films, taken as a whole, open up the question of revelation to a variety of possibilities. By representing a variety of coming-outs, Ducastel and Martineau allow gay characters the freedom to make themselves gay in the way that Didier Eribon discusses it in *Insult and the Making of the Gay Self*: 'the project of "making" oneself gay (*se faire gay*) not only means creating oneself, but creating oneself in the light of, through the inspiration of, all the examples already available in society and in history' (2004: 111–12). The characters in these four films still have a relation to a history of coming out as gay, but the cases are so unique that each one constitutes its own case of 'making oneself gay'. Etienne's visuality is highly creative and individual. In *Crustacés et coquillages*, the glass closet is rendered opaque as the 'wrong' person is suspected of homosexuality. The comedic displacement suggests that the one not suspected is suspicious and that there is something wrong with the idea that heterosexuals can determine who is and is not gay. Marc tells himself over and over that he is 'gay', lightening the process of coming out as well as the tone of queer French cinema in a broader sense. He retroactively transforms the tone of the mirror scene in Téchiné's *Les Roseaux sauvages* with seemingly tragic undertones. Everything turns out fine for the gay François in the end and any anxiety about suicide is dissipated, but Ducastel and Martineau's 2005 film replays – or reboots – the tone of the well-known 1994 scene.

The three films to be discussed next are not comedic, but they do continue the process of transforming the closet, each in its own way, by coding the idea of the secret as not gay. Ducastel and Martineau's lengthy and sweeping *Nés en 68*, beginning on a commune in rural France in the first segment, transitions into a film about the children of characters in the commune during the AIDS epidemic in France. One of those characters, Boris (Théo Frilet), survives, while another, Christophe (Edouard Collin), dies from the illness. Although these two men grew up on the commune and deal with the homophobia or sexual anxiety of Christophe's family, there is no closet, and they do not come out as gay. Instead, the film replaces coming out to family with other revelations and secrets that have a similar epistemology, displacing the gay closet into other realms, much like *Crustacés et coquillages*. The two gay characters do in fact have to come out to their families, but as HIV+, and the build-up to the revelation – with the two characters preparing in separate spaces but at the same time and in similar manners – plays off a structural similarity between homosexuality and HIV status. In addition, Boris's mother, Catherine (Laetitia Casta) falls terminally ill late in the film but does not tell her family. Her illness functions rhetorically as a secret, like the closet. Her daughter Ludmilla chastises her mother's boyfriend for not telling her and the rest of the family since, as she puts it, they have the 'right to know'. The same rhetoric is sometimes used around the gay closet: gay people who do not tell their families about their sexuality might be told that they should have told them sooner, that it is hurtful that they were not told earlier, and that as their family, they have the right to know.

L'Arbre et la forêt (literally, 'The Tree and the Forest', but translated as *Family Tree*) likewise offers a new epistemology of the closet by incorporating the Holocaust into the narrative. The father of two children, Frédérick (Guy Marchand) was sent to a concentration camp for his homosexuality, not political beliefs or actions. The film, set in 1999, takes place as his son Charles's funeral is taking place. His son, along with his wife, knew his secret but his second son Guillaume (François Négret) and his wife Marianne (Françoise Fabian) did not, nor did his oldest grandchild Delphine (Sabrina Seyvecou). Midway into the film, Frédérick tells his family his secret, to a variety of reactions. The focus in his coming out is less on his sexuality or being 'gay' than on the idea of a family secret shared by some and not by others. By not talking about why he was interned, he did not talk to some of them about his experience during the war more broadly. The revelation is a hybrid secret, about the Holocaust as repressed and undisclosed as well as about homosexuality. This double closet stands in for a cultural secret, a French avoidance of an LGBTQ Holocaust not fully recognized officially until President Jacques Chirac finally acknowledged it in 2005.[9] On one level, the closet is not Frédérick's but France's, and this story has greater import than one man's life. In the film in fact, his homosexuality exists in name only: there is no male lover, and after the war he returned to his wife Marianne after which time they had their son Guillaume. The film is very loosely based on Pierre Seel's 1994 memoir *Moi, Pierre Seel, déporté homosexuel* (*I, Pierre Seel, Deported Homosexual*). The film reimagines Seel's horrific past and places it into dialogue with a

---

9 This collective forgetting is the subject of Jean Le Bitoux's book *Les Oubliés de la mémoire* (*Forgotten by Memory*) (2002). Another key moment in memorializing the Holocaust is the publication of Jean Boisson's *Le Triangle rose* (*The Pink Triangle*) (1988). More recently, the issue is treated in Boulligny (2018).

familial present. In an interview, the directors note that they had imagined Seel today, not during the war and not in flashback (Toutleciné.com, 2010), as someone else resembling him who believed that there was no one else that had suffered the same fate as he had. Chapter 5 of the book ('Out of the Closet: A Painful Testimony') offers a different coming out than the one in the film as it takes place at a bookstore in Toulouse, not around the dinner table with family. Here, Seel tells himself: 'At last – it's out' (1995: 125). Central to the book is Pierre's witnessing the 'barbaric murder' (44) of his lover Jo, entirely absent from the film. *L'Arbre et la forêt* highlights French culture's symbolic closet, in this respect following the book which documents Seel's struggle to out a secret in broad terms for French culture.[10]

The French title of the film refers to a tree that Frédérick plants after the war, a tree he vowed to plant while in the camp if he survived. The tree is located just outside the window of the house and figures prominently in numerous scenes, functioning semantically on a number of levels. It is a family tree – as per the English title – a rooted plant allowing him to be seen as part of a biological family with children and grandchildren. It represents his own growth out of the trauma of the Holocaust, rooted in a free space and branching outwards. But the image is queer as well. The French title refers not only to the tree, but to the large forest on the estate. The tree is and is not part of that forest: on the one hand Frédérick might seem like part of the familial collective, and no one may be able to separate the (heterosexual) forest from the (gay) tree. But on the other hand, the tree is separated, not part of that collective. Frédéric's experience in the Holocaust means that he cannot fully be in a normative collective. Near the end of

---

10 Seel made a number of television appearances before the publication of his important book (see Gavillet, 2018: 174). In 2005, Christian Faure's telefilm *Un amour à taire* (*A Love to Hide*), very freely adapted from the story of Pierre Seel, came out.

the film, he and his wife decide to sell the forest for their family members Guillaume and Delphine (Charles's daughter) and for their children. This act separates the symbolic tree from the broader forest of which it is no longer a part. The tree figures prominently in the title and in a key scene near the end of the film: Delphine and her partner Rémi (Yannick Renier) rotate around it, as the new generation has incorporated it into their familial practices. The past has been revealed to the family – and by extension to a new generation of French people – and now can be at least partially integrated into family life and familial futurity. Delphine and Rémi's playfulness suggests the future of children for whom homosexuality will be no issue.

As the sole cast member who is not, or has not been, officially part of the family, Rémi stands in for the future ear of French culture around the LGBTQ Holocaust. Unlike many other characters in the family, he is low key with respect to affect, often listening patiently and gently asking questions. His interactions with Frédérick are neutral and the two share a mutual, intergenerational affection. By virtue of skipping a generation and incorporating family members not defined by blood, past and present connect and a form of futurity is invented.

Marianne's birthday happens around the time of the funeral and Frédérick sells a section of the forest to purchase a first-class trip to Antarctica for her. In a brief shot, the continent is shown as all white, devoid of green, a kind of tabula rasa that repositions nature from scratch. The white reconfiguration means that trees and forests can be resignified at home, can be rewritten not as about past trauma but about futurity. The forest has been semiotically cleared and readied for new signification in the twenty-first century.

Queer discomfort: *Juste la fin du monde*

Ducastel and Martineau's made-for-TV film *Juste la fin du monde* is not at first glance a queer narrative, but looks to be all about impending death. Their script follows the play of the same name written by French playwright Jean-Luc Lagarce (1990), completed five years before his death from AIDS. The main character, prodigal son Louis (Pierre Louis-Calixte), returns to his family home to see his brother, sister, and mother 'to announce, tell, just tell' them of his 'upcoming and irremediable death ... to be its only messenger' (Lagarce, 2018). In so doing, he notes at the end of the prologue before he is actually with them, he will offer to himself and to others 'one last time, the illusion of being a responsible person and of being, until the very end, [his] own master'. Louis never does tell them of his impending death, and, as he tells us in the epilogue, he dies 'a few months later, one year at most'. He adds, along with a final image of himself walking on train tracks at night over 'an immense viaduct ... suspended over a valley' in southern France, that he is unable to 'let out a big and beautiful scream ... that would resonate through the valley'. He cannot or will not tell his family his secret, he cannot communicate loudly to them, and he goes forward 'hearing only the sound of [his] steps on the gravel'. There is no ultimate utterance about death, only small utterances that do not communicate his news. The movie and the play narrate instead the inability to speak loudly to one's family, to 'announce, tell, just tell' a life-changing piece of news that has the potential to transform the dysfunctional way in which they all communicate with each other. The script focuses on the interactions between Louis and his family, with a series of underlying but explicit tensions between them. An amorphous lack of open communication is the result of pre-existing interpersonal issues that are never fully clear or explained. Unlike the characters not in the know, the spectator is told from the start that Louis will die (though from what is not revealed), but we do not know what exactly has transpired in the past between the family members. The communal past is both present and not present in discourse, both available and not available to us. In the film, these awkward discursive interactions contrast with the images of the characters, routinely shot by Ducastel and

Martineau in medium shots or in medium-closeups. The largely traditional camerawork has the effect of moving the emphasis away from the visual to confusing, linguistic elements of the film that hide and suggest a familial past.

The cinematic characters in essence are split into two selves, sometimes functioning externally and at other times internally. Louis delivers a speech in front of a bathroom mirror about his family loving him, but his mirror image delivers part of his speech as well. As a speaking subject, Louis is split, he is two men speaking because he comes with a past that cannot be bracketed but cannot, either, be brought out directly into the open. The reflection is not really his mirror image, as the two of them move in different ways, but rather the two men are two facets of the same person. As Louis is taking the taxi to his family's house at the beginning of the film, he delivers the prologue in his head, but at one moment he speaks out loud the phrase 'dire, seulement dire' ('say, only say'). The prologue reveals not only why Louis is going to see his family, but also that what will transpire in characters' minds and what they will speak out loud will be connected, without being identical. There will be two levels of language in the narrative with a kind of hypertextual relation between inside and outside. And more broadly, the film will function on two registers, with an inside and an outside. Not everything will be spoken aloud. And not all that is spoken aloud will have meaning.

The discourse of both the play and film is composed of many elements that do not make immediate sense. In a reading of Lagarce's play, Catherine Brun describes a 'poetics of detour' ('poétique du détour') (2009: 184), a discursive art that moves away from what looks to be clear meaning towards a somewhere else.[11] As Louis's mother notes when Antoine storms off

---

11 This detour for Brun is similar to classical tragedy in the sense that catastrophic events happen off stage and 'words are used as the final and irreplaceable possibility to die in beauty' (2009: 184). Sarrazac describes the play as an 'aesthetics of the disjointed' (2016: 14).

in anger, 'ils reviennent toujours' ('they always come back'). She is talking about coming back after a spat, but she is also talking about the language of the play which always comes back to where it began even if innumerable moments do not make sense or express a transparent meaning or represent a clearly identifiable signifier. The concept of poetic detour is expressed by the two ways of speaking mentioned: Louis detours from interior to exterior, or from himself to his reflection in the mirror. But in fact, it is not always clear whether a character or their second self is speaking. We never fully know if what characters say are detours from their own interior monologue or vice versa. Detour relates as well to perception and to listening or hearing: in his final emotional speech, Antoine (Louis's brother played by Laurent Stocker) stands in a fixed position to deliver his final words, but the camera shoots him from multiple angles and quickly cuts from one shot to the next, somewhat like a Cubist painting. His speech is lengthy, but the perception of his words is in movement as much as what he – and by extension the other characters – recounts. No one hears anyone in a single predictable manner. Hearing is as much a poetics of detour as speaking.

Could detour be a form of closet, an avoidance of outing? It is never directly articulated (like his impending death), but Louis may well be gay and estranged from his family because of his homosexuality. Despite the absence of articulated homosexuality, there is something queer about the communication. The heteronormativity of the family is not linked to a stable form of discourse that asserts normativity over a queer character, since it is in motion, constantly detoured. In an early scene as all the characters are assembled in the living room, Antoine and his wife talk about their two children, Suzanne is visibly pregnant, and of course Louis's mother has her three children in her house. It might appear that there is an awkward assault on queerness by heteronormativity. But heterosexual childrearing does not fully occupy the discourse in the remainder of the film. Catherine talks about her children, whom

Louis has never met, and about her son Louis, whose name was given in honour of Antoine and Louis's father who has died but also links Louis to her son. Although Louis's possible homosexuality is never actually spoken, Catherine may refer to it when she notes that he does not and will not have children. Later, as he thinks about leaving the house, Louis mentions that 'she' touches him in order to show that she forgives him for 'whatever those crimes might be' and 'those crimes that I am not aware of committing, I regret them, they fill me with remorse'. The spectre of homosexuality and the closet permeates the film, but is never spoken or even affirmed.[12]

Louis may well be a figure for Largarce himself. The arrival of Louis, textually speaking, may interrupt heteronormativity as he seems to bring queer detour to the house on his visit, which itself seems to be a major detour from his life elsewhere. His homosexuality or his illness – possibly AIDS – may be the instigator of this poetics of detour, turning the narrative away from normative expression. During the conversation about children, Louis notes three times that he feels 'mal à l'aise' ('uncomfortable'): there is a discomfort at this moment because of the heteronormative topics being discussed and because of the tacit suggestion that something is wrong with Louis because he is not raising children. Discomfort may be queer in this case, an affect produced by the confrontation between queerness and normativity that resembles a detour from normative comfort.

This discomfort, however, defines the entire narrative as Louis is not the only character who conveys the affect. Antinormative discomfort functions as what Lydie Parisse calls 'un

---

[12] Quebecois director Xavier Dolan's 2016 adaptation of Lagarce's play, much less faithful to the original than Ducastel and Martineau's version, makes Louis's homosexuality central to the film. In their study of the queer time and space of the film, Grandena and Gagné describe a '*queer aesthetic of absence*' (2009: 93, italics in original) and describe Louis's return as 'a forced return to the closet' (95).

acte de résistance aux certitudes assénées par les discours totalitaires' ('an act of resistance against the certitudes asserted by totalitarian discourse') (2018: 1). Those hegemonic discourses could take a number of forms, but the queer act of resistance to the normativity of familial certitude, and especially to the idea of a happy nuclear family, can be characterized as queer. Louis's discomfort is, on one level, a form of awkwardness – in language, in affect, and in interpersonal relations broadly – that inscribes a non-normativity that lingers over the course of the entire narrative.[13] Brun describes the play's 'uncomfortable place of emptiness' as the locus of possibility ('la place inconfortable du vide est aussi celle de la vie, celle des possibles') (2009: 195). What is rendered possible for me is the inscription of a way to be in a family that is not closeted or hidden away as homosexual or non-procreative, but that takes the form of radically unfamiliar discourse and uncomfortable human relationality gesturing towards queer ways to speak and act without delineating them. Ducastel and Martineau's telefilm follows the awkwardness in Lagarce's script as characters often speak in detours, but frequently conveys discomfort or angst on faces in highly visible ways.

The emphasis on 'dire, seulement dire' of the prologue emphasizes that Louis is coming to announce or to say for a second time, regardless of whether he actually did come out previously. It seems likely – or at least possible – that Louis came to see his family to come out as gay at some point. References to Louis not being loved and being absent recur, suggesting that perhaps his homosexuality caused affective problems in or for the family. His younger sister seems sad, and she seems to have missed him during his long absence. His mother asks him how old he is, as if she does not know much about him, perhaps because she has disowned him in her own

---

13 For a discussion of a queer model of awkwardness in neoliberal culture, see Reeser (2017).

mind. Temporality may be suspended for her in part because the current familial interactions take her back in her mind to the return home of the prodigal son to announce his homosexuality. But of course, he does not come out this time either.

This second 'coming out' is displaced from a single character into interactional discourses that are uncomfortable detours that never end, enunciative acts that do not always make sense. To be closeted in discourse can be way to be in a constant state of detour: as one is asked if one is gay, one may skirt around an answer. One might put off coming out until a better moment. As heterosexuals talk about normative sexuality, a gay person may try to avoid discussing the topic. The discomfort in the film does not arise because one person announces that he is gay, rather an interpersonal discomfort is inscribed through a queer character onto an entire series of interactions and speeches that might have been normative, totalitarian discourses without his presence. Even the heterosexual characters are subject to discursive detours, uncomfortable in the way in which they speak. Queer detour and discomfort, in the end, call attention to the normativity that necessitates coming out and to the assumption of transparent meaning and comfort that characterizes heterosexuality. In so doing, *Juste la fin du monde* resembles *Crustacés et coquillages* in which heterosexual closets transpose an epistemology of the closet onto everyone. Both films universalize a trait or a process that might be tagged as queer only, in the service of not isolating queer characters.

New narratives on the horizon: *Théo et Hugo dans le même bateau*

Ducastel and Martineau's *Théo et Hugo dans le même bateau* recasts HIV-AIDS representation in reference to their own earlier AIDS films, particularly *Jeanne et le garçon formidable*.

Unlike with *Juste la fin du monde*, this film's tone is optimistic, and death does not hang over the characters in a heavy-handed way. Unlike in *Jeanne*, no one dies, and unlike in *Félix*, HIV-AIDS is central to the love story, not incidental. Here, HIV-AIDS is a disease that the two main characters can live with together and that creates affective possibility for the two titular men instead of dread, fear of death, or death itself. The film's creative possibility resides, above all, in a radical revision of one of the most foundational Western myths of heterosexual love and loss, the ancient myth of Orpheus and Eurydice. In this section of the chapter, I focus on the directors' queer use of the Orphic myth to open up new narrative options in a way that heterosexual characters may be unable to do, or at least have traditionally been unable to do. By transforming the myth, this sophisticated film continues the directors' earlier reconfigurations of basic human organizational constructs, such as kinship and heterosexuality.

Théo et Hugo concludes on an Orphic note. As the two titular characters leave Théo's studio at dawn just before 6 a.m., Théo (Geoffrey Couët) realizes that he has forgotten his phone and starts to return for it. Hugo (François Nambot) stops him from behind, telling him: 'Si tu te retournes, si tu regardes en arrière, tu perds tout ce que je t'ai promis' ('If you turn around, if you look back, you will lose everything that I have promised you'). The reference, of course, is to Orpheus's losing his beloved Eurydice while bringing her back to earth from the underworld because he ignored Hades's order not to turn back to her until he reached the light of the upper world. But while Orpheus famously looked back and lost his beloved, Théo looks forward, not backward. 'On va de l'avant' ('We are moving forward'), Hugo then tells him. The final shot of the film shows them descending five flights of steps together into the dawn instead of one of them ascending alone without the beloved to the earth's light. With Théo not looking back, the young men can and likely will be together for the long term – as Hugo promised Théo in the previous scene. In an interview published in the French magazine *Têtu*, Martineau remarks that, as he began the script, he 'wanted to work on the [Orpheus] myth'.[14] The film gestures forward to an entirely new interpretation of the story, refusing to look backward on many of the traditional elements of the myth.

Concluding with such an explicit Orphic reference may seem odd in light of the rest of the film. The first seventeen minutes are constituted by explicit sex in the basement of a gay sex club, certainly not part of the tradition of the myth. A key part of the story, too, is that Théo learns that Hugo is HIV+, and because the two had unprotected sex in the club, he seeks preventive treatment at the hospital to destroy any potential virus. The rest of the film treats their budding relationship as they move through Paris on foot, on bicycles, and in the metro, ending on a very optimistic note far removed from the tragedy of Eurydice's double death. The film seemingly rejects the basic elements of this hyper-canonical myth of male–female love as presented by such artists as Ovid, Virgil, Monteverdi, Haydn, Valéry, Gluck, Stravinsky, Rilke, Rodin, Anouilh, and many others. The myth circulates in innumerable popular texts, including Robert Graves's *Greek Myths* (published as *Les Mythes grecs* in numerous editions since 1958) and a 2016 children's version titled *Orphée l'ensorceleur* ('Orpheus the Enchanter'). On screen, director Jean Cocteau made an Orphic trilogy, including the classic 1950 film *Orphée*. Ducastel and Martineau's contribution to the tradition diverges substantially from its predecessors in ways not limited to the sexuality of the main characters: the film does not focus on triumph over death

---

14 He says: 'Quand j'écrivais le scénario, je partais en balade autour de ma maison en Normandie et j'écoutais *L'Orfeo* de Monteverdi. J'ai eu envie de travailler sur ce mythe' (Naselli, 2016) ('As I was writing the script, I would go for walks near my home in Normandy and I would listen to Monteverdi's *Orfeo*. That gave me the desire to create a version of the myth').

or the underworld or on the anguish of the male poet in the face of his human limits.[15] It does not follow theorist Maurice Blanchot's interpretation of the myth as Orpheus's mistake in trying 'to exhaust the infinite' by 'possess[ing]' Eurydice 'while he is destined only to sing about her' (1981: 101). Nor does it seek to establish or reaffirm a male poetic voice as anchored in the loss of the female beloved. What then does this same-sex love story do to the foundational myth?

While homosexuality and the Orphic myth may strike one as incompatible in the twenty-first century, the lengthy literary tradition does not lack same-sex sexuality. The ancient Greek poet Phanocles notes in a fragment that the Thracian women killed Orpheus because he spurned them but loved Calais instead (Hopkinson, 1988: 45–6). After the poet loses his beloved in Ovid's highly influential version in the *Metamorphoses*, he turns to pederasty – much as he had turned to look at his beloved. As the Latin poet writes: 'He set the example for the people of Thrace of giving (*transferre*) his love to tender boys, and enjoying the springtime and first flower of their youth' (1984: 70, 71). The Italian Renaissance humanist Angelo Poliziano continues the Ovidian tradition in his important play *Orfeo* (1480), referring to pederasty as 'the sweetest and mildest love' (2004: 273). Virgil, however, offers an antidote to the Ovidian tradition in *The Georgics*: after his loss, Orpheus does give in to pederasty but remains firmly chaste: 'No thought of love or wedding song could bend his soul' (1999: 255).[16] Ovid's inclusion of 'transferred' love provokes anxiety, is censored, and is condemned in the European middle ages and Renaissance (Crawford, 2010; Ingleheart,

---

15 Sword describes the reception of Orpheus as 'enacting ... the situation, anguished yet articulate, of the modern poet' (1989: 407). See also Strauss (1971); Hassan (1982).
16 Charles Martin translates the passage to maintain the idea of 'transferring' in the original Latin: 'Among the Thracians, he originated / the practice of transferring the affections / to youthful males, plucking

2015; Mills, 2015; Puff, 2006), but then it is largely forgotten in later works.

While no one transfers their love to tender boys, Ducastel and Martineau's film does reopen the largely lost tradition of a male-loving Orpheus. Part of the reason for reopening that tradition is related to the reason why Orpheus turns to boys in the first place. On one level, he cannot have the woman he loves so deeply, so he turns to boys to never 'cheat' on her with another woman. He can still enjoy the physical aspects of sexuality without being with another woman (Makowski, 1996: 29).[17] Ovid writes that Orpheus 'shunned all love of womankind' (1984: 71) because of the bad experience with Eurydice or because he had 'made a promise' (70), either to her or to himself. His poetry subsequently becomes a replacement for lost love, channelled into his lyre and inventing the very idea of poetry as loss. But on another level, his queer turn upends a system of male–female love – resembling what we might today call heteronormativity. In becoming a pederast, Orpheus leaves behind a constraining system of gender and sexuality predicated on the ideal of eternal, true love. The longest portion of Ovid's Orpheus narrative in the *Metamorphoses* is constituted by a series of his songs after the turn to boys: 'But now I need the gentler touch (*leviore lyra*), for I would sing of boys beloved by gods, and maidens inflamed by unnatural love and paying the penalty of their lust' (75, 74). Orpheus turns his back on heavy-handed or normative narratives of

    the first flower / in the brief springtime of their early manhood' (Ovid, 2004: 344). Though the detail is often ascribed to him, Ovid does not invent the turn to pederasty, classicists note, and while Virgil's competing version in *The Georgics* (Book 4) does not register this transformation, it may be aware of references to Orpheus's turn to boys. See Fox (2015); Makowski (1996).

17 Anderson writes that in Ovid 'boy-love ranks far below heterosexual love in terms of affection, mutual concern, and chances for extensive happiness' (1982: 45).

lost love in favour of new lighter narratives, beginning with the story of Jupiter and Ganymede. *Théo et Hugo*, too, refuses the Orphic narrative of eternal heterosexual love in favour of a new narrative of love predicated on potentiality instead of on the necessity of loss. If queer cinema works against the grain of what Nick Davis calls 'epistemic buttresses' of 'normative models of sexuality' (2013: 8), here it is the episteme of the foundational myth that is refused.

In many ways, the film follows Frankfurt School theorist Herbert Marcuse's idea in *Eros and Civilization* that Orpheus is a generative figure opposed to the 'performance principle' (1966: 161). Reason and suppression, he writes, are antagonistic to 'whatever belongs to the sphere of sensuousness, pleasure, impulse' (161). Orpheus recalls 'the experience of a world that is not to be mastered and controlled but to be liberated – a freedom that will release the power of Eros now bound in the repressed and petrified forms of man and nature' (164). Marcuse concludes his discussion with the role of Orpheus's 'homosexuality' in this liberation: 'he rejects the normal Eros, not for an ascetic ideal, but for a fuller Eros [and] he protests against the repressive order of procreative sexuality' (171).[18] Orphic Eros is what Marcuse calls 'the Great Refusal', or 'the negation of *all* order' which 'reveal[s] a new reality, with an order of its own, governed by different principles' (171, italics in original). For Marcuse, it is in aesthetics that the 'reality principle must be sought and validated' (171), and Ovid's version succeeds in serving this function. Ducastel and Martineau's film – I would argue – appropriates and reconfigures elements of the Orphic myth, refusing a normative love story based on loss and repression and crafting a Marcusian 'order' not grounded in the woman's dead body. The film reorders mythic elements and gives them new meaning by queering not so much

---

18 Marcuse theorizes homosexuality but lacks interest in actual homosexuals. On this issue, see Floyd (2009: 140–5).

the characters as much as the traditional narrative elements of the myth themselves, including Ovid's.

Turning the back on Orpheus

If Marcuse reads Ovid's Orpheus narrative as refusal, the cinematic refusal is not strictly speaking a story about refusing the performance principle. While the Ovidian narrative begins with the lovers' wedding and later leads to refusal with Orpheus's transferred love, the opening scene in the film establishes anti-repression first, reversing the entire direction of the classical narrative and frontloading Marcuse's liberating power of Eros. No character ends up in a state of negation since negation is established from the start as the precondition of the narrative. The opening shot follows a middle-aged naked man heading downstairs to the cave-like underworld of the sex club. Here, the underworld is not a space to dominate, but one in which to experience pleasure, corresponding to Marcuse's idea that Orpheus's 'deed … ends the labor of conquest' (162). The scene sets the stage for the rest of the film's 'non-repressive erotic attitude toward reality' (167). Beginning instead of ending with non-repression opens the cinematic narrative up to new textual sequencings and to new gendered possibilities, all free of repressive tradition from the start. For this reason, the striking scene is so very different in content and tone from the love story to come in the rest of the film: it does the labour of establishing a new order that will permit the ensuing love story to be liberated from Orphic convention. With this opener, Hugo and Théo do not have to become pederasts or to 'transfer' their love to males in order to un-repress the reality principle, as Marcuse's Orpheus does. In fact, they are not a pederastic couple at all. The film evokes the possibility to discount it: Théo may seem younger, doing an internship as part of his education, while Hugo has a job as a notary and looks a bit older. But any possible age-based opposition never holds. Most visibly, Théo penetrates Hugo in the sex club, but in a broader sense neither character has an age-based role of any kind. The younger Théo pays for their food, to give but one example. Freed from the constraints of the Ovidian narrative trajectory, pederastic representation does not have to serve the function of refusing sexual normativity. But the liberation also functions more broadly. Sex and gender roles are not predetermined by mythic structure. The opening scene reconfigures the gender order, signalling that neither character will always parallel Orpheus or Eurydice. Théo may not turn to look at Hugo in the final scene, but he does not equal Orpheus in the film overall. Instead, then, after the opening scene, the film recasts Marcuse's Great Refusal in favour of recurring, diffuse refusals that do not force gender or sexual roles on any individual character.

What may be the most mythic element of the film in visual terms is the dramatic change from the scene in the sex club to the outside world. After Hugo and Théo decide to leave the basement together, they quietly ascend the dark, steep stairs, hand-in-hand, to pick up their clothes and pay for their drinks. At first, it may look as though an Orphic Théo is leaving the dark underworld for the upper world. Ovid describes the way up as 'a steep path, indistinct and clouded in pitchy darkness' (1984: 69), and in his book of myths Robert Graves describes 'le sombre passage' (1985: 44), or 'the dark passage' (1957: 112). But in this case, although the passage suggests the mythic movement, no one looks back on the beloved while making his way through the darkness, overturning the Orphic turn and correcting the tragic nature of the myth.

But, in fact, this playful moment comments on the use of the myth itself as Hugo performs infidelity to the mythic topos. They exit the club, and Théo moves along the street but cannot locate Hugo. It appears first as though Hugo has disappeared and that Théo has lost him unexpectedly in the ascent from the basement club.[19] Hugo appears from his hiding place with outstretched arms, like Eurydice as she fell back to Hades. But the gesture is anti-Orphic, evoking a detail to show that the myth will be employed in new ways. As the two lovers leave the hospital after Théo's treatment, they navigate numerous halls, exit the building, and then close a large gate as they leave the enclosed building grounds for the outside world. They close the gate and walk out together, with no turn and no look back, turning a blind eye to the mythic transition from the underworld to earth. Ovid's Orpheus made a promise and turns to boys, but no one here has made a promise to the Orphic tradition. A shot of the two ascending side-by-side from the basement club focuses on their naked buttocks, avoiding reference to genitalia, because this Orphic narrative will resist gendered roles based on sex. No single character will be Orphic or hold a single gender role taken from the myth.

Looking is a recurring action in *Théo et Hugo*, but in ways that transform the infamous look back. During a scene in the metro late in the film as the two characters head to Théo's apartment, they fix their gaze on each other for the duration of the ride from one stop to another. With the ride a kind of spatial transition not unlike Orpheus's ascent, looking upon the other in this case does not lead to the disappearance of the beloved and it is not an act of any one person. As they leave

---

19 In an interview, Martineau offers the following caveat about the use of the Orpheus myth in this scene: 'je n'ai pas voulu sous-entendre que Hugo sortait Théo de l'enfer du sexe pour l'emmener vers l'amour. C'est complètement autre chose, c'est plutôt une image de l'amour' (Naselli, 2016) ('I did not want to suggest that Hugo led Théo up from some kind of sexual hell toward love. It is something else entirely. Instead, it is an image of love'). This idea of mythic elements as 'images of love' corresponds closely to my take on the film here.

the metro station, Théo gratuitously turns and faces Hugo in the exit door, reinforcing the idea that looking back on the beloved at the exit of an underground space does not have to end tragically. Their initial sexual act in the club emerges out of an orgiastic scene with indistinct bodies and develops into sex between the two of them, where they gaze upon each other in an exaggerated way, each shown as if in a spotlight or halo. The heightened homoerotic gaze serves the function of transforming the Orphic look back, its recurrence replacing the single tragic error with an ongoing image of connection. If Orpheus looks back because he was, according to Ovid, 'afraid that she might fail him' (1984: 69), here the characters' gaze is one of faith in connection instead of anxiety over human loss. Conversely, not looking is not the issue that it was for Orpheus who feared not looking at Eurydice. As they begin having sex in the club, Hugo says that keeping his eyes closed helps him be with Théo. His first words of the film reveal that not looking can be a form of presence and intimacy, not a cause of anxiety about potential loss.

The film dismantles the topos of Eurydice following Orpheus to the light of earth. Virgil notes that Proserpine imposed the condition of her 'following behind' (1999: 253), and as she falls back she is 'stretching towards [him] strengthless hands' (255), an image taken up by many other purveyors of the story. In a different register, leading by hand-holding plays a key role in the repositioning of the two figures: Hugo takes Theo's hand as they go into the room with the intern at the hospital, for instance, but it is a gesture of possibility, not loss. The concept of leading the other is removed from gender: neither equals Orpheus leading his beloved since no one always leads the other. Much of their walking is side-by-side instead of with one person following the other. While walking along the street, they realize that they are not heading in any direction, and Hugo says to Théo: 'Je te suis' ('I am following you') to which Théo responds: 'Moi aussi, je te suis. On va tourner en rond' ('I am following you too. We're going in circles'). Random circulation replaces the spatial linearity of the myth, the movement from the underworld to the upper world. In some cases, the camera follows the two characters as they walk next to each other, with the viewer placed in Eurydice's position, but neither are we lost by any character's turn, further distancing the mythic roles from any single body. Anyone, including the viewer, can appropriate a mythic position. Numerous sombre passageways suggest the path to the upper world from Hades: the long halls of the hospital, the hallway leading to Théo's studio, the streets on the way to an all-night kebab shop, a stairway leading from one sidewalk up to another, and more broadly the streets of Paris in the middle of the night. There is no single movement to the upper world as the narrative turns in spatial circles unfaithful to the myth. Instead, the entire film and its night-time setting, ending as the sun begins to rise, embodies the path to the light of the upper world from Hades, making time, not space, the new narrative passageway.

If time takes over space's role, the film removes time's mythic function as well as space's. At certain moments, the screen displays the time of night. We are made aware of time and its passage, and the film ends precisely at 6 a.m. on Monday morning, which the viewer learns when Hugo tells Théo to stop and look at his phone and the time changes from 5:59.[20] But the point is not that time is passing or that time is regulating the characters' actions, rather that time exists in a queer mode. For Marcuse, the Orphic mode refuses 'the inevitably repressive work-world' (1966: 195), a key element of unrepression since labour and work help keep unfettered sexuality at bay. Here the characters resist a temporality that would in a repressive order be

20 The use of real time in Paris evokes Agnès Varda's *Cléo de 5 à 7* (*Cléo from 5 to 7*) (1962), as suggested in part by the rhyme 'Théo'/'Cléo'. The film's French title refers to Jacques Rivette's *Céline et Julie vont en bateau* (*Celine and Julie Go Boating*) (1974).

defined by work and work time, a Sunday night preparation for Monday morning work. While discussing their jobs, Hugo tells Théo that he is a notary but that he is not working on this particular Monday and that he has some freedom from normal work hours. What Marcuse calls 'play' replaces normative labour: the film is largely made up of random movement, conversations without function or goal, flirtation, and other playful elements, affirming Marcuse's idea that 'play is *unproductive* and *useless* precisely because it cancels the repressive and exploitative traits of labor' (195, italics in original).

Telling stories of gender

After Orpheus becomes a pederast in Ovid, he sings about 'boys beloved by gods, and maidens inflamed by unnatural love' before the Maenad women dismember him. There are no songs per se in the film, unlike in *Jeanne et le garçon formidable* and *Crustacés et coquillages*, but the parallel with Orphic song is embedded in the form of encounters with three characters: the hospital intern that takes care of Théo's potential infection, the Syrian immigrant working at the kebab shop, and the maid taking the metro to work. As the two main characters leave the hospital, they remark that there seem to be only two types of people at this time of night, women and gay men, or as Théo puts it in terms reminiscent of Ovid's boys and maidens: 'La nuit appartient aux femmes et aux pédés' ('The night belongs to women and homos'). Hugo and Théo do not recount the characters' stories, but these non-normative narratives of people functioning very late at night or very early in the morning have the valence of Orpheus's songs. They do not prove or reveal poetic virtuosity or replace lost love, as Orpheus's songs do, but instead they suggest stories about other types of people in terms of profession, gender, age, and ethnicity. The competent intern is assigned the night shift at the hospital and clearly knows much about HIV. The Syrian man talks suggestively about the lack of freedom in Syria where he used to live, and the woman in the metro talks about her need to work because of a lack of a sufficient pension and refers to her past life of amorous excess. The maid in the metro mentions that she is from Yvetot, a Norman village known as the hometown of novelist Annie Ernaux whose work famously bridges the gap between sociological descriptions of lived daily life and poetic prose. Her novels *Journal du dehors* (*Exteriors*) (1993) and *La Vie extérieure, 1993–1999* (*Things Seen*), in particular, describe snippets of daily life, many of which take place on the metro or the RER (suburban commuter train). As this connection intimates, there is a quotidian naturalness to the maid's narrative – as there is to the other two narratives – all three of which convey something suggestively poetic behind or around the encounters in the hospital, the kebab shop, and the metro.

The three representative encounters differ from the mythic tradition in an important way: these poetic moments are not created by Orpheus. If – as Sword writes – 'Orpheus' transformation into the paradigmatic modern poet takes place only, so to speak, over Eurydice's dead body' (1989: 409), or if in Ovid Orpheus goes on to sing stories of boys and maidens after – or because of – the death of his beloved, in the film the poetic moments do not come from the poet after the death of the beloved but from the actual individuals. The maid on the metro, above all, is a figure of a poetic storyteller, an Annie Ernaux who tells her own story through relations to the 'outside' world. Instead of proving Orpheus's poetic virtuosity, these external narratives create a sense of shared experience between the two main characters. If Orpheus's songs convey new kinds of amorous metamorphoses that do not exist in his own story or in his life and love with Eurydice, these three narratives contribute to producing the relation between the two lovers, as a narrative form of Marcusian Eros. After the woman on the metro leaves, the two characters stare at each other for a long time, making clear that looking at each other does not mean that they will be lost but that they are creating something by watching each other. Yet, the look replaces the woman character – literally, since she was sitting where Théo is now sitting. They are not looking backwards onto a previous narrative, but forward towards a potential one with new, common experiences. Their metamorphosis is a connective narrative act in itself, buttressed by other narrative voices instead of only the male poet's own songs based on absence and loss. In fact, the metro scene highlights Ernaux's idea that the self is defined dialogically and that the inner self and external interactions cannot be separated, as summed up by her epigraph from Rousseau in *Journal du dehors*: 'Notre *vrai* moi n'est pas tout entier en nous' (1993: 9, italics in original) ('Our *true* self is not entirely in ourselves').[21] The film is in part a story of encounters with people that the characters do not know but that help define them through random meetings. This inclusion of non-Orphic voices serves Ernaux's political aim, as expressed in *Retour à Yvetot* (*Return to Yvetot*): 'écrire littérairement dans la langue de tous' (2013: 34) ('to write literarily in the language of everyone') in order to 'détruire des hiérarchies' (34) ('destroy hierarchies'). The narrative hierarchy established by the myth (male poet and his poetic subjects) is destroyed in part by the inclusion of three voices on their own terms – voices that take the viewer beyond the singleness of one love story into the idea of a dialogic love narrative.

More broadly, however, the move away from a single male Orphic voice re-visions Eurydice's role in the tradition and offers a feminist way out of Western culture's obsession with the silent woman whose loss gives a poetic voice to the male

---

21 On this key aspect of Ernaux's writing, including the idea of a 'je transpersonnel' ('transpersonal I'), see for instance Boehringer (2000); Hugueny-Léger (2009); Ionescu (2001); Johnson (1999).

poet. Early Greek sources of the Orpheus myth leave her anonymous (Bremmer, 1991: 14–17). In Ovid, Eurydice says only one word: 'Farewell' ('Vale') (1984: 69; 70), as she dies her second death. If losing the beloved woman is to lose the ability to conquer death, or to lose the phallus itself, Eurydice may not even be a woman at all but a placeholder for an Orphic principle. Blanchot takes her as 'the limit of what art can attain, concealed behind a name and covered by a veil' (1981: 99) – his own version of the eternal feminine. This sexism is also predicated on traits of hegemonic masculinity: Orpheus attempts to triumph over death like other heroes, he wants to possess Eurydice, and his poetic oeuvre seeks to replace the absent woman. As an uncaring man, he may be blamed for Eurydice's second death, and revised versions of the myth give her a voice to challenge Orpheus, including H. D.'s poem 'Eurydice', Adrienne Rich's poem 'I Dream I'm the Death of Orpheus', Margaret Atwood's poem 'Orpheus 1', or Sarah Ruhl's play *Eurydice*. In French letters, Camille Laurens's wrote a short play, *Eurydice ou l'homme de dos* (*Eurydice or the Man from Behind*) (2012) and Michèle Sarde a novel, *Histoire d'Eurydice pendant la remontée* (*The Story of Eurydice's Return to the Upper World*) (1991). In such cases, Eurydice may have her own poetic voice or she may challenge Orpheus for his actions or for what Virgil's Eurydice calls his 'dreadful madness' (*furor*) (1999: 255, 254), but there is still no full exit from the mythic construct of male poetic gifts and male control over the absent female body through art. *Théo et Hugo dans le même bateau* opts out of that gendered story with a male–male couple and reboots the myth in a way that feminist writings that give Eurydice a voice cannot do. It allows the myth to neither lay blame for the look back nor produce stable gender constructs that assign traits or roles to men and to women. In this sense, the same-sex couple does not stand in for homosexuality or rewrite the myth as about two gay characters, but rather rewrites the myth as a story not necessarily related to gender.

Homosexuality queers the gender binarism produced over time by the myth, affirming sociologist Pierre Bourdieu's idea in *Masculine Domination* that homosexuality has great potential to unseat symbolic gender domination and help establish a new representational gender order (2001: 118–24). The new narrative is a new voice – part of Ernaux's 'language of everyone' that has the effect of breaking an ancient gender hierarchy apart and opening up the myth beyond gender fixity.

Turning loss and death

The topos of losing the beloved is repeated in the film, but not as something that happens once and for all. As he heads towards the hospital, Théo tells Hugo that he does not want to be accompanied, and the two separate. But Hugo appears later at the hospital as Théo is waiting to see a doctor and attends the consultation because he does not want Théo to be alone. Later, the two have an argument related to who was responsible for their unprotected sex, and an angry Hugo begins to leave Théo. But they reconcile. Again, Hugo leaves Théo in the final scene in the studio apartment, but then returns. The repetition of leaving-returning transforms the idea of love as loss or as total absence into the idea of loss as a regular, recurring part of a human relation and not mythic in stature.

Closely related to the film's portrayal of loss is the transformation of the relation to death. At bottom, the story recounts Théo's reaction to having had unprotected sex with an HIV+ partner, which he first imagines as a possible death sentence. But the hospital worker and Hugo convince him over the course of the film that the disease can be conquered, in the unlikely event that he has even contracted it in the first place, and Hugo promises to escort him through any treatment towards a normal happy life defined as a future together. With the narrative, broadly speaking, composed of a death sentence that is subsequently recuperated (in Théo's mind at least), the character of Théo reinscribes the figure of Eurydice as having never been in a real life-or-death situation to begin with. Death is not an absolute in the film, not what must be conquered by returning from Hades, but is instead a purveyor of potentiality and a springboard to love. Marcuse writes that Orpheus reconciles Eros and Thanatos, that he is 'committed to the underworld and to death', and that he does not 'convey a "mode of living"' (1966: 165). Such is the relation that the two characters develop not in spite of – but because of – HIV-AIDS, meaning that the virus incarnates the mixture of Eros and Thanatos and rejects death as fully negative. In a sense, the film depicts Orpheus when he is reunited with Eurydice in Hades after his own death – the final element of some versions of the story, including Jean Anouilh's French play *Eurydice* (1941). Ovid describes their reunion: 'Here now side by side they walk; now Orpheus follows her as she precedes, now goes before her, now may in safety look back upon his Eurydice' (1984: 125). Hugo and Théo, too, walk this way, alternate following each other, look in safety upon each other, but they do so in life, not death. That they follow each other ('Je te suis') suggests that they have already landed in the same place as in Ovid, but without having to go through the entire myth. Their equality does not require them to have died and to be dead in Hades. A key representation of the mixture of Eros and Thanatos is the St. Martin Canal in northeast Paris along which they run at one point for no real reason. As they stop, Théo notes their 'romantic sprint'. The canal evokes a key sign of the barrier between life and death and between the living and the dead that Orpheus has to cross to regain his beloved – the River Styx. Much of act 3 of Claudio Monteverdi's opera *L'Orfeo* (1607), for instance, is devoted to the poet's attempt to cross the river. In Virgil's version, Eurydice vanishes and Charon the ferryman did not 'suffer him again to pass the barrier of the marsh' (1999: 255), and the River Styx signifies the limit behind which Orpheus cannot go again to rescue his beloved a second time. But in this case, the canal is a boundary that the characters move along, not across, because there is no linear crossing, no sense that death is an absolute outside the realm of Eros. Death does not belong to a single person nor is death the fault of a single person. Rather, the potential for death is communal, not a fate reserved for the woman: Hugo and Théo both admit that they are responsible for not using a condom, with no single person to blame, unlike Orpheus who unambiguously is to blame for looking back. In a notable image in the hospital, Théo takes pills to prevent viral transmission and the medical kit includes a madeleine, the Proustian symbol of memory, to take with his pills. Its ingestion does not bring back the memory of the mythic intertext however, but ignores it, forgets it in favour of a new narrative defined by potential death and its link to Eros.

The film tells another story related to death that moves in a new direction: it participates in bringing Jacques Demy, Ducastel's mentor, back from the underworld by virtue of extending his Orphic work into a new cinematic direction. The film refers back to one of Demy's lesser-known films *Parking* (1985) about a French rock star named Orphée who loses his Eurydice.[22] The film recounts the story in a modern setting, including references to same-sex love through the character of Calaïs, Orpheus's lover in Phanocles's ancient version, played in the film by Laurent Malet, who had played the role of Roger Bataille in Rainer Werner Fassbinder's queer film *Querelle* (1982). The two men kiss in *Parking*, and Orphée twice sings the song 'Entre vous deux' ('Between you two'), which centres on his heart swinging between two people ('mes deux enfants de l'amour'; 'my two children of love') and culminates in 'Comment choisir? Pourquoi choisir?' ('How to choose? Why choose?').

---

22 The film is in turn in dialogue with Cocteau's *Orphée* (1950), which lacks explicit queer elements. Cocteau's Orpheus, Jean Marais, plays the role of Hadès in Demy's film. On this link, see Waldron (2015: 100).

Calaïs admits to himself that he is jealous of Orpheus's relation to women.[23] For Waldron, the film juxtaposes heterosexuality 'within the hellish subterranean universe' with same-sex desire 'in the comparatively idealistic upper-world' (2015: 104). Demy's Orpheus has in a sense conquered or moved beyond the constraints of the underworld by virtue of having been there and come back to a place where he can be partially queer – not unlike Marcuse's Orpheus. Waldron cites Demy: 'il faut réinventer le romantisme, réapprendre à aimer' (2015: 103) ('romanticism must be reinvented and we must relearn how to love'). Ducastel and Martineau appropriate and transform this idea, extending it by means of rendering homosexual love – not bisexual love – a new form of Orphic love. In so doing, Hugo and Théo out the queer mythic elements much more than *Parking* does. Demy's version may have brought bisexuality back into the story, but the basic elements of the myth remain largely intact despite the new setting and the appearance of Calaïs. Hugo and Théo's homosexuality queers Demy's Orphic myth in a way that transcends sexuality per se in favour of same-sex love as full-on potentiality and as reinvented romanticism.

Because Demy died of complications from HIV-AIDS and Hugo is HIV+ in the film, it is difficult not to link Hugo and Demy. The *garçon* in *Jeanne et le garçon formidable* is played by Demy's son Mathieu Demy, evoking the possibility that the content of the film pertains to the director. For Hugo to embody potentiality with respect to love and death in an era when the illness can be treated and lived with is to open up the possibility of a reference to Demy's illness. If the illness evokes the spectre of death, Demy is retroactively made a spectre, a kind of Eurydice both lost and returned at the same time by

---

23 Waldron writes: 'More than any other Demy film, *Parking* depicts a configuration of love and desire that is neither monogamous nor exclusively heterosexual' (2015: 103). On Demy's work as queer, see Waldron (2009: 64–6, 146–9). On the 'Demy revival' in recent queer film, see Rees-Roberts (2008: 109–12).

the Orphic film. But he is also a lost Orpheus whose cinema sings songs that remain present in the twenty-first century as the film's hopefulness vis-à-vis the illness resurrects Demy's cinematic songs and inscribes them into a new narrative.

Fragmented bodies

One of the most well-known parts of the Orphic story is the destruction of the poet's body into pieces. The Maenads celebrating Bacchic rites rip his body into pieces because they desire him and are frustrated that he is not willing to love them erotically, either because he is devoted to Eurydice or because he has become a pederast. Ovid writes that 'the poet's limbs lay scattered all around' (1984: 123) and the poet's head famously floats along a stream singing until Orpheus's 'shade fled beneath the earth' (125). No one's body is fragmented in this way in the film, but it does make reference to corporeal fragmentation in the final scene. Hugo asks Théo to take off his clothes, and as he stands there naked, Hugo begins to describe his body part by part, including his ear, nipples, stomach, penis, and testicles. Hugo fragments his lover's body by describing its parts, but he then reassembles it back into a fully clothed body as Théo gets dressed so they can go out for breakfast. Fragmentation is not the result of jealous women's punishment for pederasty, but rather is part of an incorporation into a corporeal Eros. During this corporeal moment, Théo stands naked explaining to Hugo why he has an odd cell phone number. He had to change his number because of his father who was calling him in part to harass him with homophobic rants. The homophobia of the Maenads – or in contextual terms, their violently anti-pederastic attitude – is transferred onto Théo's father, and the concept of fragmentation is transferred from its link to homophobia onto Eros. Fragmentation, then, embodies a story about potential Eros instead of death: Hugo tells Théo how much he likes his body parts, such that fragmentation produces eroticism instead of representing its impossibility. Hugo's fragmentation corresponds to Marcuse's idea of a resexualization of the body in the reality principle and its result, 'a reactivation of all erotogenic zones' and 'a resurgence of pregenital polymorphous sexuality' (1966: 201). The penis is one body part mentioned by Hugo, but one among many, making the 'decline of genital supremacy' (201) a reality. A queer polymorphous fragmentation is also a symbolic mechanism for potentiality. Orpheus's bodily destruction is not the end of his life, but Théo's fragmented body points to the beginning of a love relationship whose future is clear but also yet to be determined. Marcuse takes Orpheus's dismemberment as punishment for 'the establishment of a very different order' (170), but here the fragmentation affirms a new order in which two people do not have to follow normative myths of sexuality in the first place.

Erotic fragmentation has another representational function: it parallels the film's fragmentation of the Orphic story. Corporeal fragmentation does not end the film's narrative – as it ends Orpheus's life – but rather reveals how the ancient narrative has now, at the end of the film, been recast as pieces. Those pieces – as should now be clear – have come to constitute the film's narrative. The concept of fragmentation is transferred to narrative, with the fragmentation of the myth functioning as the renewal of the myth itself. The scene emphasizes potentiality in Théo and Hugo's relationship, but it also indicates the potential for new ways to rewrite mythic constructs for new ways of living, loving, and being.

The horizon of the upper world

With its suggestion that there is an optimistic future for the two characters and for the use of myth, the film considers queerness not as disruption or anti-social, but as potentiality itself. José Muñoz takes up Marcuse's idea of refusal in *Cruising Utopia* and considers him as a queer theorist: 'Queerness ... is more than just sexuality. It is this great refusal of a performance principle that allows the human to feel and know not only our work and our pleasure but also our selves and others' (2009: 135). This queerness is aesthetic too, and such an aesthetic 'can potentially function like a great refusal because art manifest[s] itself in such a way that the political imagination can spark new ways of perceiving and acting on a reality that is itself potentially changeable' (135). I take the film as a radically new perception of the Orphic myth, which has always been changeable and changed to a certain extent but usually while maintaining elements taken as structural and necessary. Muñoz takes Andy Warhol's art as an example of 'queer utopian aesthetics' (135), but for me it is *Théo et Hugo* that is imbued with such an aesthetic. Muñoz describes his own methodology as 'a backward glance that enacts a future vision' (4) – a phrase, needless to say, that suggests the Orpheus narrative. It is not the case that Orpheus's backward glance ends the love story, but in a queer aesthetic, it looks towards a new utopian future and a new narrative of love.

The final scene of the film embodies what Muñoz argues that queerness can be, 'a structuring and educated mode of desiring that allows us to see and feel beyond the quagmire of the present' (1). What interests him is 'a forward-dawning queerness' (21) or a 'horizon' (19). From this perspective, then, the film is not about same-sex love at all, but about seeing a queer mode of loving Orphically. As a result, the end of the film gestures towards newness itself. It is another world that the film wants to move towards, not the other world of the underworld. The end of the film allegorizes forward-dawningness as Hugo leaves to head home and Théo opens the only window in his studio apartment. The view over Paris is the dawn, literally, as a new day is beginning (plate 3). All Orphic reconfigurations can now be seen as the dawn of the dawn. Théo looks out on the horizon of the city because he is looking out on the queer horizon of potentiality. There is no need to get Eurydice to the light or to the dawn. That is why Hugo has to be elsewhere during this cinematic moment: the dawn cannot be the dawn of a relationship or the dawn that one lover romantically shows his lover in the window. Not turning its back on humans, dawn is about futurity itself. More than any other of Ducastel and Martineau's films, I would argue, *Théo et Hugo* embodies a forward-looking queer dawn that reconfigures not only melancholic queer cultural representations and the history of HIV-AIDS but also French queer film before it. Neither a comedic or simple love story, the film brings the ancient myth along with other elements to create a queer world that shines on the horizon in a new way.

A new day: *Haut perchés*

Ducastel and Martineau's *Haut perchés*, translated as *Don't Look Down* (literally, 'Perched High'), which came out three years after *Théo et Hugo*, ends with a horizon, though this time not in the context of a gay love story. The five characters of the film (four queer or gay men and one woman) end up looking out over the city of Paris from the balcony doors of the apartment where the entire film has taken place, from the twenty-eighth floor. The directors film the characters from outside, such that the sunset is reflected in the glass doors of the balcony (plate 4); the visual effect emphasizes that the characters together embody a new horizon linked to eroticism, desire, and love. The five characters spend the night together in this apartment and a man with whom they have all had an erotic relation of some kind is locked in the bedroom, likely chained down. Each character, one by one, enters the bedroom and does something presumably violent that the viewer cannot fully understand but hears echoes of. The final character to enter, Lawrence (Lawrence Valin), comes out of the room and gives a flowery, literary speech about the purity of his love for this man and his eventual realization that the man was in fact a void, that he saw only himself in the man, and that he was just a reflection of his own subjectivity ('I was reflected in him. Nothing more'). The reflection in the glass door allegorizes his idea that one's subjectivity is reflected in someone else and mirrored back. Images of the other necessarily create who we imagine ourselves to be, including in terms of gender and sexuality, and domination by the other may reflect a desire to be defined by them.

But the reflection does not remain one, for the film ends by projecting the characters out into the space of the city. Once Lawrence finishes his monologue, he notes to the others where in the city of Paris he lives. Each of the other characters does the same thing, indicating where they live, with the film projecting the characters out from autoreflection into the city space itself. The urban space functions as a sign of a new way to think about intersubjectivity, one not based on a blind notion of love or eroticism or based on domination of or by the other. There is a horizon into which the characters will enter, or more precisely, there is a horizon of love and desire possible outside the constraints of this form of love and eros. Lawrence notes that he did with the man what they had all decided to do, presumably finish him off after a series of torturous acts by the other four characters. As is the case with *Théo et Hugo*, here love is opened up to a new form. This connection between the two films is emphasized by virtue of the fact that the actors who played Hugo and Théo (Nambot; Couët) also play two of the characters here, Louis and Marius. Early on, Marius touches Louis in a flirtatious manner and nothing comes of it, as if to suggest that this story will not be a gay love story as in the previous film, but a very different story still related to love and desire.

What precisely this form of love or desire is never becomes clear. It is described as 'perverse' and we hear something like chains from the bedroom. The characters' stories suggest that it may not even be the same person that they go to see in the bedroom: some characters think that he talks loudly to them, others that he whispers to them. It may not be a specific person in the first place. Rather, it may be the embodiment of unequal relationality itself between two people with respect to desire. Each of the characters has their own speech in which they recount details of their affair based on inequality in some way, but the specifics of that relation differ.

The claustrophobic apartment setting and the focus on power dynamics suggest the film's relation to other narratives. In German director Rainer Fassbinder's film *The Bitter Tears of Petra von Kant* (1972), a sadomasochistic relationship between two women falls apart when another woman enters the scene, and the film is composed of a series of long takes in a single domestic space, much like this film. It is difficult not to see Ducastel and Martineau's theatrical film as channelling Jean-Paul Sartre's well-known existentialist play *Huis clos* (*No Exit*) (1944). Ducastel notes in an interview on the DVD that the script is not based on this play directly, but that there is perhaps an 'unconscious' influence on the film (Ducastel and Martineau, 2019). While the claustrophobic setting of *Haut perchés* resembles the confined space of *Huis clos*, the famous line from Sartre's play that 'hell is others' applies to the man in the bedroom. The characters may be victims of existentialist 'bad faith' as they refused to accept that they should take control of their subjectivities since they are 'condemned to be free' (Sartre, 1948). The five of them have ended up in situations in which they might not have accepted their existentialist freedom in love and did not take agency as desiring subjects, along the lines of Sartrian existentialism. But the opposite is true as well: the characters collectively reject the very idea that 'hell is others', or at least that hell is the man in the bedroom. The end of the film, then, gestures towards a form of optimistic futurity not based on the hell of relationality and not located in a space that seems like a prison cell, but represented by the dawn over Paris.

In this case, what is developed in place of existentialist relationality is equality and fraternity. *Haut perchés* is structured around a meal that the characters are loosely preparing to eat together, and when they arrive at the dessert course, they end up with an apple tart in front of them to cut into pieces. A discussion ensues around how to cut the tart and whether to cut it into five or six pieces, in other words whether to include the person in the bedroom. Mathematical solutions are proposed because the characters refuse to cut the tart in six pieces, which would be easier to do. The characters are invested in an equal part or portion for each of them, but they reject the man in the bedroom's inclusion in that equality, not allowing him his piece of the pie. The idea of equality and fraternity implies, in particular, putting aside sexual orientation. At one moment, the characters turn on music and turn down the lights to dance. The relations between the characters suggest that orientation is not clearly defined: it is true that the male characters' relations with the man in the bedroom might seem to be defined as 'gay', but the category of homosexuality is not an expressed part of these characters' relations. Their equality is based on lacking explicit or expressed orientation. It is not fully clear if the male characters are gay or not. The man in the bedroom does not have a piece of the equality pie because his approach to sexuality is different from theirs. *Haut perchés* constructs a queer relationality that rejects the stability of sexual relationality as organizing principle – the form left for dead in the bedroom. In a sense, too, the film queers Ducastel and Martineau's oeuvre to date, offering a way to be with others that differs from the inventive homosexual relations of *Théo et Hugo dans le même bateau*, *Crustacés et coquillages*, *Drôle de Félix*, and *Ma vraie vie à Rouen*. The dawn on the horizon looks forward to queer film with relationality not necessarily defined by 'homosexuality', but as unchained queer forms whose future remains to be determined.

References

Anderson, W. S. (1982), 'The Orpheus of Virgil and Ovid: *flebile nescio quid*', in John Warden, ed., *Orpheus: The Metamorphoses of a Myth*, Toronto, University of Toronto Press, pp. 25–50.

Archer, Neil (2013), *The French Road Movie: Space, Mobility, Identity*, New York, Berghahn Books.

Arroyo, José (2001), 'Drole de Felix', *Sight and Sound*, 11, 1, 47–8.

Blanchot, Maurice (1981), *The Gaze of Orpheus, and Other Literary Essays*, trans. Lydia Davis, Barrytown, Station Hill Press.

Boehringer, Monika (2000), 'Paroles d'autrui, paroles de soi: *Journal du dehors* d'Annie Ernaux', *Etudes Françaises*, 36, 2, 131–48.

Boisson, Jean (1988), *Le Triangle rose: La Déportation des homosexuels*, Paris, R. Laffront.

Boulligny, Arnaud, ed. (2018), *Les Homosexuel.le.s en France: Du bûcher aux camps de la mort*, Paris, Editions Tirésias.

Bourdieu, Pierre (2001), *Masculine Domination*, trans. Richard Nice, Stanford, Stanford University Press.

Boyle, Claire (2012), 'An Ethical Queer Cinema? Hypervisibility and the Alienated Gay Gaze in Ducastel and Martineau's *Ma vraie vie à Rouen*', *Modern & Contemporary France*, 20, 1, 53–69.

Bremmer, Jan Nicolaas (1991), 'Orpheus: From Guru to Gay', in Philippe Borgeaud, ed., *Orphisme et Orphée*, Geneva, Droz, pp. 13–30.

Brun, Catherine (2009), 'Jean-Luc Lagarce et la poétique du détour: L'Exemple de *Juste la fin du monde*', *Revue d'histoire litteraire de la France*, 109, 1, 183–96.

Catullus (1921), *Catullus, Tibullus and Pervigilium Veneris*, London, William Heinemann.

Chrétien de Troyes (2015), *The Complete Story of the Grail: Chrétien de Troye's Perceval and its Continuations*, trans. Nigel Bryant, Cambridge, Brewer.

Crawford, Katherine (2010), *The Sexual Culture of the French Renaissance*, Cambridge and New York, Cambridge University Press.

Davis, Nick (2013), *The Desiring-Image: Gilles Deleuze and Contemporary Queer Cinema*, Oxford and New York, Oxford University Press.

Ducastel, Olivier and Jacques Martineau (2011), 'Avant-propos', in Rémi Lange, *Journal d'Omelette: Suivi d'un dossier de réactions au film et d'un entretien en 2011 sur le parcours de Rémi Lange depuis 1992*, Paris, ErosOnyx, pp. 5–8.

Ducastel, Olivier and Jacques Martineau (2019), 'Rencontre avec Jacques Martineau et Olivier Ducastel', *Haut perchés*, Epicentre Films, DVD.

Eribon, Didier (2004), *Insult and the Making of the Gay Self*, trans. Michael Lucey, Durham, NC, Duke University Press.

Ernaux, Annie (1993), *Journal du dehors*, Paris, Gallimard.

Ernaux, Annie (2013), *Retour à Yvetot*, Paris, Editions du Mauconduit.

Floyd, Kevin (2009), *The Reification of Desire: Toward a Queer Marxism*, Minneapolis, University of Minnesota Press.

Foucault, Michel (1978), *The History of Sexuality: An Introduction*, I, trans. Robert Hurley, New York, Vintage Books.

Foucault, Michel (1997), 'Sex, Power, and the Politics of Identity', in Paul Rabinow, ed., *The Essential Works of Foucault 1954–1984, Volume 1, Ethics: Subjectivity and Truth*, trans. Robert Hurley et al., New York, New Press, pp. 163–73.

Fox, Matthew (2015), 'The Bisexuality of Orpheus', in Mark Masterson, Nancy Sorkin Rabinowitz, and James Robson, eds, *Sex in Antiquity: Exploring Gender and Sexuality in the Ancient World*, London and New York, Routledge, pp. 335–51.

Franklin, James (2015), *The Science of Conjecture: Evidence and Probability before Pascal*, Baltimore, Johns Hopkins University Press.

Gavillet, Isabelle (2018), '*Moi, Pierre Seel, déporté homosexuel*, Carrière et fortune d'un témoignage', in Arnaud Boulligny, ed., *Les Homosexuel.le.s en France: Du bûcher aux camps de la mort*, Paris, Tirésias, pp. 171–89.

Grandena, Florian (2009), 'Zooming In, Coming Out: Languages in Olivier Ducastel and Jacques Martineau's *Ma vraie vie à Rouen/ The True Story of My Life in Rouen* (2003)', *Studies in French Cinema*, 9, 1, 75–86.

Grandena, Florian and Pascal Gagné (2009), 'Xavier Dolan's Backward Cinema: Straight Spaces, Queer Temporality, and Genealogical Interruptions in *Tom at the Farm* and *It's Only the End of the World'*, in Andrée Lafontain, ed., *ReFocus: The Films of Xavier Dolan*, Edinburgh, Edinburgh University Press, pp. 80–98.

Graves, Robert (1957), *Greek Myths*, I, New York, George Braziller.

Graves, Robert (1985), *Les Mythes grecs*, Paris, Fayard.

Hassan, Ihab (1982), *The Dismemberment of Orpheus: Toward a Postmodern Literature*, Madison, University of Wisconsin Press.

Hopkinson, Neil, ed. (1988), *A Hellenistic Anthology*, Cambridge, Cambridge University Press.

Hugueny-Léger, Elise (2009), *Annie Ernaux, une poétique de la transgression*, Oxford and New York, Peter Lang.

Ingleheart, Jennifer (2015), 'The Invention of (Thracian) Homosexuality: The Ovidian Orpheus in the English Renaissance', in Jennifer Ingleheart, ed., *Ancient Rome and the Construction of Modern Homosexual Identities*, Oxford, Oxford University Press, pp. 56–73.

Ionescu, Mariana (2001), '*Journal du dehors* d'Annie Ernaux: "je est un autre"', *The French Review*, 74, 5, 934–43.

Johnson, Warren (1999), 'The Dialogic Self: Language and Identity in Annie Ernaux', *Studies in 20th & 21st Century Literature*, 23, 2, doi.org/10.4148/2334-4415.1468.

Lagabrielle, Renaud (2016), 'Représentations (dés-)enchantées du sida: *Jeanne et le garçon formidable*', *Revue critique de fixxion française contemporaine*, 12, 153–63.

Lagarce, Jean-Luc (2018), *Only the End of the World*, trans. Lucie Tiberghien, in Arcola Queer Collective, eds, *Global Queer Plays*, London, Oberon Books.

Laurens, Camille (2012), 'Eurydice ou l'homme de dos', in *Guerres et paix. Huit pièces courtes*, Paris, L'avant-scène théâtre, pp. 111–26.

Le Bitoux, Jean (2002), *Les Oubliés de la mémoire*, Paris, Hachette Littératures.

McGonagle, Joseph (2007), 'Gently Does It: Ethnicity and Cultural Identity in Olivier Ducastel and Jacques Martineau's *Drôle de Félix* (2000)', *Studies in European Cinema*, 4, 1, 21–33.

Makowski, John F. (1996), 'Bisexual Orpheus: Pederasty and Parody in Ovid', *The Classical Journal*, 92, 1, 25–38.

Marcuse, Herbert (1966), *Eros and Civilization: A Philosophical Inquiry into Freud*, London and New York, Routledge.

Marks, Laura U. (1998), 'Video Haptics and Erotics', *Screen*, 39, 4, 331–48.

Marks, Laura U. (2000), *The Skin of the Film: Intercultural Cinema, Embodiment, and the Senses*, Durham, NC, Duke University Press.

Mills, Robert (2015), *Seeing Sodomy in the Middle Ages*, Chicago, University of Chicago Press.

Muñoz, Jose E. (2009), *Cruising Utopia: The Then and There of Queer Futurity*, New York, New York University Press.

Naselli, Adrien (2016), 'Martineau & Ducastel nous racontent *Théo & Hugo dans le même bateau*', *Têtu*, tetu.com/2016/04/24/martineau-ducastel-racontent-theo-hugo (accessed 26 August 2021).

Ovid (1984), *Metamorphoses: Books IX–XV*, trans. Frank Justus Miller, Cambridge, MA, Harvard University Press.

Ovid (2004), *Metamorphoses*, trans. Charles Martin, New York, W.W Norton and Company, www.overdrive.com/search?q=3F0AD951-0802-47DD-AF5B-60654788481C (accessed 21 July 2021).

Oyallon-Koloski, Jenny (2014), 'Genre Experimentation and Contemporary Dance in *Jeanne et le garçon formidable*', *Studies in French Cinema*, 14, 2, 91–107.

Parisse, Lydie (2018), '*Juste la fin du monde*: Processus d'écriture et négativité', *Skén&graphie. Coulisses des arts du spectacle et des scènes émergentes*, 5, 1–12.

Poliziano, Angelo (2004), 'The Fable of Orpheus', in Kenneth Borris, ed., *Same-Sex Desire in the English Renaissance: A Sourcebook of Texts, 1470–1650*, New York, Routledge, pp. 264–6.

Pratt, Murray (2004), 'Félix and the Light-hearted Gay Road Movie: Genre, Families, Fathers and the Decolonization of the Homosexual Self', *Australian Journal of French Studies*, 41, 3, 88–101.

Provencher, Denis (2008). 'Tracing Sexual Citizenship and Queerness in *Drôle de Félix* (2000) and *Tarik el hob* (2001)', *Contemporary French and Francophone Studies*, 12, 1, 51–61.

Puff, Helmut (2006), 'Orpheus after Eurydice', in Basil Dufallo and Peggy McCracken, eds, *Dead Lovers: Erotic Bonds and the Study of Premodern Europe*, Ann Arbor, University of Michigan Press, pp. 71–95.

Pullen, Christopher (2008), 'The Films of Ducastel and Martineau: Gay Identity, the Family, and the Autobiographical Self', in Robin Griffiths, ed., *Queer Cinema in Europe*, Bristol and Chicago, Intellect, pp. 49–62.

Rees-Roberts, Nick (2008), *French Queer Cinema*, Edinburgh, Edinburgh University Press.

Reeser, Todd W. (2017), 'Producing Awkwardness: Affective Labour and Masculinity in Popular Culture', *Mosaic: An Interdisciplinary Critical Journal*, 50, 4, 51–68.

Roth-Bettoni, Didier (2007), *L'Homosexualité au cinema*, Paris, Musardine.

Sarde, Michèle (1991), *Histoire d'Eurydice pendant la remontée*, Paris, Seuil.

Sarrazac, Jean-Pierre (2016), 'Préface', in Jean-Luc Lagarce, *Juste la fin du monde*, Besançon, Les Solitaires intempestifs, pp. 7–18.

Sartre, Jean-Paul (1948), 'Man is Condemned to Be Free', from the lecture 'Existentialism is a Humanism', trans. Philip Mairet, wmpeople.wm.edu/asset/index/cvance/sartre (accessed 21 July 2021).

Schilt, T. (2007). 'Hybrid Strains in Olivier Ducastel and Jacques Martineau's *Drôle de Félix* (2000)', *Contemporary French and Francophone Studies*, 11, 3, 361–8.

Sedgwick, Eve Kosofsky (2005), *Epistemology of the Closet*, Berkeley, University of California Press.

Seel, Pierre (1995), *I, Pierre Seel, Deported Homosexual: A Memoir of Nazi Terror*, trans. Joachim Neugroschel, New York, Basic Books.

Strauss, Walter A. (1971), *Descent and Return: The Orphic Theme in Modern Literature*, Cambridge, MA, Harvard University Press.

Swamy, Vinay (2006), 'Gallic Dreams: The Family, PaCS and Kinship Relations in Millennial France', *Studies in French Cinema*, 6, 1, 53–64.

Sword, Helen (1989), 'Orpheus and Eurydice in the Twentieth Century: Lawrence, H. D., and the Poetics of the Turn', *Twentieth Century Literature*, 35, 4, 407–28.

Tarr, Carrie (2005), *Reframing Difference: Beur and Banlieue Filmmaking in France*, Manchester and New York, Manchester University Press.

Toutleciné.com (2010), 'Interview d'Olivier Ducastel et Jacques Martineau', www.youtube.com/watch?v=a0nPKB5wPIY (accessed 21 August 2021).

Virgil (1999), *Eclogues, Georgics, Aeneid, 1–6*, trans. H. Rusthon Fairclough, Cambridge, MA, Harvard University Press.

Waldron, Darren (2009), *Queering Contemporary French Popular Cinema: Images and Their Reception*, Oxford and New York, Peter Lang.

Waldron, Darren (2015), *Jacques Demy*, Manchester, Manchester University Press.

2

Alain Guiraudie: queering space, age, relationality

In a 2013 interview on the television show *Des mots de minuit*, Guiraudie tagged queer as an 'opening onto the world' ('ouverture sur le monde'), a necessity since the world must be redone (Guiraudie, 2013a). With otherworldly reinventions manifested in a variety of ways in his cinematic corpus, he differs from the four other directors treated in this book who are more rooted in the world in which queer people live or have lived. His cinema is, as he puts it, an 'attempt to create possibility, to modify relations among men' ('créer du possible, de modifier les rapports entre les hommes'): if life cannot do this, then 'let's broaden horizons' via film (Guiraudie, 2001: 4). He makes films to 'reinvent the world' in the way that he wishes it was (Boussageon, 2014; Guiraudie, 2013a; Guiraudie, 2017). He is 'attached to the idea that cinema draws from reality to head toward an elsewhere' (Guiraudie, 2016b). In reference to select films of his corpus, Weber uses the French term '*uchronie*' ('uchronia' in English), an imaginary temporality located outside of our current present that still has 'concrete enough structures in place to function according to a set of rules' (2013: 6). Quasi-fantastic settings and stories that seemingly take place outside of the twenty-first century but that also gesture towards today's world, pertain especially to two films: *Du soleil pour les gueux* (*Sunshine for the Poor*) (2001) and *Voici venu le temps* (*Time has Come*) (2005).[1] This characteristic relates to varying degrees and in varying ways to all his films as temporal setting is generally difficult to pin down. A defining element of Guiraudie's uchronia is queernesss related to cisgender male bodies: broadly speaking, queer sex acts and desires come and go in worlds that do not support stable sexual orientations. A number of his male characters fall outside the binarized categories of heterosexual/homosexual, and the categories themselves are seemingly not of concern to anyone. Guiraudie's queer uchronia defines a world that did not participate in the white, Western discursive construction and imposition of binarized sexual categories in the nineteenth century and is thus more open to certain molecular possibilities related to gender.

By putting another sexual regime in play, Guiraudie's queer-worldmaking suggests that other types of regimes can exist, particularly ones not subtended by what we might today recognize as capitalism. A world defined by capitalist critique dovetails with homoerotics and gestures towards another economic system in *Ce vieux rêve qui bouge* (*Real Cool Time*) (2001). *Pas de repos pour les braves* (*No Rest for the Brave*) (2003) questions what constitutes reality and what takes place in a dream, with queer desire one defining element of a dream-like state. Guiraudie's three more recent feature-length films – *Le Roi de l'évasion* (*The King of Escape*) (2009), *L'Inconnu du lac* (*Stranger by the Lake*) (2014), and *Rester vertical* (*Staying Vertical*) (2016) – all radically reinvent human relationality or ways for men to be desiring or gendered subjects through the medium of queerness. Most all of the characters in his films

---

1 His early-career short *La Force des choses* (*The Force of Circumstance*) (1998) would also fit this category.

'remain very white' in part because, as Guiraudie noted in an interview, he does not know 'how to integrate the figure [of the foreigner or immigrant]' and while he wanted more diversity, such difference is not 'part of [his] world' (Guiraudie, 2006: 27). In the three films just mentioned, play with time is less central than in Guiraudie's earlier films, but as non-urban spaces redefine or have an influence on the reinventions that Guiraudie proposes, geographical forms of subjectivity play a major role. If a homosexual/heterosexual binary does not define the earlier films, the rural spaces of these three later films offer a setting that permits another narrative about homosexuality to be told. The capitalist system allowed men to function economically outside the realm of the family and thus for gay identity to take root, formed in urban areas as workers found jobs in the city and could develop a gay consciousness in communities of like-minded people. A substantial body of work in LGBTQ studies considers the meaning and presence of queer rurality and debunks the assumption that homosexual identity or queerness has to be – or has to be imagined as – an urban phenomenon, critiquing 'metronormativity' as a concept for LGBTQ peoples (e.g., Crawford, 2017; Gray *et al.*, 2016; Halberstam, 2005; Herring, 2010; Johnson, 2013). Still, the idea that queer and urban fit together naturally remains widespread in many people's minds, and the image of Paris as a gay capital looms large in a French cultural context. Guiraudie in 2006 noted his desire to bring cinema out of a limited Parisian milieu 'between four walls' to the countryside and include a broader range of people, including unknown actors (Guiraudie, 2006: 27). He himself is from the region Occitanie in south-central France, where his family held a farm, and his cinematic corpus suggests that non-urban spaces – often those of his home region – foster new gendered relationalities or new ways to be a gendered subject. Not only does male queerness not have to be – or to be seen as – an urban phenomenon, but rural spaces can themselves be coded queer, located where fluid desires and sexual acts take place beyond the realm of identity-driven cities. The rural is the locus of queerness, and conversely the rural itself is queered. Dalton reads the natural spaces in a number of Guiraudie's films as embodying 'a potentiality for queer ecosystems and ecologies' (2019: 67) and 'initiat[ing] processes of queer rewilding that open queer ecologies up to unknown futures' (70). Even more broadly, the queering of and in the rural can have even broader implications. Guiraudie has had a long-standing interest in how by talking about himself and his rural world, he can 'rayonner sur le monde' (Guiraudie, 2006: 26), or extend cinematic content out into the world more broadly. His settings are not about a given region's culture, but resemble an elsewhere or a nowhere beyond time and place. That world is not unrelated to the genre of the western since the landscape of the American West resembles the French landscape of some of these films, even as the content of the films is quite different. Still, the generic resemblance remains one aspect of the way in which Guiraudie, as he puts it, 'multiplied genres' (Guiraudie, 2013a) or in this case queered the western while referring back to it.

Also central to Guiraudie's queer cinematic reinvention is intergenerational desire and sexual acts and desires between men from different age groups. While queer relations across generational lines might have the potential to map onto classic notions of pederasty, erotic attraction in these films is not embodied by a middle-aged man and a young man, but frequently a middle-aged man and a significantly older man. Often standing in for new forms of relationality tout court, not simply gay intergenerational ones, these relations cannot be separated from considerations of death and eros. Guiraudie has noted in interviews that he is influenced by the work of theorist Georges Bataille (Guiraudie, 2013b: 52; Guiraudie, 2014c: 17), whose most famous work, *Erotism: Death and Sensuality*, posits the now-canonical idea that eros and death are not antithetical but are in close relation with each other. The book begins with an often-cited 'formula' about eroticism: 'Eroticism, it may be said, is assenting to life up to the point of death' (1986: 11).[2] Numerous are the representations in Guiraudie's cinema in which queer eroticism signifies an approach towards death, a recurring image of which is a young man's sexual act with, or erotic attraction to, a much older man (*Ce vieux rêve qui bouge*; *Pas de repos pour les braves*; *Voici venu le temps*; *Le Roi de l'évasion*; *Rester vertical*). In these cases, it is not so much a kind of gerontophilia at play as much as it is the case that the older man embodies Bataille's concept of eros as approaching death. The move towards death, however, as will be discussed below in the context of specific films, often produces new forms of subjectivity not trapped in static or normative ways of being. For Bataille, eroticism allows one to say 'I am losing myself' (31). By virtue of moving towards death in eros, in some cases at least, a character loses investment in the self, including stable or normative ideas on what gender or sexual orientation is or has to be, opening gender and sexuality up to new configurations more broadly. In some cases, the loss of the self opens up into a universalist conception of gender or sexuality – a key element of Guiraudie's cinematic reinvention. One element of that loss might be fear, as Bataille notes: 'Beyond the will to leave one's narrow being for one that is more vast, there is – very often mixed with this first will to loss – a will to loss ... that takes advantage of the fear it provokes in order to become all the more inflamed and delirious' (1985: 250). This addition of fear to a death–eros mixture is central to the functioning of eros in *L'Inconnu du lac*, but it pertains to other films as well.

This intergenerational link factors into Guiraudie's 2014 novel, *Ici commence la nuit*, translated as *Now the Night*

---

2 Guiraudie cites this very phrase in an interview in *Cahiers du cinéma* (Guiraudie, 2013b: 52).

Begins, which won the Sade Prize in 2014 (given for undoing the constraints of literature). Early in the novel, the narrator Gilles finds Pépé's ('grampa's') underwear on the clothesline and masturbates with it on, and then returns the underwear to the clothesline. The police come to investigate the incident, which puts the plot in motion and reveals not so much a desire for this particular man but a desire for an approach to death via eroticism that an old man signifies. As Gilles puts it to the ninety-eight-year-old man: 'I really liked jerking off in your underwear ... But I don't actually want you' (Guiraudie, 2018: 44). At one point in the novel, grampa speaks to Gilles in Occitan, as a sign that he is archaic in the modern world, a throwback to a former time. Guiraudie has noted that his book was 'situated between *The King of Evasion* and *Stranger by the Lake*' (Guiraudie, 2016a), and that the young man/old man sex act in *Staying Vertical* resonates with a similar relation in his novel. In these three films, Gilles's declaration could pertain as well to other male characters who either have sex with much older men or are in what look to be erotic situations with older men, but do not in the end 'actually want' them. Rather, as will become clear here, those relations emblematize non-normative male–male relations more than a specific relation and aim to open up new relational modes.[3]

L'Inconnu du lac: drowning relationality

Though he had already made five feature films, it was Guiraudie's *L'Inconnu du lac* that gave him exposure to a broad audience in France and in the US. The film was presented at the Cannes Film Festival in 2013 where it won the Queer Palm and where Guiraudie won the award for best direction. In 2014, lead actor Pierre Deladonchamps won the César for

---

3 For readings of the novel along these lines, see McCaffrey (2016, 2018).

most promising actor for the film. It was selected as the best film of 2013 by *Cahiers du cinéma* and as the second-best film of the year by the readers of the magazine. The film also made numerous top ten lists in that same year. Given its importance in the reception of French queer cinema, I will begin by discussing the functioning of queer in this film before turning back in time to Guiraudie's other films and concluding with the most recent film discussed in this chapter (*Rester vertical*).

Guiraudie himself noted in an interview about *L'Inconnu du lac* that in his previous films he 'had not gone all the way in terms of desire' ('Je n'étais pas allé au bout du désir') (Guiraudie, 2013b: 50), suggesting that this film does in fact go all the way. Despite the broad accolades outside the LGBT community, *L'Inconnu du lac* looks on the surface to be – simply put – a very gay male film, and certainly the most identity-driven in Guiraudie's corpus. The entire setting of the film takes place at the titular lake, a well-known and widely used gay cruising spot where white gay men go to have casual sex, strictly delineated from other parts of the lake coded as heterosexual. Frequent male nudity is combined with very explicit gay sex acts (including a penis ejaculating), and the setting during the AIDS era suggests that the film is, at least on one level, about gay sexual liberation despite the epidemic. Characters are conscious of condom usage in casual sexual encounters. No woman or non-male character appears at the lake, and non-gay male characters stand out as aberrations: a presumably heterosexual man comes to cruise for women at one point, almost comically, and he is told that he is in the wrong place. He may well arrive as the exception to the rule, to incarnate the 'stranger' of the English title or the sexually 'unknown' (the strict sense of '*inconnu*'). The presumably heterosexual police inspector who enters the space to investigate a suspicious death that takes place in the lake also seems out of place as he asks many questions related to male–male intimacy and sex acts, at times spying on the men and appearing out of the brush to surveil them. The most major non-gay character, Henri (Patrick d'Assumçao) seems to have an affective attraction to other men, and to the main character Franck (Deladonchamps) in particular, as if coming to the beach on the lake has an effect on his heterosexuality, at least with respect to affect. The plot, such as it is, revolves around Franck's reaction to witnessing the murder of a gay man in the lake by another gay man, the handsome and rugged-looking Michel (Christophe Paou). Franck increasingly desires him, or in his own words he falls 'in love' with him, but it is not clear if his feelings are because of or in spite of the murder. Gay male criminality, following a French tradition made most famous by writer Jean Genet, is ambiguous with respect to desire and sex, as the approach to death is erotic.[4] Trailers for the film do not attempt to hide the homosexuality at all, and in fact the film provoked controversy because of a publicity poster that made clear to the public that the film was about gay cruising and sex acts (see Piper, 2020: 84–6).

Nonetheless, the film was often not received as a 'gay film' and its wide success suggests that the message of the film went well beyond homosexuality as topic. Guiraudie himself noted that, even though most of the action takes place in a delineated gay space, the film was not meant to depict a 'homosexual microcosm', but 'to speak about humanity in general' (Melbourne International Film Festival, 2013). How, then, can such a gay-seeming film not really be about homosexuality? How does the film end up as a universal narrative, beyond

---

4 Guiraudie notes that he reread Genet's *Querelle* and watched the film version by Fassbinder while he was preparing the film, but that what he wanted to portray 'was completely different from *Querelle*' (Guiraudie, 2014c: 18). In *Cahiers du cinéma*, he describes Fassbinder as not a model or a source of inspiration, but as a 'compass' (Guiraudie, 2005: 28). In the interview, Guiraudie situates himself 'rather far from Fassbinder' and notes that he did not 'directly inspire' him (28). One difference between them is that the German director 'talks directly about things' whereas he speaks 'through poetry and lyricism' (28).

homosexuality? How does the human go 'all the way' in terms of desire? And what does that universalizing process have to do with inventing new ways of being in the world?

L'Inconnu du lac is a film about the surface of the lake and about the menace of depth. Most of the action takes place around the lake, including up in the bushes behind the beach, but the murder itself takes place on the surface of the lake when Michel drowns his lover that he wants to get rid of for reasons that are never clear. In a striking long take, the lover disappears into the depth of the lake and is never seen again on screen.[5] Homosexuality in a sense is drowned in the depth of the lake as the action on the surface takes on deeper meaning. The reason for the murder, however, becomes extraneous to the narrative and Franck does not seek to know the motive, suggesting that the film is not ultimately about some deep, psychological motive or inner drive on the part of Michel.

But on the other hand, depth is not fully extraneous to the film. There is a rumour in circulation that there is a *silure* in the lake, a human-sized omnivorous catfish, that would presumably eat the dead body and perhaps live swimmers as well.[6] While depth is menace or threat, dangerous for the men on the beach, it is also something to be avoided in making sense of the film. To not read superficially, to take the signs of the film as deeper than they seem denotes a dangerous reading practice. One should not enter into the depths of the lake just as one should not enter into the depths of the characters' psyche to determine motivation or to make sense of what they do and why. This is not a film about the depths of the mind: it is a film that signifies in other ways. Damon Young concludes his book on sex in public with a reading of the film, suggesting

---

5 Although much less central to the novel *Now the Night Begins* than to the film, a similar scene is witnessed by the main character Gilles (2018: 96–8).
6 The imagined catfish also makes an appearance in Guiraudie's novel (2018: 58–9).

'murderous violence is a strangely deracinated operation of the drive ... which operates autonomously, without reason, and detached from any apparatus of repression, thus forestalling any repressive hypothesis' (2018: 233).[7] Guiraudie has noted that he first conceived of the story as 'a simplistic geometric and geographic schema' and as an 'architectural' space (Guiraudie, 2014b). Because the entire film takes place at the lake and never leaves the space, the sub-spaces in the film (the water of the lake, the beach, the cruising beach, the non-cruising beach, the bushes behind the beach, the dense vegetation behind the bushes, the parking lot) play as much of a role in the narration as the characters.[8] Characters have meaning by virtue of where they are in space, or by virtue of their relation to the natural world, or as Nathan Friedman puts it, they should be 'read as abstract points and vectors' (2016: 183). He takes the film as 'diagram', 'not illustrations but abstract machines, capable of producing novel relationships of desire between site, activity, and matter' (183). Without deep psychology as a concern, the characters are free to diagram new ways to be unconstrained by social constructs of gender or sexuality that may exist more firmly in urban settings or that constrain cinematic characters to have a gender or sexual identity. Like Friedman, I take the film as about potentiality, inventing ways to be a gendered subject, not about character motivation.

The focus on gay cruising suggests relational potentiality. As one of the precursors of late twentieth-century queer theory, French theorist and activist Guy Hocquenghem describes cruising (*la drague*) or what he calls the 'pick-up machine' in

7 See also Young's nuanced view of surface/depth in the film (2018: 235–6). He sees 'a certain crisis, a certain negativity, of the surface' (235), represented by not knowing what Michel will do to Franck.
8 On non-urban space as queer, see Dalton (2019). Weber (2013) studies space 'released from urban-centrism' in Guiraudie. See also Fournier (2015).

a section of his book *Homosexual Desire* (1993: 130). Gay cruising might be imagined by heteronormative culture as a form of sexual lack: the gay man is unable to have the kind of stable, monogamous, heterosexual love that he supposedly wants, so he can only go cruising to substitute for that lack. For Hocquenghem, cruising could also be taken as quite the opposite, as a form of freedom that throws off the shackles of normativity and liberates the human being: 'everything is possible at any moment: organs look for each other and plug in, unaware of the law of exclusive disjunction' (131). The pick-up machine for Hocquenghem is not so much gay or queer as much as it 'corresponds to the mode of existence of desire itself' (132). Part of the potentiality of the *L'Inconnu du lac*, then, is that homosexual acts and desires – incarnated by *la drague* as central image – open up a space in which a mode of human desire can be represented in new ways. From this perspective, it is never fully clear to what extent the film is about homosexuality or about humanness broadly, the borders between the gay and the non-gay are not entirely clear, and Franck's cruising and desire remain potential metaphors for human desire. At one point, a random man on the beach tells Franck that he knows 'the local queers' who would 'screw the planet if they could' and that he should not try to steal the man that he is with for sex. Franck responds that they are in a cruising space, and the man responds that he has gone beyond the cruising limit delineated by a group of trees. Cruising has limits, this exchange suggests, but it's not entirely clear what those limits are and they depend in part on hypothetical and arbitrary limit-setting that may or may not be agreed upon by all parties present. If cruising stands in for a mode of desire broadly, it is not entirely clear where cruising starts and where it stops. Part of the film's content is the opening up of gay male sexuality into the realm of sexuality broadly, creating a fluidity between sexual borders.

One way to understand Hocquenghem's non-normative 'mode of existence of desire itself' is through the character Henri, an older divorced (presumably) heterosexual man, who nonetheless comes to the lakeshore for reasons that are never fully clear. Is he a closeted gay man? Does he want only same-sex sex acts? Does he have an affective orientation towards gay men? Or something else? The inability to pin down what kind of desire he has suggests that though he does not cruise per se, Henri too incarnates a 'mode of existence of desire itself' outside the bounds of stable sexual orientation. He sits off to the side of the centre of the action in the film, away from the main cruising area but within clear sight of the cruising areas. He and Franck sit awkwardly and silently together early on during one of their first encounters as they talk together on the beach. Their interaction begins with a silent moment that could potentially express eroticism on one or both of their parts, and could lead to a sexual act. But in fact, it does not lead anywhere, for their attraction is of another order, neither heterosexual, homosexual, nor simply friendly. It is an awkward affect that calls attention to a non-normative way of relating that cannot easily be described or put into language.[9] Both men later admit that they do not want to have sex with each other, but that they do want to be together. Henri does not think that 'you have to fuck someone to sleep next to them' and wonders why he and Franck cannot be together in a mode that is not based on erotic love or sexual acts but on another affective form that nonetheless has energy behind it. He finds 'friendship' boring, and Franck makes his heart race, 'like when I'm in love'. 'I can't go a day without seeing you', he tells him. Not only is Henri's orientation never really clear, but the very idea of what orientation means is

---

9 For a model of awkward affect that gestures towards new masculinities, see Reeser (2017). See also Reeser (2019).

put into question through his character and his relation to Franck. Is orientation based on affect, sex act, erotic desire, or something else? Michel believes at first that he and Franck are a couple because they are together on the beach, but his assumption articulates a cultural assumption that two men together on a gay beach are likely a couple. Henri expresses hostility towards Michel, perhaps out of jealousy, but even that jealousy is not clear in terms of what he is jealous of (Sex? Emotion? Time spent together?). Does Henri inscribe the non-gay viewer in the film? Does he sit on the shore of the lake, as the titular 'stranger', watching what transpires from another sexual perspective? Does he express an orientation beyond gay and heterosexual? His location on the beach, the liminal space between the lake and the bushes where most sex acts take place, figures his sexual liminality as well. He is murdered by Michel late in the film, but in the bushes behind the beach, precisely because it is a space for gay sexual acts where he does not belong and where he should not be located. Michel struggles with this ambiguity, his erotically liminal location vis-à-vis Franck, replacing it with a more substantial and radical ambiguity (another 'mode of existence of desire itself') that he himself incarnates. Even the ambiguity of orientation and affect is not radical enough for Michel's gendered mode, the cornerstone of the film's universalizing message.

In an interview, Guiraudie explains that he considered systematically filming with a fixed camera and a hand-held camera so that the film could be seen both from an objective point of view and from Franck's point of view. In the end, he settled for a fixed camera most of the time (Melbourne International Film Festival, 2013). The director's desire for two cameras indicates that the film was meant to convey an oscillation between the viewpoint of Franck as a single gay character and a broad universal 'fixed' perspective not belonging to the main character who defines the point of view of the film. In fact, Franck's queer desires have the potential to become the general viewer's at any time. Even in moments when the point of view is clearly Franck's, the camera at times films from another perspective to allow for the general viewer's presence and to account for the two viewpoints. The general viewer is, in a sense, always present, able to witness, leaving the film questioning whether it is about male homosexuality at all.

The possibility of a 'fixed' camera angle taking over gestures towards the possibility that the particularism of 'homosexuality' disappear. The police inspector cannot understand why Franck is not more worried about the murder of another gay man and about the likelihood that a homophobic murderer is on the loose. He assumes an idea of community in which gay men would act in a certain way and would think in communal terms. But this is not the case. Franck aside, it is never clear if the other men identify as 'gay' or 'homosexual' and if they feel any affiliation with a group defined by sexual orientation at all. Henri tells Franck early on that the men there are generally married, closeted, not gay-identified men. The film's temporal location in the 1980s, with the cars as the only real indicator of decade, clashes with the more communitarian temporal context of the film itself (2013), the year in which 'marriage for everyone' became legal in France, as if to disband the communitarian, gay-centred arguments that were taking place around marriage. Michel points out that Franck's car is a model that he has not seen for a long time. His car comes from out of the past, just as the setting of the film comes out of the past, and dismantles to an extent gay communitarianism of the twenty-first century. Schoonover and Galt read the film as interrogating the concept of gay community: '*Stranger by the Lake* refuses to settle whom the concept of the social serves, and it implicates the spectator in a questioning of community' (2016: 215). For them, instead, the film imagines 'radical forms of social being' beyond identitarianism – a take on the film with which I entirely agree.

At no point is the move from individual to general more evident than in the murder scene, the most emblematic scene of the film. In a video made for the *New York Times*, Guiraudie comments on the camerawork: 'there's a change of point of view during the shot': it begins from Franck's point of view and then 'slowly we slide into a point of view more objective, the point of view of everybody, of a spectator, of a director' (Murphy, 2014) (plate 5). Franck's viewpoint then returns at the end of the take. Witnessing the murder leaves Franck in a state where he does not know if Michel will drown him as well. It also leaves him in a state where he can imagine that Michel can love him in a way that transcends pleasure-only sex at the lake. Developing deeper feelings, Franck keeps seeing Michel until he tells him that he wants to spend the night with him, an idea that he strongly rejects. As a result, Franck begins to lose sexual desire for him and has trouble having sex. Yet, he does not turn Michel in to the police inspector, who returns over and over to the beach, since as Michel puts it after he covers for him, he loves him 'a little'. Killing his previous lover may be a sign that he wants some other kind of love or some other kind of relation. Or it may be a sign of a desire for another kind of relationality itself. Franck does not know what the murder means about Michel's approach to relationality, but he is willing to keep him from being arrested for murder to find out.

But who exactly has witnessed the killing off? Who has seen the act that might embody new relationality? It is Franck, of course, on the surface, but it is also the general spectator, or 'everybody', as Guiraudie said in the interview. The act of seeing the murder may leave a 'spectator' in a quandary about what the act of murder means with respect to love and desire. The viewer is invited to broaden out from queer to general: the gay lover (whom we can barely make out from our far-away vantage point) is killed off, becoming a general lover. What is drowned is queer perspective itself as the general viewer witnesses the murder of queer relationality. This movement from specific to general sets up an interpretive lens for the rest of the film.

The act of killing, and Franck's subsequent erotic attachment to the killer, will not pertain to Franck alone in the logic of the film, but to the general viewer who may have any orientation. What happens to Franck from this scene on happens to 'everybody'.

The murder scene follows an explicit, random sex act between Franck and another character, which culminates in a shot of his ejaculating penis as the man kisses him (though the actual penis belongs to a body double). The juxtaposition of murder and orgasm opens the question of whether the murder itself is orgasmic, a kind of *jouissance* or a moment in which Franck moves outside himself and outside of his own subjectivity.[10] This ejaculatory move outside subjectivity establishes that the next scene, the murder, will lead to loss of subjectivity. In this sense, the film is reminiscent of approaches in queer studies that take sex, and gay male sex in particular, as a willed loss of subjectivity. Most famously, Leo Bersani's canonical essay 'Is the Rectum a Grave?' concludes with a sentence that pertains to this aspect of the film: 'Male homosexuality advertises the risk of the sexual itself as the risk of self-dismissal, of losing sight of the self, and in so doing it proposes and dangerously represents *jouissance* as a mode of ascesis' (1987: 222). In Guiraudie's film, the risk of being with a murderer who might murder again at any time is linked directly to the self-destruction or *jouissance* of orgasm. In the ejaculation scene, the man fears unprotected sex and masturbates Franck with his hand: avoiding the risk of HIV-AIDS with this sex act moves risk out of this scene into the realm of the murder in the following scene. There is not a risk of death on Franck's part, but a risk of 'losing sight of the self', much as Franck loses sight of the drowned body.

The murder scene returns in an altered guise later when Michel asks Franck to come swimming with him in the lake,

---

10 For a different reading, see Dalton who takes this scene as about 'distance and disaffection' (2019: 73). See also Walton (2018).

as they 'have the lake to [them]selves'. Concerned after what he has seen, he resists going swimming, for fear of being drowned, but he gives in and enters the water. Michel swims over towards him quickly and forcefully, and then instead of drowning him kisses him, as a sign of the affective indeterminacy between eros and death. The kiss refers back to the previous scene where the anonymous man kissed Franck as he ejaculated: Michel's kiss in the water is itself a lower-level kind of ejaculation as well, as fear and eroticism seamlessly join together into ecstasy. The camera takes a very different angle this time around however, shooting from the perspective of Franck on the surface of the lake. The spectator is of course meant to experience Hitchcockian suspense along with Franck, as we have been trained to look through Franck's eyes during the murder scene. But the perspective moves to a general one again, very similar to the one during the murder itself. The camera does not move, or 'slide' as Guiraudie put it, from Franck to the general spectator in a subtle way, but in a dramatic manner. It cuts from Franck's viewpoint on the water to that of a general spectator on the hill up above. Gone are the trees or brush that had framed the murder shot. Nothing blocks the view this time around, no trees frame the act in the lake. The light is different too this time, more visible on the water and not so couched in twilight. It is unclear what the locus of seeing is: the shot embodies unframed pure objectivity, outside a metonymic connection to Franck. The mixing of eroticism and criminality becomes everyone's, even more than in the murder scene, radically broadening the subjectivity of the single gay character into the realm of objective subjectivity. Any erotic link between homosexuality and criminality is no longer proprietary. The move towards general subjectivity and away from homosexuality is represented by a double orgasm, or a double *jouissance* of the two men. The scene cuts from the objective perspective to Franck and Michel having anal sex on the beach, the former on the bottom. It is obvious why Franck is orgasming on the beach: the mix of murder and eros has created a boundary-breaking subjectivity. There is no handjob or condom because the danger of infection parallels the danger of potentially being murdered. No one can know if Franck will contract HIV from Michel, just as no one can know if he will ever be murdered by him. There is a double danger, a double *jouissance*, and a double break with the specificity of gay subjectivity.

In this model of subjectivity, what about Michel? Why does the man on top orgasm? He is not just a murderer for he is moving towards a more ambiguous sexual subjectivity that might incorporate casual sex acts as well as affective relations along the lines of those that Franck desires and had with Henri. The double orgasm might be, in part, a result of Michel's domination on top, as a potentially murderous man dominates the more submissive Franck, but it is a double *jouissance* because both men experience boundary-breaking. While Michel knows that Franck knows about the murder, he does not know whether he will cover for him or turn him in. He is in a state of unknowing as well, not knowing what Franck's relation to criminality and murder is. This is the first moment of a movement for Michel towards another way to be, even as in the following scene he refuses to spend the night with Franck elsewhere since he fears that they will grow tired of each other. His subjective boundary may have been moved, but he still maintains queer boundaries that resist normativity.

The film ends after Michel kills Henri and the inspector, and Franck realizes what his lover has done. He runs away from Michel, who calls to him in the near darkness to tell him that they can spend the night together. After a silence, Franck calls for Michel in the final words of the film. The film closes in total darkness because Franck and the viewer both end up in a situation of not knowing. The spectator cannot see any longer, they are in the dark about where things stand. The darkness raises the question: can the threat of danger be intimacy? Has the murderous man become a loving man? Do all these murders, taken as a unity, constitute love? Although Michel may be tracking Franck down to kill him, he may well want to spend the night with him too. His sex-only regime has been broken in favour of a more affective one that has the potential to be more traditionally intimate. Has he killed off Henri because he is jealous of the continuing affective relation that he has with Franck and that he now wants? Does killing the inspector imply the end of a normative, state-sanctioned form of investigation that does not and cannot capture or recognize their unique relation? Michel may be moving in an affective direction in part because Franck, by virtue of covering for his criminality, has shown that he is willing to move out of homonormativity into a new mode of loving. When the inspector questions Franck after night has fallen and warns him that there may be a homophobic killer on the loose in the area, Michel is waiting in the darkness and appears to Franck after the inspector leaves, clearly aroused by what he told the inspector. A moment of affective intimacy follows as the two men move towards each other, towards a mid-point between criminality and affective intimacy. In their reading of the film, Schoonover and Galt write that the film deploys 'disparate affective regimes' in order to force the viewer to 'experience exclusion from the social and reflect on that experience' (2016: 215, 216). The camerawork forces the viewer to take over Franck's viewing position so that they can have the affective relation that Franck has vis-à-vis Michel, an affect in which he is 'falling in love' at the same time as he knows that the object of love and desire is a criminal. 'Darkness', Schoonover and Galt write about this scene, 'is simultaneously a space of ethical caring and a space of threat and death' (216). The film ends, for them, with a call for 'the need to invent and experience new modes of sociality' (217). In an interview, Deladonchamps revealed that Guiraudie filmed a second ending in which Franck goes off with Michel at the end of the film (Deladonchamps, 2013). While that ending was not of course selected in favour of the final ambiguity, it does suggest that the final darkness allowed for the possibility that the two men can be together in a new way that embodies 'new modes of sociality'.[11]

Hitchcock by the lake

The film has been considered as Hitchcockian because of the suspense around the question of whether Franck will be murdered by Michel.[12] Guiraudie has stated that he was not thinking particularly about the British director when making the film, but that he has been a general influence on him and on the cinematic context in which he has worked (Guiraudie, 2013c). More specifically, the film may recast Hitchcock's most gay film, *Rope* (1948). In both films, there is a gay murderer (a murderous duo in Hitchcock, Brandon and Phillip) whose murder comes very early in the film: neither film leaves ambiguity as to guilt and neither film is a whodunnit. Rupert (played by James Stewart) figures out that the murder has taken place, though at what precise point is not clear, and there is some suspense about whether he will be killed with their gun. In the opening scene, the dead body of their strangled friend David is put into

---

11 I am indebted to Schoonover and Galt's reading of the film here. Another way to consider this abandonment of the self is through the images of the landscape and of nature that serve as distractions from the human. McCaffrey reads these images as 'the source of a shared intimacy ("surplus") that exceeds the personal'. He continues: 'In the absence of personal(ized) relations, Guiraudie finds in the forms of the outside a way of exploring an ontology of queer intimacy as a form of abandonment – a leaving of the self that is accompanied by an abandonment to the materiality of the earth' (2019: 393–4). McCaffrey's excellent analysis discusses this idea through Deleuze and affect, with the idea of 'becoming-animal' as cornerstone.
12 See for example Brody (2014); Migration User (2014); Pendleton and Grundmann (2014: 17).

a *cassone*, an Italian marriage chest that often had elaborate decoration, for the duration of the film.[13] The two men, coded as a gay couple, invite the victim's family and girlfriend over for dinner, along with Rupert, a former schoolmaster of theirs, and they serve a buffet dinner on the top of the *cassone*. Their goal is not to kill and hide the murder, but to keep it always on the verge of being discovered. When Rupert finally deduces what has happened and opens the *cassone*, he shoots a gun off out the window, de facto calling the police to the apartment. For Greven, *Rope* is Hitchcock's 'coming-out' film (2017: 125), and the film makes a statement about the cultural status of the closet in the 1940s and of post-war white wealthy homosexuality (2017: chap. 4). Innumerable innuendos are made about the murder and about homosexuality, which may be structurally equivalent since finding the dead body could be taken as the coded outing of the two gay characters. Rupert functions as a kind of heterosexual investigator, a precursor to the investigator in Guiraudie's film, embodying in both cases a non-queer social order that might normalize gay male culture (though it is not entirely clear that Rupert is not himself queer). In Guiraudie's film, the normalizing force does not succeed in normalizing either, but is literally killed off by Michel, while in Hitchcock, the social order is re-established as the final scene suggests that the crime will be punished. In Hitchcock, the two main characters attempt to self-annihilate, wanting their crime to be revealed to David's heterosexual friends and family, desiring to out themselves. They are attempting to do violence to the heterosexual social order and to Oedipal normativity by killing off a man and forcing those around him to be transformed by their act. Their attempt to reconnect David's girlfriend with her ex-boyfriend points to their desire to reconfigure heterosexuality in

13 Walton (2018: 261) in an endnote sees 'intriguing parallels with *Rope*', including the *cassone* as a precursor to Guiraudie's lake (both with a dead body inside).

a way that they see fit. Still, in the end, the social order exerts itself and ends up annihilating them (see Greven, 2017: 135). In *L'Inconnu du lac*, attempts at gay self-annihilation are not contained, but get mixed in with erotic intimacy to incarnate a queer way of being, not part of normative fabric. The film is three steps ahead of Hitchcock's film, beyond the world of the closet but also beyond the sexual liberation of the 1970s and the communitarian movements of the twenty-first century, rejecting a post-closet gay world of cruising and of gay rights in favour of other ways to be a sexual subject. The very public nature of gay sexuality allows Guiraudie to do something else with suspense that does not require him to think about homophobic representation or the establishment of normativity despite the pre-gay-equality setting. As Young aptly sums it up, 'the battles of gay liberation already having been won, Guiraudie is free to be Hitchcock' (2018: 231).

Hitchcock's film takes place from the perspective of the two main characters, not from Rupert's point of view. Despite embodying the law, Rupert is not simply a signifier of a heteronormative order, for he brings, as Greven puts it, 'an increasingly emotional urgency to the role and to the film ... He ... shares in the queer anguish he promulgates' (2017: 23). The film may, broadly speaking, invite the non-queer viewer in to their 'criminality' and to a situation in which it is unclear if they will be caught. Richard Allen writes that Hitchcock's interest is not in rendering homosexuality abject or abhorrent, but 'in staging the performance of a gentlemanliness beneath which the darkest secrets are harbored in a manner that renders them alluring and often sympathetic' (2007: 128). As with *L'Inconnu du lac*, all viewers are brought along for the suspenseful ride with queer subjectivity. As a character who spends time observing and is not directly part of the action as a body more corpulent than the other bodies, Henri may be a directorial figure literally sitting in for Hitchcock. Consequently, Henri's murder late in the film in a sense kills off *Rope* as a Hitchcockian intertext, allowing Guiraudie's innovative ending to move queer cinema in a direction in which gay characters do not have to get arrested and in which social normativity does not have to assert itself at the end of the narrative. While Brandon and Phillip do not have a future except as inmates, calling attention to their fate points towards a future where homosexuality will not have to be criminal, but Guiraudie recasts gay criminality in a context in which criminality is not opposed to legality but represents in another register altogether.

On the hunt: *Du soleil pour les gueux*

Before his first feature film came out in 2001, Guiraudie made three short films: *Les Héros sont immortels* (*Heroes are Immortal*) (1990), *Tout droit jusqu'au matin* (*Straight Ahead until Morning*) (1994), and *La Force des choses* (*Force of Circumstance*) (1997). In an interview, the director described the basic elements of *L'Inconnu du lac* that already could be found in *Héros*, namely 'someone who comes every day to the same place' (Guiraudie, 2013b: 50). In the short, two men sit and talk each night waiting for someone to come, prefiguring the way in which the men spend much of their time in *L'Inconnu du lac* sitting on the beach. Guiraudie also made a film for TV titled *On m'a volé mon adolescence* (*My Adolescence was Stolen*) (2007), very much unlike the rest of his corpus as a story about a family, heterosexual adolescence, and divorce.

Guiraudie set his one-hour *Du soleil pour les gueux* on a limestone plateau (*causse*) in south-central France. The film resembles *La Force des choses* in atmosphere, both taking place in a uchronic rural setting. As will be the case in *L'Inconnu du lac*, more than a decade later, the characters seem to be seeking self-annihilation in a natural world firmly outside of urban time and space. A young woman named Nathalie Sanchez

(Isabelle Girardet) is searching for a shepherd that tends to flocks of animals called 'ounayes'. She locates a laid-back shepherd, Djema Gaouda Lon (Michel Turquin), but he has lost his flock. Finding these beasts has been a dream of hers since she was a kid in another world where she grew up, an elsewhere very much unlike the setting of the film. This world is, as she puts it, 'another world, full of monsters' that she had set out for a number of times on her bicycle while a girl but in the end never approached because of fear. She wants to have sex with the shepherd that she finds, even though he is married and substantially older than she is, and the two do end up having sex in the grass of the plateau. She discusses cross-cultural differences with him, including the legality of suicide and the nature of justice. Nathalie and the shepherd continue searching for the flock as they meet other characters, and the film concludes with Nathalie finally locating an ounaye. She wants to pet it, but, as she was told earlier in the film, the animals, when they are sick, live vampirically by sucking human blood, potentially transmitting a disease called borondale, to humans. The shepherd had shown her his forearm with ounaye bites and she touched it out of curiosity to see if the wound hurts. To have sex with the married shepherd was to have contact with a potentially diseased shepherd who had his blood sucked out by the mythical creatures. In the final shot, Nathalie, who finds the animals 'cute' and smaller than she imagined, walks out of sight of the camera to go touch one, though warned that she should not and that she may become infected. The film closes, then, on the loss of blood and infection in this world in which she did not grow up. In hindsight, it would seem that she has been seeking this vampirism all her life, that she wants to give energy to a mythical beast by being bitten and becoming diseased.

This curative vampirism leading to her own illness reveals a desire to be infected by a world with its own rules and logic, one that would allow her normative world to be transformed in turn once she returns back to it. In the world from which she comes, she is bored by her life as a hairdresser since her income only affords her basic necessities for living, nothing more. While she does not fully understand the rules of this otherworld, her body opens up an alternate form of exchange not predicated on a service-based economy or the world of labour that she cannot otherwise escape. Her infection to come is not negative, for the disease, in exchange for her blood, will infect the oppressive capitalist economy that only allows her to survive and not thrive or prosper.

Alongside Nathalie Sanchez's transformation relating to disease, there is a second narrative, relating to death. An outlaw-bandit Carol Izba, played by Guiraudie himself, roams the plateau, but he is being tracked by a hired 'pursuit warrior' (*guerrier de poursuite*) named Pool Oxanosas Daï (Jean-Paul Jourdàa), who wants to capture him for the client that has hired him. If he succeeds, he will be paid handsomely and he will be able to leave for a tropical island and not work for much of the rest of the year. Whether the crime that Carol Izba has committed deserves this treatment is unclear (Nathalie thinks not, and the shepherds of the area are happy that someone who oppressed them has been killed by Carol Izba). Not only is the need for justice ambiguous, but it is not fully clear that the pursuit warrior is even performing his duty at all. He is unable to complete his mission successfully, perhaps as he tells some unknown person on the phone, because he is not well and is suffering from jet lag. The two men are always proximate in distance, both talking to Nathalie and the shepherd at multiple points. In one scene they perform a dance-like push-me-pull-me chase, mocking the very idea of a linear chase in which one man should be running after the other. The warrior is so exhausted from the chase scene that he falls to the ground, shirtless and wearing loose shorts, as Carol Izba stops and returns to look at his body (plate 6). This scene follows the one in which Nathalie and the shepherd have sex, as if the men's movements across the prairie are as sexual in nature as the two heterosexual characters' sex act. The homoerotic gaze of the character-director suggests that the follower–followed relation is recast in a new way: the man being hunted should not return to gaze on his pursuer's erotic body. The economic relation between a paid hunter and his victim is queered, putting the idea of paid labour into question. Guiraudie's outlaw character (also shirtless) – and by extension the film itself – is aroused by virtue of being pursued for money. The pursuit might not be related to justice or money at all, but an erotic exchange that renders the stated reasons for the pursuit suspicious in the first place and reconfigures the relation between the two men, questioning relationality in broader terms. The queer reconstruction of relationality in *L'Inconnu du lac* via eros and murder is here in nascent form as the pursuit warrior is a desired, and not feared, male body – much like Michel.

This homoerotic gaze is not the only element of the film that calls into question the meaning of relationality. The bandit cannot escape the plain at all: though he is pursued, he remains in the area, returning again and again to where he should not be if he values his life. He cannot run off to Montpellier because, he says, the local beverage that he loves is not good there. For both Nathalie and Carol Ibza, the plateau is the space of the reconfiguration of subjectivity, reflecting Deleuze and Guattari's description of the plateau (via Gregory Bateson) as 'a continuous, self-vibrating region of intensities whose development avoids any orientation toward a culmination point or external end' (1987: 22). Only here do logical rules of normative culture and identity not apply as capitalism is deterritorialized and Guiraudie's movement is a line of flight away from the molar, not a linear flight from pursuit. Were Carol Ibza to go to the city of Montpellier, he would be unable to reconfigure anything, preferring to remain in this queer rural world. Conversely, Natalie comes to this world from elsewhere in order to have a mythic transaction that would reconfigure capitalism. The bite will infect, above all, normative assumptions in the world outside this one. This is the sunshine for the poor (*gueux*) of the title, the possibility of systemic transformation in this natural setting.[14] The bright spot is not that the poor get money or become rich, but that the concept of economic transaction is transcended in the first place.

Negotiating structures: *Voici venu le temps*

Guiraudie's *Voici venu le temps* contains many of the same otherworldly elements as *Du soleil pour les gueux*, and the temporal context remains unclear as medieval, feudal elements are juxtaposed with industrial and capitalistic ones without any line of demarcation. The rural setting and character of the film evoke American westerns as well, putting genre into question. The main character, a 'guerrier de recherche' (search warrior) named Fogo Lompla (Eric Bougnon), works for men with money to track down whomever they want. In the opening scene, he locates two men who presumably owe the man that has hired him money and he then captures them. After counting the amount of money that they had on them, they begin to negotiate with Fogo Lompla about the money that he needs to return to the man who hired him, even though they are tied up. The ways in which negotiation and currency function in this environment have their own set of rules that do not make sense to outsiders. It seems odd on one level that Fogo would negotiate with the men he has tied up. But on another level, the set of rules specific to this uchronia suggests that the entire film could be taken as about negotiation, with respect not to money but to identity. The film will ask how humans could negotiate identity in new ways. Fogo Lompla's homosexuality is never an issue as such, as if the sex/gender system

---

14 The word *gueux* also suggests a space that lacks ornamentation, an appropriate sense for Guiraudie's plain setting.

functions beyond homophobia or heterosexism, and the world is subtended by a form of gender negotiation that follows rules unlike ours today.[15] Further, the hero's two lovers are both older, one significantly, suggesting that eroticism around age has already been reconfigured as well.

The question of negotiation is not simply related to sexuality per se however, but to political and economic structures. Major questions in the film are how and whether the shepherds of the region should be 'liberated', whether those resisting hegemonic power forces should be able to resist in any way possible, and – for the main character – what to do about love that looks to be impossible. Should he liberate himself from impossible queer love? Fogo Lompla has two older male lovers, a man who works at the bank in town that presumably hired him to collect the money in the opening scene, and a second man who is married to a woman. Fogo Lompla is a well-respected warrior, but he has many questions about local politics, his profession and, especially, about his love affairs. The inability to have the kind of love that he desires parallels his inability to fully participate in the socio-economic context that he critiques. There is a Marxist element to the film, Guiraudie himself notes on an interview on the DVD (Guiraudie, 2009), a revolutionary aspect to the main character even as he 'asks himself questions' about the theory and practice of power and revolution. To ask questions about same-sex love is to ask questions about power, to consider non-normative ways to negotiate in love is to consider other ways to negotiate in terms of class, economics, and power.

---

15 Cheval (2016: 166) makes similar comments about the film, positioning it within a French cultural context in which the PACS (legal domestic partnerships) had existed for six years but same-sex marriage and full equality were beginning to be possible. The full integration of queer desire and love in this world suggests the world to come in the gay world of 2005.

The hero has no sure answers on either score since the film only asks questions about how desire and power could or should function, not offering any definitive answers. The queerness of the film, in the end, pertains less to sexuality, and more to the series of questions that are opened up but not answered.

This focus on queer questioning explains why the love story does not end happily. When one of the objects of his desire is aroused by Fogo Lompla's sleeping in his house and goes outside to masturbate, Fogo Lompla follows him and they begin to have sex, but the older man dies during the act. In addition, Fogo Lompla decides to leave his other lover, Toba Louhan, even though they have a physical relationship, meaning that in the end he is without any lover at all. Lacking love and questioning the foundations of his cultural context, he asks himself at the tail end of the film if he should remain in the area or leave for some unknown place. He is a man of questions, embodying the queer questioning of normative regimes. This final openness is not unlike the dark final scene of *L'Inconnu du lac* as both films ask but do not answer questions about how subjectivity might be reconfigured in the dark or in a state of unknowingness.

Moving queer reality

In *Ce vieux rêve qui bouge* (*Real Cool Time*, literally translated, 'That Old Dream that Moves'), queer relationality is inextricably linked to the closing of a rural factory and, by extension, to industrial capitalism. The 50-minute film reveals how capitalism helps maintain normative erotic relations while the symbolic dismantling of capitalism creates erotic possibilities that might not exist or might not exist as much under traditional capitalism. This dismantling is metaphorical, but it is also literal since a man who does not work at the factory comes there for no other reason than to take apart a machine so that the factory can definitively close. Unlike *Du soleil pour les gueux* and Guiraudie's later films, *Ce vieux rêve qui bouge* does not take place in nature or in rural outdoor spaces, but inside and around the nearly abandoned factory.[16]

The film begins with a series of male workers entering a factory while the man the spectator will soon learn is not a long-standing employee of the factory waits for someone. The scene references the Lumière brothers' famous exit of male and female factory workers in Lyon ('Workers Leaving the Lumière Factory' (1895)), which launches the idea of film in France and of movement as cinematic concept. The short conveys the sense of the working class leaving work at the very same moment. As German director Farocki says about this influential scene, the movement of the workers was symbolic of 'the absent and hidden movements of goods, values, and ideas that were in circulation in industry' (2002: 72).[17] On one level, Guiraudie offers another take on this familiar scene, with the 'hidden movement' of homoerotics a fresh take on an old theme: his film will entail working-class movement predicated on the idea of entry, not exit. Guiraudie's characters are entering something new, not leaving work for what is presumably their post-work leisure-time. The male characters are coming into a new representational space, one in which male homoerotics will be highlighted front and centre. The factory, as a redefined space, functions as a kind of nowhere space beyond daily life: we never see any of the characters at home, only at

16 The French film's title evokes a line from the song 'Les Barbares' by Bernard Lavilliers (1976), with the addition of 'vieux' ('old') which is not in the song. The song is about miners and their dreams of leaving their laborious jobs. The men are 'militant' in their determination to obtain 'this dream that moves' ('ce rêve qui bouge'). The song also refers to locker rooms in which the workers 'steal five minutes' from their work, not unlike the men in the film who drink or gaze erotically at male bodies in the locker room.
17 On this scene, see Peyrière (2012). As evidence of the scene's influence, German director Harun Farocki put together a hundred years of scenes with workers leaving factories (1995).

the factory, and when the characters have leisure time in the form of *apéritif* (before-dinner drink), it takes place in a green space within the factory complex, not at one of the characters' homes. The factory is a special space not defined by work (we do not actually see them working), but by the reconfiguration of sexualities. If the Lumière brothers' scene inaugurates film, here is the inception of a combination of factory labour and queerness. The workers will not do what the manager wants them to do, since their labour is representational and not physical. Instead, as Fabienne Bullot describes the film, Guiraudie is opening 'a field of possibilities' (2014: 320).[18]

The factory is in the process of closing, and the workers are working for their last week, but there is no actual work for them to do during this transition period. Jacques, played by Pierre Louis-Calixte, has come to the factory to dismantle a machine named the 'Ubitona' for management. The machine is a nonsensical machine whose function cannot be understood, even as the characters discuss its workings. The machine, however, resembles an old-time reel film projector: what is being dismantled in a sense is an old-fashioned form of cinema predicated on old-fashioned forms of gender and sexuality. The Latin word '*ubi*' (meaning 'where') suggests, too, that what is being dismantled is place itself, or the factory's traditional associations with work alone and that the space is redefined as a space of eros.

This film, more than any of Guiraudie's others, relates to the thesis put forward by John D'Emilio, that capitalism is at the root of the development of gay identity. As more and more people with same-sex desires moved to cities to work as industrial capitalism developed in the West, they increasingly experienced a sense of similarity with other people whose sexualities

---

18 I also agree with Bullot that the film 'transforms the genre of social realism into a working-class poetics' (2014: 318).

they perceived as like their own, and as a consequence, something resembling what we now label 'homosexuality' began to arise and to solidify as a category of identity. D'Emilio writes: 'two aspects of capitalism – wage labor and commodity production – created the social conditions that made possible the emergence of a distinctive gay and lesbian identity' (1999: 48). He very carefully explains that he is not positing that 'capitalism causes homosexuality nor that it determines the form that homosexual desire takes' (48). Capitalism 'has made possible the formation of urban communities of lesbians and gay men and, more recently, of a politics based on sexual identity' (50). One might imagine men and women moving to Manchester in England or Lyons in France to work in factories and meeting among the other men and women who came there to work, some people who preferred to have what we now call homosexual sex or affective relations with people of the same gender. These people, no longer necessarily constrained by the heterosexual family and the cultural link between sexuality and procreation, had new sexual options not available in the same way in an agrarian-based or family-based economy. What Guiraudie's film suggests, however, is a shift from homosexuality linked to industrial capitalism (albeit it in a small-town, quasi-rural form) to anti-industrial forms of queer male sexuality that reject traditional, stable notions of male homosexuality as like seeking like. Dismantling industrial capitalism produces new ways of being a sexual subject, much as the invention of industrial capitalism had originally allowed for 'homosexual' to be invented as a new way to live, to be, and to love. When Jacques dismantles the machine, 'homosexuality' is taken apart so that an economy of queer masculinity can take its place. The converse is true at the same time: to queer sexuality is to reconfigure the economy. As Preciado puts it, 'the new political organization of labour cannot be achieved without a new political organization of gender and sexuality' (2018: 13) since capitalism is organized through heterosexuality. Queerness here aims to create a new organization of labour.

A key element of that new queer space will be forms of desire predicated on differences between men, especially age. Jacques is presented as a kind of travelling dismantler, someone who moves around taking machines apart and not staying in the same place for too long. He notes that he had to spend a year at one factory, and he was very ready to go after that length of time. Not held down by heteronormativity or by homonormativity, he embodies movement itself, but movement predicated on queer erotics as capitalism comes down. He makes it clear that he has erotic desire for Donand (Jean-Marie Combelles), the manager of the factory who is quite a bit older than he is, but who is also part of the managerial class. Donand may or may not be 'gay', but he hesitatingly comes in to see Jacques repeatedly on several occasions, leaving quickly in some cases. Despite the obvious attraction, Donand's desire is linked to dismantling. In one scene, he comes to see Jacques in the middle of the factory and stands next to the Ubitona, right next to a phallic-looking tube section of the machine. Jacques is aroused by him and begins to touch his crotch with his hands. It is unclear what is going to happen, but then Donand pulls away from him. Jacques tries again later to touch him, and he refuses a second time, again for ambiguous reasons. In another scene, he invites Jacques to have coffee with him and they begin talking about personal matters. Donand tells Jacques that he is a 'beau garçon' and he returns the compliment, noting that women are not his 'thing' and that he has an emotional life with men.

Jacques seems to be dismantling binarism and to be producing a queer heterosexuality that cannot be labelled. Donand tells him late in the film that it is 'impossible' for them, even as he admits that he has some feelings for Jacques. It is a fantasy that anything can happen, he tells him, and he should not believe in 'things that do not exist' and he has 'extrapolated' from the situation in ways that do not correspond to reality.

Conversely, the older worker Louis (Jean Segani) comes into the locker room and makes a move on Jacques whom he has desired for several days. Jacques refuses him but agrees to have dinner at his house. Louis embodies real-life, concrete gay possibility, unlike Donand. In the final scene, echoing the opening scene, Jacques and Louis leave the factory, talking about why the former does not desire the latter. Jacques is invested in another form of non-capitalist queerness, not a corporeal homosexuality based on Louis's shirtless body, revealed in an earlier scene. Louis wants to know if the issue is his age or his size, but Jacques avoids these questions as his investment is not in how desire functions in such physically oriented terms but in queering relationality itself.

The dismantling has an aesthetic element: Donand stands for the queer eye of the camera, or rather he becomes the queer eye. The factory locker room with the shower room behind is filmed as male bodies including Jacques's are shown naked, or dressing or undressing with a fixed eye gazing from the same vantage point. There would seem to be a queer male gaze unattached to any body. In the penultimate scene, Donand appears in the workers' locker room where he does not normally go. Guiraudie flips the perspective, and the camera eye looks from the shower room to the locker room. Donand stands where the camera had been: he is retroactively made into the queer eye. He has perhaps been there all along, aesthetically speaking. His comings and goings to see Jacques may have taken place in the locker room as well as in the factory. Or have they? Is that gaze the one imagined by Jacques? Has Jacques created in his mind a queer eye that has 'seen' him naked in the locker room? Is he the one responsible for dismantling or transferring Donand's normative sexuality? In short, Jacques's dismantling process may create new ways to see as much as to desire queerly.

As the film opens and closes on credits, an all-male chorus sings Berlioz's three-verse 'Villanelle', the text taken from a poem by Théophile Gautier (1841). In the verses, the male singer and his 'belle' will, as spring comes, gather lilies-of-the-valley, listen to blackbirds, 'talk of [their] beautiful love', affirm their love's eternal nature, and then 'bring back home wild / Strawberries' (2000). The words suggest a heterosexual peasant narrative defined spatially, man and woman leaving home, going out, reaffirming their love, and coming back again to where they began. The movie, by contrast, is not circular in structure: a 'new season' has in a sense come, but love here is not 'forever' nor is it domestic, not returning back to the domestic sphere. The two characters Louis and Jacques in the final scene head back to Louis's house for dinner where there will be no sex and where they will not bring back erotic symbols such as wild strawberries. They have not gone to the forest to collect food or flowers but are returning home empty-handed as the factory closes for the last time. Love here does not collect or accumulate, for queer relationality takes place beyond the realm of capitalist narratives of accumulation or heteronormative narratives of natural and eternal love. It may well be a 'new season', but that season is the closing of the factory and thus the representational end of the dominance of industrial capitalism's hold on homosexuality.

Sleeping queerly: *Pas de repos pour les braves*

As Guiraudie's first film over an hour long, *Pas de repos pour les braves* is presented in the opening scene as a metaphysical narrative about sleep and waking hours. Basile (Thomas Suire) sits in a café with another young man about his age named Igor (Thomas Blanchard) and recounts that if he goes to sleep, it will be his next-to-last sleep ('avant-dernier sommeil') and that he will then die after that. Presumably, then, he needs to remain awake forever and cannot enter into sleep mode. He reacts negatively when he believes that Igor does not take him seriously, getting up in anger and leaving the café. His departure suggests not so much that he is angry at Igor, but that he is entering into a dream about not sleeping – what will be the rest of the film. He enters an alternate world that is neither fully dream nor fully reality. Lying outside normative realms of space, time, and sexuality, it is a uchronic world not defined by capitalist time with an eight-hour workday, leisure time after work and on the weekend, and eight hours of sleep during the night to rest up for work the next day. Basile does not work as much as he does not sleep. He explains at the end of the film that he remains awake until 4 a.m. and cannot get up early, but also that he cannot work, in part because of his location outside normative time. His leisure time is not in opposition to work time, and he does not even really have leisure time per se, even as he does activities that could be considered leisurely (dancing, playing pool, watching television).

In a number of scenes, Basile lies awake at night, not asleep or resting. He repeatedly goes to visit Roger (Roger Guidone), a much older man that loves him and lives in the '*village-qui-meurt*' (the village that dies). They do not actually have sex at any point, but erotic tenderness and loving companionship between the two is very palpable. Basile caresses him as he lies shirtless in bed in one scene, and Roger caresses Basile as he lies shirtless outside in a natural setting, as a sign of mutual non-sexual erotics pointing towards a relation not named as gay or intergenerational. To get to Roger's home, Basile has to walk across a plateau of some kind, often at night, and the camera follows him across this plateau, as if he is entering a dreamworld akin to Deleuze and Guattari's 'self-vibrating region of intensities'. There is something representationally queer, then, about entering into a night-time dreamworld that deterritorializes the molar identity of male homosexuality. It is a queerness not defined by sexual acts, but by cross-generational erotic and affective connections. The night is not a time for sex or sexual acts as much as for queer alternate realities.

That Basile has to journey, very visibly, to get to the 'village that dies' and enter another space very separate and distinct from the village where much of the action takes place (the '*village-qui-vit*', or the 'village that lives') suggests that queer – broadly speaking – is not just defined through time, but through space as well. Basile is in his own physical world as much as he is in his own temporal world. One of the characters, named Johnny Got (Laurent Soffiati), decides to track down and kill Basile because he has supposedly killed many members of a neighbouring village. When he finally locates Basile, he points his gun at him, but cannot kill him because he is located in an alternate universe of some kind. As he notes this, he calls him a 'faggot' (*pédé*), and then Basile takes off randomly down a series of corridors, as if in a funhouse, to show that he is not so much running away but in some other space that cannot quite be defined. His alternate universe is a queer one separate from the mostly heteronormative world and the non-queer characters around him (e.g., Igor, Johnny Got), but it is a world of dreams or illusions that do not last or survive. Dressed as a pilot, Basile begins to prepare a small plane to flee in one scene, but it turns out that the plane is out of gas. When he enters a random café set in the middle of a field, the locals make jokes at his expense, and they refuse to give him petrol as he is not a local. He is a stranger to them in this normative dreamworld. He cannot take off away from those who surround him, stuck in a world that he cannot escape and that does not support his alternate world.

Queerness, then, does not ultimately dismantle normativity: for Basile's own spatiality remains separate from other spatial configurations. The film can be taken as a story of the transition from a queer, alternate world into the realm of other worlds neither queer nor normative. About halfway through the film, Roger dies (though Johnny Got later tells Basile that he is not really dead) and the explicitly queer elements of the film drop out. The narrative transitions to a mock thriller story (or a *film noir*, as Guiraudie called it (Boffet *et al.*, 2003)), in which Johnny Got – accompanied by Basile and Igor – is pursued by outlaws for reasons that are never fully comprehensible and the line between reality and dream is unclear. In the final scene, Basile sits in a village square delivering a monologue in which he explains his own space in his world. After all, he notes, 'this place is my home' and people are what he wants to focus on. His future might not be clear and he might not be able to work now since he stays up so late at night, but 'with time' everything 'should work out'. The opening premise of the film, that if he sleeps it will be the penultimate sleep and he will then die, has been proven false since he has slept and still lives. Instead, Basile has invented a third world, in which he is not alone queerly on the other side of an invisible wall or alone with Roger elsewhere.

This film makes implicit reference to Calderón's classic play from the Spanish Golden Age, *Life is a Dream* (1636) through the character Basilio. Not a queer play, it is a key literary text about the indistinction between dream and reality: Basilio, the King of Poland, has kept his son Segismund locked away in a tower so that he not act tyrannically were he to assume his rightful place as king. Basilio decides however to let him out for a while to see if he can act as a just king should, but allows himself an out should the experiment not work out: he will tell his son that life is a dream and becoming king was nothing but a dream. Segismund however has his own discourse on life as dream that puts into question the nature of reality in broader, metaphysical ways than simply his father's attempt to control him. 'The insight life's experience gives / Is that, until man wakes, he lives / A life that only dreams contrive' (Calderón de la Barca, 2006: 78). This idea puts into question all aspects of life, including – above all – whether Basilio is dreaming that he is king in the first place: 'The king dreams he is king and reigns / Deluded in his full command' (78).

In Guiraudie's film, likewise, it is never fully clear what is reality and what is a dream taking place while awake. Does Roger really die, for instance? A giant wave comes up on the beach and takes him away in a very dream-like sequence, but Johnny Got later tells Basile that Roger did not die. When Basile falls asleep with Johnny Got in the room, he dreams that the clock that is supposed to wake him up gets stolen. The scene ends however back in what looked to be an earlier scene in which he was in a hotel room with Johnny Got. He may well be dreaming, but that possible dream is not verified as a dream. The fluid line between reality and dream explains, in part, the non-linearity of the film as well as its lack of coherent narrative and may explain why critics of the film called it 'the most formally experimental of Guiraudie's works' (Pendleton and Grundmann, 2014: 16) and his 'most overtly zany feature' and 'also his patchiest and most self-indulgent' (Romney, 2014: 66).

That fluidity might explain – or be explained by – the film's queerness, a fluid homoeroticism that never involves sex acts but does become a springboard to enter the dream-like state bordering reality. Guiraudie in a sense queers Calderón's play, replacing royal power with homoerotics as the dream-reality element. For a viewer to see homoerotics represented on screen but not to see it lead anywhere sexual is to destabilize the line between the real and the non-real. By the end of Calderón's play, Segismund does become king of Poland, meaning that his father Basilio's attempt to control him through the life as dream manipulation ends up failing. The conclusion of *Pas de repos*, too, abandons the idea that sleep will lead to death, and thus that the dream-like state avoiding sleep has to be maintained. It is not exactly true that reality fully takes over at the end of the film, but the dream-like qualities of Basile's experience appear less dream-like. The end of the Spanish play parallels Basile's final monologue, which gestures towards a future reality beyond the scope and logic of the film. Basile may wake up from his dream-like state, as the conclusion of Calderón's play suggests. Segismund concludes the play, as King, by noting that his dream may return and he will 'awake to find [him]self / Imprisoned once again' (Calderón de la Barca, 2006: 120).

When Segismundo responds to the question 'What's life?' with the response that it is 'not anything it seems. / A shadow. Fiction filling reams' (79), he could definitely be talking about *Pas de repos pour les braves* and indeed about Guiraudie's cinematic corpus – a series of queer fictional worlds that may be reality or dream-like, may be neither here nor there.

Queer lines of flight: *Le Roi de l'évasion*

Taken together, the two opening scenes of *Le Roi de l'évasion* convey – in comic fashion – the film's take on sexual subjectivity. In the first scene, the main character Armand (Ludovic Berthillot), a successful and well-liked middle-aged salesman of tractors and farm machinery, is making a sale with an older farmer named Robert (Pierre Laur). The discussion centres not on which tractor to purchase, but on the colour of the tractor that Robert wants to buy. He cannot decide. His mother comes out on the deck where they are discussing the issue, irritatingly interrupting the discussion between the two men. It then becomes clear that the two men have an erotic connection, and Robert wants Armand to come back for lunch when his mother is not there. Immediately, the film 'evades' traditional images of gay desire. On one level, this erotic scene between rural, older men talking about tractor purchases rejects, as Rees-Roberts puts it, 'gay narrative clichés by presenting (and later eroticizing) character types and body shapes that are wholly neglected by contemporary cinema – bodies that are worn out by age or no longer in perfect physical condition' (2015: 451). This will not be a film about chiselled gay urban youth. The rainbow of possible tractor colours adds another kind of queer subjectivity to the LGBTQ rainbow on screen.

Yet, the additions to queer sexualities on screen are more than simply age and body type, Robert cannot decide, and in fact does not settle on a colour for a tractor. As he walks Armand to his car, he tells him that he cannot decide between the blue and the red, caught between two choices. The film, in the realm of sexuality, likewise will avoid selecting with respect to sexuality. Although gay, Armand will end up with a lover named Curly, a young (underage) woman who quickly becomes attached to him when he saves her from a group of harassing young men on the city street. Curly is played by French actress Hafsia Herzi, who is of Algerian/Tunisian descent, known for her role as Rym in Kechiche's 2007 film about a couscous restaurant, *La Graine et le mulet* (*The Secret of the Grain*) for which she won the most promising actress César in 2008. Armand moves between homosexual and heterosexual and between older men and younger women, as well as between white and non-white bodies. Late in the film, Armand will change his mind yet again about sexuality and leave Curly, reversing course and fleeing heterosexuality. There is something 'evasive' not just about Armand but also about orientation: it is never fully asserted and it resists linguistically recognizable articulations.

In the second scene of the film, Armand's boss tells him that he cannot encroach on other salesmen's territory since he is such a charming and successful salesman, and that he is stealing sales and commissions from other salesmen in 'their' territory. He crosses a clear geographical dividing line, and other salesman are angry because he is seductive and farmers might be attracted to Armand in some manner. He crosses defined borders not only of geography, but also of sexuality. Any man – whatever their orientation – might end up seduced by Armand, threatening 'fair' capitalism. Yet, what is also revealed here is that the evasiveness or fluidity around sexuality in the film as a whole will be subject to broader social forces that do not allow undefined forms of sexuality to exist. Fluid or molecular sexualities will be territorialized, made to exist within delineated or molar categories outside of which they will not be allowed to err. 'Sectors are sectors', Armand's boss tells him. Because he has had a physical relation with the underage Curly, Armand is forced to wear a tracking bracelet and during much of the middle of the film, he is tracked by a representative of law enforcement, the embodiment of normative regimes of sexuality. Being tracked through the forest and across streams for much of the film serves as a recurring metaphor for containing and stabilizing sexuality. He is surveilled as a gay man even when he 'becomes' heterosexual because it is sexuality per se that is monitored, not a given orientation. His quick movement through the natural territory of rural France parallels his errancy with regard to sexuality as well as normalization. The law officials cannot understand how Armand moves so quickly through the forest, or in Deleuzian terms how he evades the territorialization of molar sexuality so well with lines of flight.

The conflict between territorializing and deterritorializing, however, takes a third turn in the final scene, involving the two men of the opening scene, a man named Jean (Jean Toscan), and Armand's boss (presumably heterosexual, but whom Armand convinced to give oral sex). While having oral sex with Armand, Jean, seemingly the oldest man present, does not want to orgasm or ejaculate, preferring instead to save himself for more sex (plate 7). If he does not orgasm, he notes, his 'love stays alive'. It took him seventy years to learn this, he tells Armand. Sex becomes open-ended, not defined by the linearity of male ejaculation, but by a process. Jean asks Armand if orgasm makes him happy afterward, and Armand responds with a strong desire to kiss him – a sign of a new form of desire yet to be articulated, decidedly outside an ejaculatory framework.

Jean is holding out for something more, much as the narrative is holding out for new sexual possibilities as well. The metaphor of Robert's inability, or unwillingness, to settle on a tractor colour returns here, as he too is present in the scene, transformed into an unwillingness to finalize the sexual act, to let it remain open-ended. The final shot of the film is of the four men in the cabin in bed, turning off the light, with Jean calling to Armand not to go too far away from him. Rees-Roberts describes this scene as the film's 'climax in the interchangeable communion of bodies and the human need for affective comfort, in relational modes structured around an erotic reconfiguration of sexual friendship as an experimental form of sociability' (2015: 453). The setting of the final scene is an abandoned house in the woods, a kind of temporary step (*gîte d'étape*) on a wayward flight that will continue after the scene and the film both end. Dalton reads this final scene as a 'modest queer utopia' (2019: 88) based on a connection to the natural world that surrounds it: it is 'a dwelling of neither self-shattering transgression nor dystopian non-futurity, but rather the quiet potentiality of a queer cultivation of hermeneutic and epigenetic interactions with non-human surroundings' (88). Before he arrives at the cabin, Armand leaves the forest and sits in the middle of a winery, grapes growing all around him. He is a sexual subject resembling the grapes of the winery, free in the natural world on the one hand but also on the way to 'cultivation'. The cabin in the woods is the locus of the mixture, much like the vines in the vineyard, at the intersection of nature and culture, neither fully contained by molar subjectivities nor fully wild and molecular either. Armand evades sexual stability, but it is an evasion that still has a relation to the molar that chases him and will continue to chase him. In the end, sexuality is a negotiation that allows for cultivation of new queer forms, but within constraints that keep sexuality from flowing freely.

Vertical queer: *Rester vertical*

The question of deterritorializing is central to Guiraudie's next film, *Rester vertical*. As a new kind of queer pastoral, it eschews traditional or classical shepherd/homosexual connections in favour of a radical opening up of erotic relations in nature where new types of queer masculinities emerge. Even more than with Armand in *Le Roi de l'évasion*, Léo (Damien Bonnard) cannot be pinned down with respect to sexuality. When asked if the character was 'bisexual', Guiraudie responded that the category does not interest Léo and that he would find it irritating to 'define him as heterosexual or as homosexual' (Guiraudie, 2016a). On the one hand, he operates in a heterosexual framework, albeit a non-traditional one. Soon after randomly meeting Marie (India Hair), a farmer/shepherdess, he has sex with her, and they later have a child whom he takes primary responsibility to raise when Marie leaves him and the farm with her two other kids. A loving caretaker of his baby throughout the film, Léo takes on the 'maternal' elements of childrearing in the face of the failure of the seemingly heterosexual relationship. On the other hand, Léo has a visible attraction to the young man Yoan (Basile Meilleurat). Nothing sexual happens between the two of them, but the erotic element, at least on Léo's part, is palpable. The film, in fact, begins with a travelling shot of the road along which Léo drives as he cruises Yoan, not knowing who he is, and he stops to ask if he would want to do a screen test. The film is presented from the opening scene as about queer cruising and Léo may be cruising or on the hunt (as a 'lion') the entire film. His desire for Yoan does not end here, even as Yoan refuses his advances. Later, he penetrates Marcel anally (Christian Bouillette), an old homophobic presumably gay man on his deathbed, who at the same time takes a drug to die – an act that Léo describes as 'assisted suicide'. Marie's father Jean-Louis (Raphaël Thiéry) wants to have sex with Léo, who does not return his advances. Queer male eros is widespread, and no man's sexuality is ever categorically clear. A key element of the narrative is that Léo, a scriptwriter for films, is unable to write a script for the producer who is after him. Literally tracking Léo down, the producer at one point paddles a canoe down a river to find him, hidden in the water.

In this queer rural world without sublimation, work or production cannot operate normally and a final product cannot be created. Léo cannot work or produce, nor can he participate actively in a capitalist mode of work. His relation to desire and sexuality gestures towards a futurity to come, a script yet to be completed or even composed. Gender and sexual scripts do not, literally or metaphorically, exist for Léo or for the film in a broader sense. Guiraudie proclaimed that this film was his 'queerest film' of all (Guiraudie, 2016a), despite the fact that *L'Inconnu* was much more graphic with respect to sex acts. He might have meant that *Rester vertical* destabilizes stable subjectivities around gender and sexuality more radically. McCaffrey explains this queerness as radical because it transcends human bodies: 'Guiraudie is carving out a queerness that not only transgresses and traverses boundaries of subject, self, and identity but, in its capacity to "devenir-tout," Guiraudie expands how we understand queer intimacy by seeing it as extending outwards to include the natural, vegetal, material, and cosmic' (2019: 405).

The film expands long-standing ideas of the pastoral as a space in which same-sex male sexuality, originally pederastic, can function as natural, without the constraints that might exist in urban areas (see Shuttleton, 2000). In Virgil's second *Eclogue*, for instance, the shepherd Corydon, 'aflame for the fair Alexis' (1999: 31), tries unsuccessfully to seduce the young man with songs of the bucolic erotic pleasures of the countryside. His attempt evokes natural desires from the animal kingdom in parallel with his desires: 'The grim lioness follows the wolf, the wolf himself the goat, the wanton goat the flowering clover, and Corydon follows you' (35). While ancient Greek and Latin texts such as Theocritus or Virgil establish this tradition in Europe, it remains in less generic or classical terms in cinematic culture, with Ang Lee's *Brokeback Mountain* (2005) perhaps the most well-known example from contemporary film. In Lee's film, the bucolic naturalness of male–male love and sexual act is contrasted with the homophobia of culture itself. But in Guiraudie's film, male–male eros or sex act is not so much freed from societal constraint as much as the bucolic offers a space in which sexuality (at least for Léo) can function openly. Léo might be 'aflame' for the younger Yaon, but Jean-Louis is aflame for the younger Léo as well. Corydon follows Alexis as the wolf follows the goat and the goat follows clover, and in the film Léo (meaning 'lion') follows whatever he desires without constraint or order. It is no accident that Léo and Marie first touch each other while out watching over sheep: the pastoral offers Léo the chance not to love a younger man, but to act in heterosexual ways as much as queer ones.

Still, this waywardness does not mean that there are not stable elements to gender. Gender is not simply put into continual motion. Taking on the traditionally maternal elements of childrearing, Léo realizes over the course of the film that he does not actually want to be with Marie but wants to have a child without a woman. Though non-normative perhaps, this gender presentation is essentially stable throughout, not fully queer. Much of the film juxtaposes Léo's sexuality in movement with this stable gender construct, meaning that in the end gender for Léo is constituted by assemblages of gender and sexuality that are not fully queer.

As with Armand in *Le Roi de l'évasion*, Léo is not able to fully move on his own terms. Armand and Léo are both tracked by the state's surveillance mechanism. Because of his sex act with Marcel, the state removes his baby from him and returns him to Marie, even though she does not want him. Léo's life of wayward lines is held in check by normative elements of the culture of the nation-state. As in *L'Inconnu du lac*, the final definition of eros remains unclear, a potentially new form of being a sexual subject. Resembling Franck who may face death, Léo in the last scene may confront death head-on in the form of a wolf. The idea that wolf incarnates death on the farm had been established early on: at one point Jean-Louis and Léo find a series of dead sheep killed by wolves overnight. In the striking final scene, a pack of wolves approach Léo and Jean-Louis on the hills of the farm, with no gun in sight, as Léo holds a baby sheep in his arms. Léo wants to connect with, to touch, one of the wolves, even as there is the obvious danger that they will collectively attack the two men. Léo tells Jean-Louis that he needs to remain standing, to 'stay vertical', as per the title of the film. Léo, with his animalistic name, is becoming animal or becoming animal-like, arriving at a point where he is wayward and not static as a human subject. If the wolf metaphor in Virgil denotes the naturalness of same-sex desire, the wolf here denotes the open-endedness of Léo's subjectivity. Léo is in a sense finishing his script that he has been unable to complete, by becoming animal, or he is finishing his narrative by virtue of its open-endedness. The naturalness of the pastoral, with the animal as a metaphor for same-sex pursuit, has been turned into the pastoral queerness of becoming animal. The queer man is not like a wolf that pursues others, but he *is* wolf. Holding a baby lamb in his arms, Léo might be becoming wolf, but he is also on another level the sheep pursued by the wolf. He dismantles the metaphor of pursuit itself in Virgil's extended metaphor as he is bidirectional, pursuing and being pursued. He is sheep-like and he is lion-like. He is wayward, without linear direction. It is important too that a pack of wolves surrounds the two human characters even as Léo is in front of one lone wolf who stands still. McCaffrey reads this final scene as depicting a series of in-betweens, including 'in-between lone wolf and the pack; in-between pack multiplicity as mobility and lone wolf as stasis; in-between a straight line and a winding one' (2019: 410). The end of the film thus returns to the opening queer cruising scene, but here it puts that movement into dialogue with stasis, leaving subjectivity neither static nor entirely movement-centred. Or, to cite McCaffrey again, the film 'realign[s] queer intimacy with new lines of affect that challenge traditional Oedipal lines of filiation and the fissured sexual politics of heteronormativity' (2019: 410). As is the case across Guiraudie's corpus, *Rester vertical* concludes with a specific image of open-endedness, made possible by queer male desires that represent sexualities as much as non-normativity in broader terms, but still never fully a constant becoming either. In other words, queer representation lies in-between sexuality and normativity – a horizon bordered by constraint.

References

Allen, Richard J. (2007), *Hitchcock's Romantic Irony*, New York, Columbia University Press.

Bataille, Georges (1985), *Visions of Excess: Selected Writings, 1927–1939*, trans. Allan Stoekl, Minneapolis, University of Minnesota Press.

Bataille, Georges (1986), *Erotism: Death and Sensuality*, San Francisco, City Lights Books.

Bersani, Leo (1987), 'Is the Rectum a Grave?', *AIDS: Cultural Analysis/Cultural Activism*, 43, Winter, 197–222.

Boffet, Laurence, Moncef Zarrouk, and Didier Thiebot (2003), 'Sortie nationale du film *Pas de repos pour les braves*', *JT Locale Albi* (France 3 Albi), Archive Régions Pro, INA Notice TL00001324476.

Boussageon, Alexandre (2014), '*L'Inconnu du Lac*: Le Sexe et l'effroi selon Alain Guiraudie', *L'Obs*, www.nouvelobs.com/cinema/20130612.CIN3340/l-inconnu-du-lac-le-sexe-et-l-effroi-selon-alain-guiraudie.html (accessed 2 September 2021).

Brody, Richard (2014), 'Silence Equals Death in *Stranger by the Lake*', *The New Yorker*, www.newyorker.com/culture/richard-brody/silence-equals-death-in-stranger-by-the-lake (accessed 23 September 2021).

Bullot, Fabienne (2014), 'L'Usine vide comme imaginaire cinématographique', *Contemporary French and Francophone Studies*, 18, 3, 314–22.

Calderón de la Barca, Pedro (2006), *Life Is a Dream*, trans. Gregary Racz, New York, Penguin.

Cheval, Olivier (2016), '*Voici venu le temps d'aimer*: Les Camaraderies utopiques d'Alain Guiraudie', *Revue Critique de Fixxion Française Contemporaine*, 12, 164–73.

Crawford, Lucas (2017), 'A Good Ol' Country Time: Does Queer Rural Temporality Exist?', *Sexualities*, 20, 8, 904–20.

Dalton, Benjamin (2019), 'Cruising the Queer Forest with Alain Guiraudie: Woods, Plastics, Plasticities', in Jon Hackett and Seán Harrington, eds, *Beasts of the Forest: Denizens of the Dark Woods*, Herts, John Libbey Publishing, pp. 65–91.

Deladonchamps, Pierre (2013), '*Stranger by the Lake*: Q&A Toronto Film Fest', *Toronto Film Festival*, www.youtube.com/watch?v=UXNcWZlwxMM (accessed 5 July 2021).

Deleuze, Gilles and Félix Guattari (1987), *A Thousand Plateaus: Capitalism and Schizophrenia*, trans. Brian Massumi, Minneapolis, University of Minnesota Press.

D'Emilio, John (1999), 'Capitalism and Gay Identity', in Larry Gross and James Woods, eds, *The Columbia Reader on Lesbians and Gay Men in Media, Society, and Politics*, New York, Columbia University Press, pp. 48–55.

Farocki, Harun (1995), 'Arbeiter verlassen di Fabrik (Workers Leaving the Factory)', *Vimeo*, vimeo.com/59338090 (accessed 10 August 2021).

Farocki, Harun (2002), *Reconnaître et poursuivre*, trans. Bernard Rival and Bénédicte Vilgrain, Courbevoie, Théâtre typographique.

Fournier, Jean-Marc (2015), 'Effet de lieu, frontières et territoires sur un lieu de drague. Lecture géographique du film *L'Inconnu du lac* d'Alain Guiraudie', *Géographie et cultures*, 95, 13–28.

Friedman, Nathan (2016), 'Diagram of the Amorous Search, Generating Desire with Guiraudie's *L'Inconnu du lac*', *Scapegoat: Landscape, Architecture, Political Economy*, 9, 183–8.

Gautier, Théophile (2000), 'Villanelle', Op. 7, trans. Richard Stokes, www.oxfordlieder.co.uk/song/699 (accessed 5 July 2021).

Gray, Mary L., Colin R. Johnson, and Brian J. Gilley, eds (2016), *Queering the Countryside: New Frontiers in Rural Queer Studies*, New York, New York University Press.

Greven, David (2017), *Intimate Violence: Hitchcock, Sex, and Queer Theory*, Oxford, Oxford University Press.
Guiraudie, Alain (2001), 'Entretien avec Alain Guiraudie', film publicity brochure, *Ce vieux rêve qui bouge*, pp. 4–11.
Guiraudie, Alain (2005), 'Pas par quatre chemins: Entretien avec Alain Guiraudie', *Cahiers du cinéma*, 600, 28–9.
Guiraudie, Alain (2006), 'J'ai envie de refaire la France', *Vertigo*, 29, 2, 26–8, www.cairn.info/revue-vertigo-2006–2-page-26.htm (accessed 28 July 2020).
Guiraudie, Alain (2009), Interview with Guiraudie, *Voici venu le temps*, Epicentre Films, DVD.
Guiraudie, Alain (2013a), Interview, 'Alain Guiraudie, Jean François Sivadier, Claire Gibault et François Rivière avec A Filetta #497', *Des mots de minuit: Magazine culturel*, desmotsdeminuit. francetvinfo.fr/videotheque/alain-guiraudie-%F0%9F%8E% A5-jean-francois-sivadier-%F0%9F%8E%AD-claire-gibault-et-%F0%9F%93%9A-francois-riviere-%F0%9F%8E%BC-avec-a-filetta-497 (accessed 4 September 2021).
Guiraudie, Alain (2013b), 'Jusqu'au bout du désir: Entretien avec Alain Guiraudie', *Cahiers du cinéma*, 690, 50–3.
Guiraudie, Alain (2013c), 'Alain Guiraudie: "J'ai voulu revenir aux fondamentaux"', *L'Humanité*, www.humanite.fr/culture/alain-guiraudie-j-ai-voulu-revenir-aux-fondamentau-543575 (accessed 28 July 2020).
Guiraudie, Alain (2014a), *Ici commence la nuit*, Paris, POL Editeur.
Guiraudie, Alain (2014b), Interview with Guiraudie, *Stranger by the Lake*, Strand Home Video, DVD.
Guiraudie, Alain (2014c), 'Sunshine for the Scoundrels: An Interview with Alain Guiraudie', *Cinéaste*, 39, 3, 16–22.
Guiraudie, Alain (2016a), 'Alain Guiraudie: "*Rester vertical* est mon film le plus queer"', *Têtu*, tetu.com/2016/08/26/alain-guiraudie-rester-vertical-interview (accessed 4 July 2021).
Guiraudie, Alain (2016b), 'Alain Guiraudie: "La Frontière entre rêve et réalité est de plus en plus poreuse dans mon cinéma"', *Première*, www.premiere.fr/Cinema/News-Cinema/Alain-Guiraudie-La-frontiere-entre-reve-et-realite-est-de-plus-en-plus-poreuse-dans-mon-cinema (accessed 28 August 2021).

Guiraudie, Alain (2017), '*Staying Vertical* Q&A', *New York Film Festival*, www.youtube.com/watch?v=SB_0nN429qU (accessed 4 July 2021).

Guiraudie, Alain (2018), *Now the Night Begins*, trans. Jeffrey Zuckerman, South Pasadena, Semiotext(e).

Halberstam, Jack (2005), *In a Queer Time and Place: Transgender Bodies, Subcultural Lives*, New York, New York University Press.

Herring, Scott (2010), *Another Country: Queer Anti-Urbanism*, New York, New York University Press.

Hocquenghem, Guy (1993), *Homosexual Desire*, trans. Daniella Dangoor, Durham, NC, Duke University Press.

Johnson, Colin R. (2013), *Just Queer Folks: Gender and Sexuality in Rural America*, Philadelphia, Temple University Press.

McCaffrey, Enda (2016), '(Im)Personal Relationality in Alain Guiraudie's *Ici commence la nuit*', *Revue critique de fixxion française contemporaine*, 12, 60–71, www.revue-critique-de-fixxion-francaise-contemporaine.org/rcffc/article/view/fx12.07 (accessed 28 July 2020).

McCaffrey, Enda (2018), 'Le Retour du sexe dans le queer: *Ici commence la nuit* d'Alain Guiraudie', *Voix Plurielles*, 15, 2, 139–53.

McCaffrey, Enda (2019), 'Lupine and Zig-zag Lines: Queer Affects in Alain Guiraudie's *L'Inconnu du lac* and *Rester vertical*', *Contemporary French Civilization*, 44, 4, 387–415.

Melbourne International Film Festival (2013), 'MIFF Festival Guest Interview with Alain Guiraudie – *Stranger By The Lake*', www.youtube.com/watch?v=QXQcpBnt3jY (accessed 28 July 2020).

Migration User (2014), 'Mediocre French Thriller Keeps Getting "Stranger"', *Boston Herald*, www.bostonherald.com/2014/02/21/mediocre-french-thriller-keeps-getting-stranger (accessed 9 August 2020).

Murphy, Mekado (2014), '*Stranger by the Lake*, Anatomy of a Scene with Director Alain Guiraudie', *New York Times*, www.youtube.com/watch?v=zVlepW1KnSE (accessed 28 July 2020).

Pendleton, David and Roy Grundmann (2014), Introduction, 'Sunshine for the Scoundrels: An Interview with Alain Guiraudie', *Cinéaste*, 39, 3, 16–22.

Peyrière, Monique (2012), 'Filmer le travail, filmer contre le cinéma?', *Travailler*, 27, 1, 65–85.

Piper, Paige (2020), 'Logical "Phallicies": Challenging the Borders of Masculinity and Morality with a Male Gay/ze in *L'Inconnu du lac*', *Journal of Romance Studies*, 20, 1, 75–89.

Preciado, Paul B. (2018), *Countersexual Manifesto*, trans. Kevin Gerry Dunn, New York, Columbia University Press.

Rees-Roberts, Nick (2015), 'Hors milieu: Queer and Beyond', in Alistair Fox, Michel Marie, Raphaëlle Moine, and Hilary Radner, eds, *A Companion to Contemporary French Cinema*, Chichester, Wiley, pp. 439–60.

Reeser, Todd W. (2017), 'Producing Awkwardness: Affective Labour and Masculinity in Popular Culture', *Mosaic: An Interdisciplinary Critical Journal*, 50, 4, 51–68.

Reeser, Todd W. (2019), 'Approaching Affective Masculinities', in Lucas Gottzén, Ulf Mellström, and Tamara Shefer, eds, *Routledge International Handbook of Masculinity Studies*, London, Routledge, pp. 103–11.

Romney, Jonathan (2014), 'Dream Lovers', *Film Comment*, 64–7, www.filmcomment.com/article/stranger-by-the-lake-alain-guiraudie (accessed 5 July 2021).

Schoonover, Karl and Rosalind Galt (2016), *Queer Cinema in the World*, Durham, NC and London, Duke University Press.

Shuttleton, David (2000), 'The Queer Politics of Gay Pastoral', in Diane Watt, Richard Phillips, and David Shuttleton, eds, *De-Centring Sexualities: Politics and Representations beyond the Metropolis*, London, Routledge, pp. 125–46.

Virgil (1999), *Eclogues, Georgics, Aeneid 1–6*, ed. G. P. Goold, trans. H. R. Fairclough, Cambridge, MA, Harvard University Press.

Walton, Saige (2018), 'Cruising the Unknown: Film as Rhythm and Embodied Apprehension in *L'Inconnu du lac/Stranger by the Lake* (2013)', *New Review of Film and Television Studies*, 16, 3, 238–63.

Weber, Serge (2013), 'Délivrés de l'urbano-centrisme? Les Grands Espaces du désir dans le cinéma d'Alain Guiraudie', *Géographie et cultures*, 87, 109–24.

Young, Damon R. (2018), *Making Sex Public and Other Cinematic Fantasies*, Durham, NC, Duke University Press.

Plate 1 Ducastel and Martineau, *Drôle de Félix*, Fox Lorber Films, 2000

Plate 2 Ducastel and Martineau, *Ma vraie vie à Rouen*, Wellspring Media, 2002

Plate 3 Ducastel and Martineau, *Théo et Hugo dans le même bateau*, Epicentre Films Editions, 2016

Plate 4 Ducastel and Martineau, *Haut perchés*, Epicentre Films Editions, 2019

Plate 5 Guiraudie, *L'Inconnu du lac*, Strand Releasing Home Video, 2012

Plate 6 Guiraudie, *Du soleil pour les gueux*, Shellac, 2000

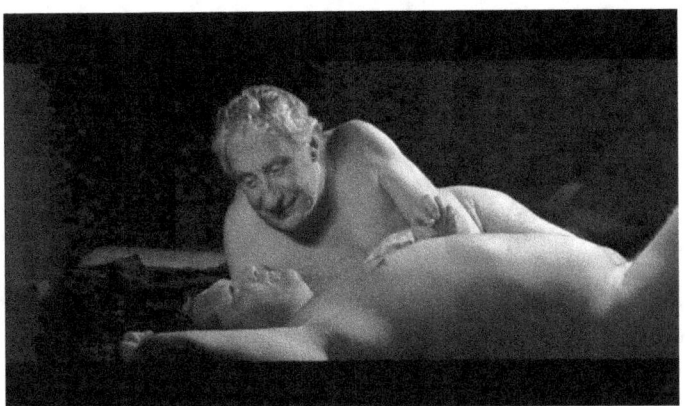

Plate 7 Guiraudie, *Le Roi de l'évasion*, Peccadillo Pictures, 2009

Plate 8 Lifshitz, *Les Corps ouverts*, France Télévisions Editions, Silver Way, 1997

Plate 9 Lifshitz, *Presque rien*, Picture This! Home Video, 2000

Plate 10 Lifshitz, *Wild Side*, Wellspring Media, 2004

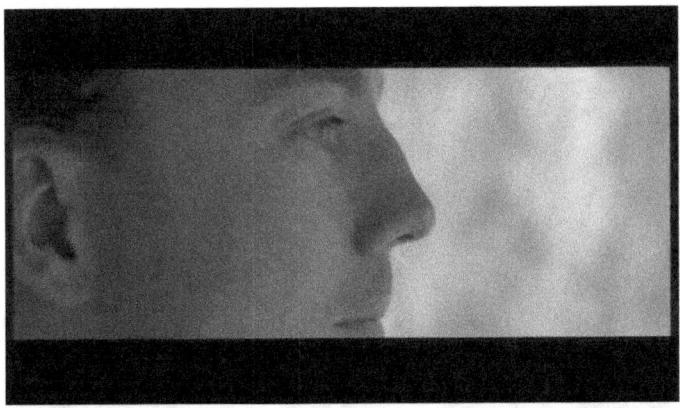

Plate 11 Lifshitz, *La Traversée*, Lancelot Films, France Télévisions Editions, Silver Way, 2001

Plate 12 Sciamma, *Naissance des pieuvres*, Slingshot, 2007

Plate 13 Sciamma, *Tomboy*, Pyramide Video, Hold-Up Films, and Productions, 2011

Plate 14 Sciamma, *Bande de filles*, Strand Releasing Home Video, 2014

Plate 15 Sciamma, *Portrait de la jeune fille en feu*, Pyramide Video, 2019

3

Sébastien Lifshitz: documenting movements in time and space

An intellectual director, Sébastien Lifshitz makes films treating journeys in time and space that lead to – or have the potential to lead to – new ways of being and of relating to others. Those journeys can be seen as beginning with photography. In an interview on the *Plein sud* DVD (Lifshitz, 2010), the filmmaker notes that he wanted to be a photographer, but then rather accidentally fell into a film career. Lifshitz's collection of photos taken by others has been exhibited: in fall 2019, for instance, he presented a photographic exhibition at the Pompidou Centre in Paris titled *Photo perdue, photo trouvée* (*Photo Lost, Photo Found*), with more than 400 images from the past. In addition to making films, Lifshitz edited a series of books of old photographs from his collection depicting LGBTQ people or expressing queer ambiguity: *Les Invisibles* (2013), *Mauvais genre* (*Wrong Gender*) (2016), the four-volume *Amateur* (2016), and *L'Inventaire infini* ('the endless collection') (2019). The photos in these books are anonymous, meaning that they may invite readers to invent narratives about the photographers and about the subjects since no information is available to contextualize the photos. In the collection *Amateur*, there is neither text by Lifshitz, nor information about each photo. Volume four, titled 'Flou' (meaning 'blurry' or 'fluid'), contains photos that suggest sexual fluidity. Lifshitz notes in his introduction to *Les Invisibles* that the person who had the film developed would have almost surely taken the film in to a store and risked homophobic reactions on the part of the film developers. To end up with these photos, people would have had to negotiate with their cultural context, meaning they were not simply closeted. As Lifshitz writes: 'what if a majority of homosexuals from these different periods had, for the most part, succeeded in living a good life, despite who they were? Perhaps they were able to negotiate something with the family, their professional milieu, or society as a whole' (Lifshitz, 2014: ii). As modern viewers of these old images, we are invited to unearth a queer past, whether of unfettered happiness, of queer negotiation, or of some other narrative that we invent around the images that we see. On one level, the books document and reclaim a forgotten queer past, but on another level, they invite the production of twenty-first-century narratives about a queer past. Undoubtedly, some of the subjects of the photos were not queer at all, but the inability to know how they actually identified or what types of people they desired or had sexual experiences with, means that queerness is invented around these vestiges of their lives. The photos also invite us as twenty-first-century subjects, in an era in which same-sex marriage is legal in France and other countries, to reconsider what LGBTQ means today by virtue of comparing or contrasting our cultural condition with what we can see of the past.

Lifshitz's interest in photography is not limited to these books and exhibits, however, for a photographic impulse permeates much of his cinematic corpus, as will be discussed throughout this chapter. Characters look into the past to locate some aspect of who they are in the present or they struggle with past images of themselves or others in their present. In some cases, actual photos play a role in the narrative of the film, whether for the characters or for the purpose of commenting on how representation functions. Pasts are unearthed, brought into the present, but as with the actual photos, the past is made into something new by virtue of the unearthing process as the present is redefined and as the past is mixed in new ways with the present. If viewers look at queer photos from the past and invent a narrative about them, that new narrative is as much about the viewer and their own cultural context as it is about the person or people photographed, suggesting a past that is not fixed or frozen in time but open to revisiting and to rethinking. Beyond photography, queerness is often made visible in Lifshitz's corpus through the process of present–past dialogue, whether in feature films or in the documentary films that became the focus of his oeuvre after 2009. The relation between past and present is central to the narrative of the films discussed here: *Les Corps ouverts* (*Open Bodies*) (1998), *Les Terres froides* (*Cold Lands*) (1999), *Presque rien* (*Come Undone*) (2000), *Wild Side* (2004), and *Plein sud* (*Going South*) (2009). It is also central to his biographical documentaries *La Traversée* (*The Crossing*) (2001), *Les Invisibles* (2012), *Bambi* (2013), and *Petite Fille* (*Little Girl*) (2020). This chapter will treat these films in roughly chronological order, beginning with Lifshitz's film shorts and his two medium-length films. I leave aside here the documentary *Adolescentes* (2019) as it not focused on questions of queerness.

Hearing voices: early shorts

Dated 1995, a forty-eight-minute interview with French director Claire Denis titled *Claire Denis, la vagabonde* (*Claire Denis, the Vagabond*) focuses on her relation to her own cinematic corpus, which she notes is hard to discuss because she does not have a solidified approach to her oeuvre or a coherent narrative about the development of her films over time. While Denis is the one speaking, a non-linear dialogue between past and present is constructed between her and her past work through embedded film clips. The complexity of the relation between the representational past and the present is one that Lifshitz carries forward in his later work that does not narrate in linear terms.

The nine-minute short, *Il faut que je l'aime* (*I Have to Love Them*) (1996), is centred on the voices in the mind of Juliette who is leaving her boyfriend for another woman. The three voices – of her mother, her boyfriend, and her lover – have already spoken to her, and the film focuses on Juliette's corporeal and facial expressions as she rehears the three voices, sometimes homophobic, sometimes distraught, sometimes angry, and sometimes loving. It is not fully clear what Juliette has done: has she left her boyfriend? Started a relationship with the woman? Is she now contemplating what to do? If there is a gap between the visual present and the auditory past of the utterances, there may also be a gap between the visual present and the visual past. The film may reflect back on Juliette hearing voices from the perspective of a future time period, meaning there are three total temporal layers in the film. Is the Juliette that we see on the screen a younger version of an older Juliette reflecting back on herself as a young woman? She may not simply be hearing voices but remembering herself hearing voices in the past. Juliette cries as the voices speak, which may suggest that she is having trouble becoming a woman who loves a woman or becoming lesbian, but it may also suggest that she is an older woman who remained with men and is thinking back on a point in her life when she could have – or should have – been with a woman for the long term or become a lesbian. At one point, Juliette's mother tells her daughter that one needs to be 'unfaithful to memory', and that she could have, or should have, left Juliette's father. It may be the case for instance that he was abusive or alcoholic, and that she is reflecting back on moments when she did not leave him. Her mother's memory raises the question whether Juliette, likewise, is in the process of missing an opportunity and is looking back on herself missing the chance like the one that her mother had. Is Juliette no longer being unfaithful to the memory of the love that never was? This is an open-ended series of representations, and no definite answer to the question of what happened or what did not happen is offered. The voices could be understood as a photographic use of voice in the sense that they are vocal snapshots of what others have said to her, snapshots that do not tell a coherent and linear narrative about coming out or about loving a woman. Lifshitz opens the film (after the credits) with a lateral tracking shot along a Parisian street, but without following a single person, a signal that the short film to come will not follow a single individual and their life story as it moves along. Movement itself will define the characters, in this case between the moment of remembering voices and the past actions to which the voices refer. The use of a character remembering elements already past and asking questions about the present prefigures later narratives about characters who struggle with their traumatic or difficult past, narratives which Lifshitz will develop in depth in his feature-length films *Presque rien*, *Wild Side*, *Plein sud*, and in the two films to be discussed next.

Beur possibilities: *Les Corps ouverts*

Les Corps ouverts and *Les Terres froides* came out in close proximity (1998 and 1999) and display a number of similarities. Lifshitz's film career takes off in 1998 when *Les Corps ouverts* wins the Jean Vigo Prize, which recognizes independent cinematic thought and high-quality direction. Both of the medium-length films were positively received and helped establish their director's reputation. In the newspaper *Libération*, for instance, a review noted that Lifshitz 'succeeds as a supertalent' ('réussit en surdoué') and 'passed his entrance exam with flying colours' ('haut la main son examen de passage') (Garnier, 1999). Approximately one hour long, each film tells a story about a male *beur* character (whose family immigrated to France from the Maghreb but who grew up in France) trying to find himself in specific ways that suggest the presence of broader cultural structures that cannot easily be resisted. Djamel – one of the three main characters in Lifshitz's later film *Wild Side* – is also *beur* and while Franco-Maghrebi ethnicity is less central to that film than to these two medium-length ones, it plays a key role there in how subjective possibilities are manifested. In all three of these films, the same actor plays the role of the *beur* character, Yasmine Belmadi (who died tragically in 2009 in a scooter accident in Paris), even as the sexuality of the three characters is not defined in the same manner.

In both of these medium-length films, Belmadi's character disrupts normative identitarian forms and opens up new gendered ways to be, asking the question how queer and *beur* can function together. In *Terres froides*, the character Djamel disrupts but also opens up new forms of sexual being in a white, patriarchal, heteronormative environment, while in *Corps ouverts*, the main character Rémi disrupts not so much gender or sexual normativity as much as narrative itself. What is transformed in this case is the way in which the story of gender is told, and more specifically how queer sexuality relates to narrative.

One of the distinguishing features of *Corps ouverts* is that it is not organized in a linear fashion: scenes closely related to each other in time or in space are not usually positioned next to each other. The film might look at first glance to be at its core about the coming out of the main character Rémi, a high school student interested in being in a film more than being in high school. His Maghrebi father is sick, seems likely to die soon, and his mother, described as 'French', presumably not Maghrebi, has died at some point in the not too recent past. Rémi tries out for a film directed by an older gay man named Marc (Pierre-Loup Rajot), and he easily lands the lead role. Rémi has sex with Marc – who looks to be taken with him – but in a scene about halfway into the film, Rémi goes to a gay porn sex club and has sex in a bathroom stall with a man closer to his age named Sébastien, played by the director himself. There are multiple scenes between Rémi and Marc: in an early scene, they are having a lovers' quarrel in a café, Marc asks Rémi if he is playing with him and doesn't care at all about him, then announces that he is leaving. Rémi tells him to stay, but not in a very convincing way. Three scenes later (but chronologically earlier) comes Rémi's screen test with Marc. Four scenes later, Rémi arrives at Marc's apartment, after something has happened to keep Rémi from coming over, and then after Marc tells him to stay or go as he wishes, he comes in and the two of them have sex. They have an argument outside a bar because Marc is jealous two scenes later. Five scenes later, a rehearsal goes bad because of tensions in their actual relationship. Then, eight scenes later, the two men spend the night together and have breakfast the next morning. During another rehearsal scene five scenes later, Rémi asks Marc what his film is about, in one of the chronologically earliest scenes of the narrative but placed at the tail end of the film.

It may be possible to establish a linear trajectory and put these scenes in chronological order, but that order will not necessarily be definitive. In addition, what the film is conveying through temporal scrambling would be lost. The scene in which Rémi has sex with Sébastien in the bathroom stall referred to a scene earlier in the film's narrative even though it takes place later chronologically. In the final scene, Rémi asks Marc if he will have to kiss a man in the film, but in an earlier sex scene with Marc and in the sex scene with Sébastien, Rémi kisses them, suggesting that he is rehearsing what he is told that he will have to do in the narrative. He kisses men of his own volition first but is required to kiss them later in the framework of the film. As these examples suggest, his sexuality is defined through a complicated non-linear movement. Most notably, Rémi does not follow a coming-out trajectory that might proceed in the following way: a series of unsatisfying heterosexual experiences, a realization of gay desire, meaningless sexual experiences with men, and then a substantive gay relationship. His scene with Sébastien not only falls out of this normative order but is in fact the most emotional and tender scene between men in the whole film. In two scenes, Rémi has heterosexual sex, the first one with a street dancer in a blond wig that he hooks up with for no obvious reason (though she may incarnate his dead mother whom he misses). If there is a moment that could be taken as a version of a coming out, it is in one of the final scenes where Rémi mentions to his presumably heterosexual friend who asks him about his exploits, while rolling a cigarette, that he has been with someone but not a woman, to no real reaction on the part of his friend. It is no secret at this point that he likes men: the scene is not telling the viewer that he desires male bodies, rather that the enunciative act around homosexuality (or of non-heterosexuality, or of queerness) falls outside of linear temporal movement and is extraneous to its narrative organization in the first place. As this scene suggests, *Corps ouverts* performs the absence of a normative temporal trajectory for *beur* homosexuality.

A second key element of the film resists linear storytelling. At randomly inserted moments, from various perspectives, Rémi walks along the streets of Paris, sometimes during the day and sometimes at night. These walking interludes could, on one level, be imagined as cruising interludes during which he is seeking men with whom to have sex, but often Rémi is so focused on his own movement (and often, the music to which he is listening) that it is clear that he is not seeking to have sex, or even to locate other gay men. Rather, these interludes convey a being out of time, and they serve as spatial markers of a temporality that is out of joint, out of the narrative, and could exist at any time in any time frame before or after the film takes place. In short, they call attention to non-linearity itself. In his study of the film as a form of what Ross Chambers calls 'loiterature', Joe Hardwick writes that 'Rémi's spatial wanderings through the streets also count as temporal deviations from his more formal daily schedule' (2004: 78). Rémi may well be going somewhere (work or home, for instance), but we do not know where. Hardwick takes Rémi's movement as a kind of age-based suspension outside of the stable time of adulthood: 'He is not ready to take up his passport for the passage to the life that others have mapped out for him' (79). Though he discovers sexuality, the film is not a story about sexual initiation in which he learns how sexuality functions or experiences eroticism that he had not experienced (81).[1] Indeed, Rémi is in movement, these scenes reveal, but they also convey that the trope of cruising opens up the concept of movement itself.

One cinematic element of this movement is the use of cuts, what I might consider queer cuts. Broadly speaking, the move from one scene to the next renders it impossible to transition from heterosexuality to homosexuality in any kind of linear way. The most striking cut takes place at the end of the third scene in which Marc and Rémi are in a café having a lovers' quarrel. Instead of some logical outcome of this quarrel, the scene leads directly to a close-up of a naked breast. A viewer might imagine that Rémi and Marc have gone to an apartment to have sex after their quarrel and that this shot focuses on the carnality of their encounter. The very short scene however makes it clear quickly that the breast belongs to a woman and not to a man. There is little else that takes place in this scene, since the jump cut itself constitutes the content of the scene. The sudden move from potentially homoerotic to female body allegorizes the lack of a linear coming-out process and the queerness of anti-linear temporality.

When Rémi is late to his job at a neighbourhood convenience store (*épicerie*) and his angry boss Rachid chews him

---

1 Hardwick notes that many contemporaneous reviews of the film mistakenly take the film as linear in terms of the transformation of Rémi's sexual identity (2004: 81–2).

out, we do not know the reason for his being late. It may be because he was taking care of his sick father or his younger sister, because he was having gay sex, or because he was with a woman. He comes to Marc's apartment very late in another scene, and we do not know why. Did the scene in the gay club come just before this scene? Is he late because he has been with another man? In one of the first scenes of the film, his father tells his son not to come home too late, and again we do not know where or with whom he has been. What the viewer can know is that time is out of joint for this character, and that he follows his own temporal code, not that of normative culture.

In taking this approach to temporality, the film mirrors the concept of 'queer time' as developed in queer theory (e.g., Dinshaw *et al.*, 2007; Halberstam, 2005). Heteronormativity functions in such a way that it controls the way in which time is constructed, and in turn links that construction to gender and sexual normativity. An important tool for heteronormative control over humans is the use of time to normalize. Such an approach to time might be related, for instance, to organization of the work week (working from nine to five so that one can go home to one's nuclear family after work and so that one might imagine work time, sleep time, and family time as three separate parts of the day and week). It might also refer to a normative life cycle in which a baby becomes a toddler, then a child, then an adolescent and an adult that has children with someone of the 'opposite' sex, all with the gendered and sexual traits from one stage to the next. The asexual boy becomes a heterosexual man after puberty. He cannot become a woman, nor can he have been a woman all along. Queer subjects on the other hand might function at night (sex work, gay sex in clubs) or in occupations that are not necessarily normative, with work hours not between nine and five.

The queerness of time pertains not only to the way in which actual human beings live their lives, but also to the way in which narratives are recounted. A standard or classic plot that begins with character introduction, moves to plot complications, and over time resolves (or not) those complications can be a kind of normative narrative structure based on recurring cultural ideas about the ways in which time is imagined to pass. Such narratives may move from point A to point B in time, in a linear fashion. They may be heteronormative as much as temporally normative as the two forms of normativity function in tandem, with one buttressing the other. A story may proceed in temporally normative ways, not playing with time, and end with heterosexual marriage to show that all is well that ends well. Or a narrative about boy meeting girl may begin with flirtation, lead to sex, then love, then marriage, then parenthood, not organized beyond what Halberstam calls 'paradigmatic markers of life experience' (2005: 2). Such linearity does not *have* to be – or does not have to be represented as – heterosexual of course, and these two forms of normativity do not have to function in tandem. As Halberstam offers as a caveat to queer time, 'not all gay, lesbian, and transgender people live their lives in radically different ways from their heterosexual counterparts' (1). People may know in advance how things will end up in a story about same-sex characters as well. A non-queer narrative can begin with a character in the closet, but then end in an identitarian, stable form of 'homosexuality', or a trans narrative about the movement from one sex to another, from maleness to femaleness, ending in the telos of stable gender, might be considered a non-queer way to tell a story. These kinds of linear temporal narratives can be bundled with other narrative organizational structures that include other movements also coded as linear. Spatial movement across territory in a linear way, from geographical point A to geographical point B, would be one example, as in the case of a text in which a character travels across space at the same time as they move towards another gender subjectivity, such as Duncan Tucker's linear road movie *Transamerica* (2005).

In Lifshitz, queer time, on the other hand, follows another direction, and corresponds to a temporal organization that leads not to a simple arrival at point B (becoming a good, stable 'out' homosexual or a good, cisgender-seeming man or woman), but scrambles linearity and produces queerness not predicated on such an organization of time. This alternate schema points to ways in which queer characters live in non-normative ways and in which their narratives are not pre-fabricated with respect to time patterns. In other words, the film's use of time allegorizes queer ways to live, even as queer lifeforms lead to alternate temporal organization.

If temporality takes a queer path in *Corps ouverts*, it is largely because Rémi signifies queer time. When Rachid yells at him for his extreme lateness and for not even offering any excuse, the grocer asks if he knows or 'sees' what time it is ('T'as vu l'heure?'). At breakfast, Marc asks him where he is headed in life and what he plans to do after high school. When Rémi tells his father that he will be acting in a film, he tells his son that he needs to finish high school and pass the French high school final exam (*le bac*) in order to have a career trajectory. Rémi does not 'see' time: the answer to Rachid's question is no (he has not literally 'seen the hour'), and he does not want to follow the trajectory of coming to adulthood that his father lays out for him.

Two opening vignettes serve as an epigraph or a poetic preface positioning Rémi as a sexual subject. In the second vignette, Rémi plays with a large spider while lying shirtless on his bed. The spider crawls up his arm and chest, but he changes what looks to be its directional movement, at one point putting the spider into motion, pushing it along. The scene is establishing that Rémi will be moving along what might look to be a natural or linear narrative movement: but also, he will let that movement run across him, or he will let movement be part of his selfhood. He is moving himself forward in time as he approaches adulthood, and he is directed by that movement which is not entirely within his control. Rémi means rower or oarsman (*rameur* in French), from the Latin *remex, remigis*. He is propelling the narrative forward by virtue of his desire to be an actor and his movement towards same-sex encounters, but he is not necessarily steering it. He plays with the spider and changes its course, but not necessarily in a way that forces it to fully deviate from its path. He is moving the path of normative time, but not radically changing it.

The image of the spider, however, has other valences that are part of what this scene is telling the viewer about the film to come. The spider has a role in the twenty-ninth chapter (surah) of the Qur'an, serving as a contrast image to Allah: 'The example of those who take allies other than Allah is like that of the spider who takes a home. And indeed, the weakest of homes is the home of the spider, if they only knew' (Quran, 29:41). This verse critiques those who venerate false idols instead of worshiping Allah, a single god. Only He knows, and He is all-knowing. Empty idols lack consistency and permanence like the web of the spider, offering no subsistence or 'provision' (29:17), while Allah is the one who gives subsistence. Thus, true believers should leave their homes and should be those who 'emigrat[e] in obedience to [Allah]' (29:26).[2] Rémi is linked in a sense to the spider: his home life is unstable because he cannot talk about sexuality at home, he is on unstable footing with respect to sexuality, and he lacks consistency, desiring various types of gendered bodies. His home life is unstable, too, because he tries to care for his sick father and to help raise his younger sister in the absence of his mother, but much of his energy is devoted to dealing with and to hiding his sexuality. He does seem to 'know' Allah.

---

2 For more on this image, see Amir-Moezzi (2007: 76–7). For a similar image in the Bible, see Job 8:13–15 (New King James Version): 'And the hope of the hypocrite shall perish ... / whose trust is a spider's web. / He leans on his house, but it does not stand. / He holds it fast, but it does not endure'.

This scene, however, is the second one presented in the film. In the opening scene, Rémi chants while looking out over the Parisian landscape. His cultural hybridity is highlighted by the juxtaposition between the words he chants, not in French, and the French space before him. We learn later that his mother was 'French' while his father speaks French with a non-hexagonal accent, suggesting that Rémi's home is between two languages. Back-to-back at the opening of the film, the first and the second scenes are linked: Rémi is introduced as a sign of the lack of 'consistency' with regard to time, but also with regard to ethnic status. What he will do to time, or what time will do to his narrative, we learn here, happens in part at least because he is a post-colonial or culturally hybrid subject.

The spider image from the Qur'an ('the weakest of homes is the home of the spider, if they only knew') suggests that those who worship idols do not know that their home is unstable. Those who live in the most stable of homes, that of Allah, know what will happen to them and they know what the sole telos of life is. The question of knowledge is central to the narrative web which implies a lack of knowing. A linear narrative – one that can be predicted because of its cultural consistency and is repeated over and over with the same beginning, middle, and end – is based on knowing in advance what will happen along the way and at the end. If a viewer knows from the beginning that a narrative is a coming-out narrative, they likely assume that in the end the character in question will become a well-adjusted or 'out' 'homosexual'. So even during the difficult moments along the way (e.g., gay bashing, internalized homophobia, relations with the 'wrong' sex, etc.), the viewer may know that they are just blips on the radar that will end and lead to a molar identity as the plot moves forward. Because the telos is predetermined, the viewer can know certain elements of what will happen, even if some of the details are not determined.

At a number of points in the film, Rémi embodies a lack of knowing or of knowledge. He lives in 'the weakest of homes' because he does not 'know'. When he announces to his father and sister that he may be in a film and they ask him questions about it, he has to tell them that he does not know anything about the film. He may be talking about the film that he will play in, avoiding a response, but he is also in a sense talking about Lifshitz's film. He does not know what *Corps ouverts* is about or, perhaps more importantly, where it will lead the viewer or how it will be organized as it moves along. During a rehearsal scene with Rémi and Marc, a line in their script provokes an argument between the two of them: 'What do you know?' ('Qu'est-ce que t'en sais?'). The line is repeated multiple times for emphasis (almost violently), and finally Rémi has to abandon the rehearsal because he cannot 'remember any more'. He has lost any knowledge of the scene and opts out of the rehearsal narrative. He has forgotten or he does not know what a normative or linear narrative might be, incarnating the film's not knowing what homosexuality is and how it should be narrated. *Corps ouverts* unknows normative homosexual narrative to produce another queer story.

The most dramatic unknowing in the film relates to the interplay between two cinematic layers that cannot always be separated. There is the film itself, of course, but there is also the film that Marc is in the process of making with Rémi. Some scenes are clearly rehearsal scenes, and they are tagged as part of Marc's film. We see the two of them filming. But there is no way for us to know whether other scenes in the film are part of that film or not. We do not even know if Marc is a character or an actor. When the two of them have sex, we do not know which film they are part of, ours or theirs. The scenes with Rémi's family may, too, be scenes from this internal film. And what of the random-seeming scenes where Rémi walks around Paris? Are these interludes or transitions between scenes, or is Rémi being filmed by Marc? Where do they belong? The camera shots are markedly different from the rest of the film in these cases, sometimes low-angle shots and sometimes level shots of Rémi. This change in angle calls attention to the filming itself. Is the change due to the fact that Marc is filming? Does the difference mean that Marc's filming is different from Lifshitz's filming, and that some of these shots belong to the actual director and others belong to Marc the director character? These questions cannot in the end be answered, but rather, I am suggesting here, they call attention to what the viewer does not and cannot know in broad terms.

The inability to know the limits of the film is complicated by Lifshitz's appearance in the sex scene. The lighting of this scene is pure red, reflecting the nature of the sexualized space, but it is also a red light that invites us to stop and rethink who is directing whom. The scene presents Lifshitz as passive; it begins rather slowly and does not easily or quickly move to sex. Rémi asks 'Sébastien' if he wants to kiss, and the latter answers 'if you want' ('si tu veux'). Though he seems to have less experience in this kind of public sex situation than his more effeminate kissing mate, Rémi appears to be directing or to be steering the erotic narrative along while the actual director is not. With Marc too, Rémi looks to be calling the relationship shots. The question being asked with both of these men is who is directing whom. We do not know who the inscribed director is at a number of points because the narrative is not controlled by a story-maker who spins a narrative web about Rémi. Directorial agency is in a sense surrendered, or left as a question, as directorial consistency is placed aside in favour of a fragmented approach to the cinematic text, like the spiderweb in the Qur'an that does not hold up.

The film's fragmentation relates to Rémi's ethnic origins. His relation to linear time is not clear with respect to his past; we do not know how he was raised or what relation he has to his own past. His father sits alone at the kitchen table looking at photos, and then we see a close-up of a photo of his wife. Near the end of his life, Rémi's father remains focused on a relation to the past and his deceased 'French' wife. Rémi, then, is unlike his father with respect to time as he signifies another relation to the past. In a brief scene in which he is playing a driving video game, the screen flashes that his time has been extended, suggesting that his relation to time is different from others'. Time for him can be moved around when he drives or steers his life.

Rémi's relation to time means that he does not 'decrypt' his past. His economics teacher announces when she comes to class to replace the normal instructor that the students need to learn how to 'decrypt' (*décrypter*) the messages with which they are bombarded on a daily basis, especially from the media. They need to find the hidden meanings in those messages in order to be good French citizens. Rémi is not particularly interested in understanding or making sense of signs however, and the teacher would seem to be talking about the hidden messages of the film itself and the viewer's role in making sense of the text. As viewers, we need to bring the signs of the film away from being hidden ('crypte', from the Ancient Greek word for hidden) into the realm of intelligibility. Yet, what the film does is not make sexuality intelligible and easy to understand. Rémi's queerness will not simply be brought out of the '*crypte*' into the narrative. The implied contrast with Rémi's father is relevant here: in looking at photos of his dead wife, he is in a sense 'decrypting' her, or bringing her back from the crypt where she lies, whether physically or metaphorically. Rémi is doing the opposite: he is not uncrypting the dead past or locating something hidden in the crypt (e.g., homosexuality), but rather he is gesturing towards the future. His encryption – and by extension, the movie's encryption – aims to create something new, something future-oriented, not something taken from the dead and buried past. In so doing, the film avoids normative structures and narratives of sexuality, making an implicit argument for new narratives or new ways to structure ethnic narratives around subjectivity. Didier Péron's review of the film in *Libération* (1998) picks up this idea: 'le travail de

Lifshitz consisterait ... à rendre crypté, obscur et silencieux ce que la télé, la sociologie et le langage courant ont rendu terriblement bavard' ('Lifshitz's work encrypts, hides, and silences what television, sociology, and everyday conversations have made incredibly verbose'). For me, Péron means that the act of confessing homosexuality is crypted, obscure and silent, but also that the film calls attention to this encryption, in a way making it the subject of the film. At two points, Rémi approaches a confession about being 'gay' or 'homosexual', once with his school friend (as noted above) and once with a girlfriend. In the latter case, she tells him that he might not like women because males his age are misogynist. When he notes that this was not what he meant, she tells him to say what he means, but he avoids continuing. Instead, he begins to recite a poem of his own that reveals that he does not know what love is, evoking poetic tropes of love instead of a gay confession. The film approaches confession precisely to perform its erasure, to not know it, to render it cryptic, or to put it in the crypt instead of in the confessional.

On one level, the new way of doing narrative creates a *beur* character who is not a fetishized object of white gay male desire, rejecting implicitly colonial stereotypes of passive Arab men that older men can use for erotic pleasure. Rees-Roberts discusses the close links between *beur* men and gay porn in French culture, writing of this film (and of *Les Terres froides*): 'Crucial to the concerns of same-sex relations, the premise of Lifshitz's project is to chip away at dominant colonial stereotypes' (2008: 36). Indeed, Rémi is driving (or rowing) the narrative and his relation with Marc is largely based on what he wants or does not want, not on the older white Frenchman's desire for the younger Arab man that he can dominate. Colonialism, too, is predicated on a certain kind of linear narrative organized by time: the colonial power traditionally positioned its African colonies as backwards in time, as uncivilized, while the forwardness of the white colonial, 'civilized' power moves forward in time towards the 'civilized' future. By scrambling time and temporality in the narrative, Rémi the character leaves that kind of tired temporal narrative in the past in favour of new ones that arise in unpredictable ways. His temporality is not the one of a colonial and racist France: he steers clear of it and moves towards queer *beur* time.

The open-endedness of narrative explains the important final scene between Rémi and Marc. The scene is radically out of order: were it part of a linear, unscrambled narrative, it would have come much earlier than at the tail end of the film. Marc slowly explains that the film Rémi is auditioning for is about a 'marginal' man with 'special' desires, pausing and then adding that they are same-sex desires. The scene is filmed in near-darkness as Marc is barely visible and as Rémi – though the lead actor – is largely in the dark. Nothing is clear here. Rémi worries that his father will not accept the queer subject matter, to which Marc responds that his father does not know that he skips classes at school. He can function, Marc suggests, without his father knowing what he is doing. Rémi continues to express hesitation, but when Marc conveys that he will not be able to do the film if he cannot express same-sex desires, he changes his attitude without simply adapting and accepting same-sex behaviour entirely. Rather, he says that he can 'try' to play the character, and that they can 'faire des essais', meaning that they can try it out (*essai* = trial or attempt) but also that they can rehearse the scene (plate 8). The end of *Corps ouverts* too is a trial, an *essai*. The narrative ends in no end, an open ending in which what is to come is unclear. In French culture, '*essai*' has a specific referent, a textual genre invented by the Renaissance writer and thinker Michel de Montaigne who wrote the *Essais* (1580), which form the basis of much later French thought predicated on open-endedness. His essays are not well-crafted answers to questions, with a coherent thesis as one might imagine in a modern argumentative essay, but a sceptical series of open-ended questions that do not get resolved. His essays are fluid and in movement, with parts referring back to other parts, much like the structure of *Corps ouverts*. Montaigne's famous sceptical motto 'Que sais-je?', or 'What do I know?', means that nothing could simply be known and taken for granted. Rémi is calling for trials and rehearsals, but he is also calling for an unending series of questions to be asked that do not produce stable knowledge but open-ended questions about how narratives of sexuality can be told.[3] He notes too that he does not know if he can do the film, and we never really know if he does. His inability to know the future parallels the inability to know how the narrative ends, a resistance to narrative teleology that would or should end in a character being 'out' and 'gay'.

It is significant that this film is being tried out, essayed, for film is an ideal medium for this trying out of new narratives and new potentiality, in part because of the fluid line between inside and outside or between film and non-film. Reality and script are not separate in the end, and narrative does not remain narrative but has the potential to become part of actual spectators' lives beyond the realm of simple representation. Trying out new ways of being rejects following a prewritten script to the letter and distinguishing life from fictional text. Rémi embodies an indifference to the separation between inside and outside, between film and life. In a scene in his economics class, the teacher explains that there are two types of growth ('croissance'), internal and external. As she begins her explanations, Rémi is asleep on his desk in the classroom. He does not know the difference between inner and outer, he remains indifferent to the binarized line between the two. This indifference encapsulates his whole character.

---

3 The idea of French film as an '*essai*' is not simply related to this particular film. On ways in which the Montaignian essay comes to define French film more broadly, see Corrigan (2011). On Montaigne as queer, see Reeser (2016: 575–80).

In the final scene, his indifference to inner/outer binarism resists the line between film and non-film and the line between being in 'homosexuality' and outside it. He is outside of a system in which one is 'in the closet' or 'out of the closet'. In his book on *beur* literature, Michel Laronde notes that because second-generation immigrants whose families have come from the Maghreb, do not themselves migrate to France, a non-migratory form of movement remains central to *beur* representation: they undertake 'internal movements' or 'little getaways around an internal, immobile centre' (1993: 185).[4] For these *beur* subjects, it is a question of a 'semblance of flight' ('vernis de fuite') (185), not actual flight. They may flee in small ways, mirroring on a reduced scale the migration of their parents or grandparents. Laronde's idea is taken to another level in this case as Rémi is in constant internal movement, but around a centre that he never fully leaves. It is not an actual flight from a conservative family or Franco-Arab culture nor from a life in the closet, it is a series of semblances of flight. The random-seeming shots of Rémi on the streets of Paris mentioned above are semblances of flight, highlighting movement-centeredness that does not in the end allow him to fully flee anything. He is circling around homosexuality, and he is in part fleeing it. Or more precisely, he is circling around a normative narrative of homosexuality while fleeing it also. This is why the film twice has Rémi approach a confession about his sexuality: he circles around it without actually confessing. But he circles around another narrative convention as well. Before the final scene, we see Rémi seeing the Eiffel Tower from afar, as if he circles around Frenchness as much as homosexuality. He is in the orbit, too, of a French universalist model of sexuality that

---

4 Laronde writes: 'les déplacements externes à l'Occident qui caractérisaient les générations précédentes (la non-fixation de l'errance) font place à des déplacements internes qui se limitent à des *escapades* autour d'un centre de fixation interne (Paris et sa banlieue)' (1993: 185).

might require him to be a citizen first and a homosexual or a queer *beur* second. His experience necessarily has a relation to this widespread model of identity, but it is also quite distinct from it, as a non-white French citizen whose relation to the concept is not easily defined.[5]

Following Laronde, I would say that these internal movements in the film related to sexuality are prompted by the main character's ethnicity. As a *beur* character, he lives sexuality queerly, not based on normative or homonormative temporalities or teleologies. The image of the character Marc as a director cannot be unrelated to Lifshitz as a director as well, and invites us to consider whether, in the same way that Marc is highlighting Rémi's marginal desires and inviting him to perform then on film, Lifshitz too is bringing out Rémi's ethnic queerness as 'marginal' for reasons related to film. While in the final scene marginal equates to homosexual, in the film more broadly 'marginal' means *beur* and queer as an intersectional subjectivity. Whether Lifshitz is directing this intersectional story or not is unclear: Rémi is an actor in both senses of the term, a person with agency and a person playing a role for representational purposes.

Fluidities: *Les Terres froides*

In *Les Terres froides*, the main character Djamel does not so much 'try out' new possibilities, as in *Les Corps ouverts*, but negotiates through normative cultural structures and opens them up from within. Time is not scrambled in this film, but instead the storyline is linear. Djamel is not really a queer character in terms of desire, rather he operates queerly with

---

5 By complicating (white) queerness itself, Rémi participates in the projects of Provencher (2017) and Mack (2017).

respect to hetero-patriarchal domestic normativity. In the opening scenes, he leaves the Parisian suburbs to find and confront the man that he believes is his biological father and that lives in Grenoble near the French Alps. Though played by the same lead actor as in *Corps ouverts*, Djamel flees in a very different way than Rémi does, heading to a traditionally white part of France, as reflected by the whiteness of winter snow. His mother is no longer alive, he had lived with his grandmother, and he seems to have no siblings or other close family members. The story revolves around his locating Monsieur Chamblasse (Bernard Verley), his assumed father who owns a factory where Rémi secures employment in a minimum-wage job. He then confronts him about his paternity. In the confrontation scene, when Djamel shows Chamblasse a photo of his mother, he is told that he must in fact be mistaken and that he should leave immediately.

If Djamel's father embodies the metaphoric 'cold lands' of the title, it is especially because of his cold whiteness. Shots of cold and snowy landscapes throughout the film highlight the racial coldness that emanates from Chamblasse. He is also cold to his wife and to his gay son Laurent (Sébastien Charles), whose sexuality he seems unwilling to accept in any shape or form. The workers at his factory are on the verge of striking, and he appears cold to their demands for higher wages and is generally not popular with them because of his icy treatment. He goes to bars by himself to drink as he is alone in his well-off world defined by homophobia, patriarchy, and industrial capitalism. His last name might suggest '*chambre*' or bedroom, thus that he is alone in his own private space and unable and unwilling to connect to others.

The white, upper-middle-class, patriarchal family is the form of normativity that Djamel will, in the final scene of the film, disrupt as he enters the home from which he has been excluded. Also excluded – albeit in another way – is Laurent who is not out to his father. Djamel, by contrast, is not a gay character in the sense that he has a girlfriend, engages in heterosexual sex, and masturbates to heterosexual pornography. Nonetheless, he imports queerness onto the normativity of the white household, reflecting in a guise different from *Corps ouverts* Laronde's idea of 'internal movement', the movement here being internal to the static household.

Conceptual queerness, as opposed to desire-based queerness, is created by Djamel through the medium of same-sex sexuality. While following Laurent one day, presumably to gain information about his half-brother and to understand how his family structure functions, he ends up at an ice-skating rink where he sees his half-brother kissing a man off in a dark corner. He follows Laurent to a gay bar, approaches him, buys him a beer, talks to him flirtatiously, and eventually tries to kiss him. While Laurent does not accept his advances immediately, he is interested and agrees to meet him the next evening for a date in a park overlooking the city. They drink champagne, talk about having sex together, and then decide to go back to Laurent's familial house for penetrative sex (with Djamel to be on top). Laurent does not want to have sex at his house because of his father, but Djamel promises before they leave the park that he will be quiet and that they will not be discovered by his parents. They have penetrative sex in Laurent's bed, with Laurent on the bottom, and Djamel spends the night in the house afterwards.[6] They are indeed quiet and their sex act disturbs no one in the household.

The queer disruption, however, takes place after Djamel gets up and leaves Laurent in bed, and takes a shower in the bathroom. Although dripping wet, he goes to explore the rest of the house, which he has not seen in daylight, including his father's bedroom where he is sleeping with his wife. In so doing, he leaves a trail of water beginning in Laurent's bedroom and continuing along his path throughout the house.

---

6 Rees-Roberts links the sex scene between Rémi and Marc in *Corps ouverts* and this one between Djamel and Laurent (2008: 36, 37). In this case, Djamel is on top, but had been on the bottom with Marc.

Getting up and heading from his bedroom for the kitchen while tying his tie, Chamblasse notices the water trail and follows it into his son's bedroom, where he sees the two of them in bed together. Recognizing Djamel from the confrontation in his office and becoming infuriated, he attacks Laurent physically, the naked Djamel comes to Laurent's aide, but the former ends up lying on the ground, face down, immobile from the blow to his body. The film avoids narrating what exactly has happened – and will happen – to Djamel however as the film cuts to the kitchen table where Chamblasse and his wife are eating breakfast. She heard the fight upstairs and says to her husband: 'Qu'est-ce que tu as? Dis quelque chose' ('What's wrong? Say something'). The father has a confused expression on his face and loosens his tie, and *Terres froides* ends.

This final scene is ambiguous with respect to what happens after the film concludes, but for me the scene asks what *beur* queerness has the potential to do to normativity in a white, domestic context. Djamel has literally and metaphorically entered into the private household (the '*chambre*' of Chamblasse), the space of domesticity, and disrupted it to its core. Djamel had spied on the household from the outside in two earlier scenes, so this scene reads as his planned penetration into the realm of the domestic space denied to him by his father. He penetrates the household from within as he penetrates Laurent from on top. Consequently, non-whiteness and queerness intersect to form the disrupting element of the film's conclusion. Sudeep Dasgupta reads the final positioning of Djamel on the floor not as death or an end to his search, but as a corporeal 'suspension … within a racial, cultural, and familiar discourse of exclusion' (2005: 176) that has been taking place throughout the film. His body on the ground is 'a physical and cultural rem(a)inder of the ideological short circuit by which family and cultural value is discursively fused' (179). Djamel destabilizes links between national exclusions of non-white or Arab subjects and the French family structure, a kind of representational nation-state with the father as leader. As Chamblasse was getting ready for work and loosening his tie, he signals that his participation in capitalism is suspended, at least for now. Knocked unconscious, Djamel is in a literal and metaphorical sense suspended, but the suspension gestures forward, as an opening up towards new, non-normative options for the normative familial/national structures. Djamel's unconsciousness equals a new consciousness for this form of normativity. That Laurent's mother tells Chamblasse to 'say something', as the final line of the film, suggests that he cannot speak, and that the normative discourses that had until now been operational are no longer able to function. He cannot speak because a force greater than language has taken over the household. Undoing his tie, Chamblasse is forced to undo what had been held together by capitalist patriarchy, homophobia, racism, and sexual normativity. A new way of being is ushered in. It is no accident that the place where Djamel is staying during his time in Grenoble is called the 'Hotel of the Renaissance': there is a rebirth coming, thanks to Djamel.

The last scene is not simply a revenge scene but is also a moment when Djamel outs his half-brother. Revealing Laurent's homosexuality is one element of this renaissance of the Chamblasse household. Djamel's reconfiguring potential might be a projected image of virility that white male homosexuality cannot accomplish. As Laurent and Djamel are on their date in the park, Laurent explains that he sees *beur* men as unflappable, always able to project an image of strength, as 'extremely physical' ('hyper-physiques'), even if things are going badly for them. Laurent admires them, wants to be hard like them ('like concrete'), and sees them as 'models'. 'It helps me', he tells Djamel, who counters the idea by citing his uncle who does not fit this image at all and tells his date that he is 'imagining things' ('Tu phantasmes'). As Laurent speaks these key lines, the camera pans the landscape of Grenoble down below. The lines are voiceovers, and the viewer does not see

Laurent or Djamel during their articulation. Word and image clearly do not correspond, and similarly, there is a gap between the perceived virility of *beur* masculinity and its reality in the world outside that perception. By extension, the very film the viewer is watching is predicated on a gap between the actuality of *beur* masculinity and the image that Lifshitz's film is putting forward. This construct is evoked and critiqued, to be sure, but the scene leaves open the option that this film, not directed by a *beur*, may be subject to the perception too. Laurent's projected image is not limited to him alone but reflects cultural projections of *beur* masculinity as virilized. Lifshitz himself has commented on this gay white 'fantasy' of *beurs* as masculine and virile. Rees-Roberts documents Lifshitz's comments on the gay 'fantasies of Arab and black men' as 'symbols of masculinity or a type of virility' (2008: 38). In a broader French context, Mack studies at length what he calls virilism, 'a mixture of toughness, hardness, unruliness, assertiveness, and sometimes aggression which is projected onto male and female immigrants and their offspring', especially the 'Arab *other*' (2017: 1). *Terres froides* asks to what extent these constructs are a cultural projection and a fantasy of anti-normativity. Djamel might disrupt normativity not simply because he takes revenge on his father who does not recognize him, but because he is a constructed character in the mind of the film or of the director.[7] Is *Les Terres froides* putting forward a cultural phantasy of Djamel's virility and using it as a cinematic tool for ends unrelated to his subjectivity? The film consciously raises but does not answer this question. In any event, the disruptive virility transcends Djamel's body and allegorizes a force, a kind of visceral intensity transferred from Djamel to Chamblasse. In the end, the virility that Laurent imagines in *beur* bodies is projected not onto Djamel's body per se,

---

7 On the other hand, Rees-Roberts (2008: 36–7) sees the kissing scene between Lifshitz and Laurent as depicting sexuality from the position of the *beur* subject, no longer the fantasy object.

but onto what his body can do to other types of bodies, in this case a white heterosexual male body.

Whether a phantasm or not, Djamel represents subjectivity in movement, not yet fixed in a national/ethnic system. When he goes to apply for a job at his father's factory, he is asked if he has a 'fixed address', to which he answers no. He is in movement spatially: one of the first images of the film is Djamel taking the train from Paris to Grenoble. This movement does not only define the character but signifies too the possibility of putting broader cultural patterns into movement. The workers at the factory are in the process of attempting to strike for slightly higher wages, and they try to recruit him to join them. Djamel is being paid minimum wage, so he says that he sees little fiscal advantage to be gained from a strike. His girlfriend Isabelle tries to convince him to join the movement, but he considers strikes as a 'a thing for whites' ('un truc des blancs'). His reconfiguration of normativity will not be a traditional or culturally sanctioned one – a strike – that in his view will not bring about substantive change. In one scene, he drives his scooter down a mountainous road but in the wrong lane. His movement creates his own left-of-centre course in the narrative, not relying on traditional political ways of disrupting normativity.

The transformation of normativity that takes place relates to the titular image of the cold lands. The water dripped onto the floor of the house floor is a key image: Djamel is in a sense melting the snow and ice of the 'cold lands' that had until this scene stood in for his exclusion. He has 'melted' ice and snow in the household, subverting it from within as he melts the coldness of Chamblasse's normativity. This metaphor is set up at the opening of the film, even before the credits. Djamel first appears as a character lying on the snow, surrounded by cold lands, his familial situation. The opening scene contrasts directly with the final one where Djamel is also lying on the ground. If lying face down in the final scene indicates that he has transmitted virility elsewhere and has transformed normative consciousness, in the opening scene Djamel lies face up because he is being invented as a character and as a signifier that will have the capacity to transmit. The sun shines on him as he lies, like a solar panel that absorbs sun and takes in energy to give off later. The environment may be cold, but he absorbs sunlight and heat. The contrast between his brown body and the whiteness of the snow already intimates that race defines his relation to, or his juxtaposition with, the environment. As he sits with an older man talking about the French nation in a café later on, the man points out that he cannot pass as from Normandy. Djamel adds that he always has his papers checked when in public, presumably unlike people that look white. The nation-state is cold to his being in France. As Rees-Roberts notes: 'The title [of the film] is a pointed reference to contemporary France as inhospitable' (2008: 35). What needs to melt, then, is both familial and social. The *beur* subject might be imagined as not from metropolitan France, or as not belonging in the Alps or as not belonging in white snow. The cold lands are imagined as not *beur* lands, and the *beur* subject cannot or should not be there. The snow–Djamel juxtaposition in the opening scene establishes the perception of outsiderness to the *beur* subject in hexagonal territory. The binary oppositions of white/*beur*, land/*beur*, family/*beur*, and nation/*beur* are all presented as stable ones that affirm racism. After Djamel confronts his father in his office and is rejected, he goes up on a hill looking down over the city of Grenoble, separated from the snowy space that he sees. The rejection of the white father is transformed into separation from the land itself as cold lands incarnate both family and nation.

If the water of the last scene suggests the melting of the cold land, it is because Djamel enters into dialogue with the cold land alongside Laurent. During their date in the park, the two of them wrestle flirtatiously in the snow. Obviously, Laurent is not cold to him – quite the contrary – so it is via Laurent that he begins to melt the coldness of the family to which he should belong. This queer moment involves the land or the environment as the beginning of the creation of a new form of relationality, the land implicated in what will be Djamel's entry into the family. The queer reconfiguration that Djamel orchestrates functions on several levels then: the social, the individual, and the environmental or ecological. Djamel brings together the outside and the inside, or the 'ecological' and its Ancient Greek origin (*oikos*, household). *Les Terres froides* brings together multiple modes of subjectivity in order for the normative to be opened up to something new. Queer futurity here incorporates a relation to the ecological, rejecting the tradition of patriarchal capitalist exploitation or domination of the land in favour of something new, queer, hybrid, and so forceful that it is yet to be known.

Gay domesticity: *Presque rien*

Lifshitz's *Presque rien* – literally 'almost nothing', but translated as *Come Undone* – focuses on how with the absence of stable domesticity the gay maturation process cannot be complete. The film has the opposite take on domesticity as *Les Terres froides*, where normative domesticity was queered: here, domesticity is the missing element in gay subjectivity that remains to be located. While same-sex domesticity might be taken as homonormative and the least queer element of LGBTQ life possible, the film should be taken in French cultural context during which same-sex domesticity was not yet sanctioned by the nation-state and domesticity could be taken as a signifier of queer futurity in a way that it may not be taken today. Debates about '*le mariage pour tous*' ('marriage for all') did not lead to the legalization of marriage for same-sex couples until 2012. Legal recognition of same-sex couples, however, was discussed in the 1990s, and in 1999 the French Parliament voted in the '*Pacte civil de solidarité*' (civil unions, or domestic partnerships), which offered same-sex couples many of the same legal rights as male–female couples but stopped short of bona fide marriage. Domesticity in Lifshitz's film, then, operates as a sign of what may come (and in fact, does come) for same-sex couples.[8] The main character's growing understanding of his own erotic desire and his need for domesticity and for a stable gay relationship, require him to move back in time and to unearth and process a relationship that did not fit that mould. In order to invent the possibility of a future, he has to queer time in order to construct a stable gay domesticity which cannot in context be created via a linear, gay narrative.

While on summer vacation with his family at their beach home on the Atlantic coast, Mathieu (Jérémie Elkaïm) becomes involved with Cédric (Stéphane Rideau) in an adolescent relationship based largely on sex, with a notable absence of domesticity. From the beginning, the two young men's families are positioned as separate from their relationship. A home/beach distinction functions as an exclusive binary opposition, as a number of scenes in the film alternate between the beach as the locus of (homo)sexuality and the vacation home of Mathieu's family as the space of domestic problems. In one scene, Mathieu complains about his family – especially his sister with whom he does not get along and his mother who has recently lost a baby and suffers from severe depression – a scene immediately juxtaposed with a Hollywoodesque sex scene on the beach. Cédric, too, has harsh words for his absent mother and keeps Mathieu separate from his presumably homophobic father, whose nearby home is never seen.

As *Presque rien* focuses on the young men's separation of familial domesticity and their developing relationship, it makes being seen as a couple a central issue in the first part

---

8 For a lengthier discussion of French gay male film in this period and the relation to domesticity, including in the films of François Ozon, see Reeser (2008).

of what could be considered Mathieu's coming-out process. It is Cédric that watches and seduces Mathieu, whose anxiety of being seen as gay provokes a refusal to be in public with Cédric, particularly near his family. Mathieu later apologizes for his homophobic behaviour, and the two again have sex on the beach, after which they spend much time in public as a couple. One of the final steps in the process of becoming a visible couple takes place when Mathieu tells his mother that he loves Cédric and that he plans to move with him to Nantes where he will begin university, instead of to Paris as planned. Significantly, Mathieu frames the issue for his mother as one of 'loving' Cédric, not of telling her that he 'is gay'. The process through which he is going is not so much defined by sexual categorization (with visibility or the 'closet' as one of its defining aspects) but is transforming into the issue of his relationship to relationships.[9]

As a result of this psychological shift, Mathieu begins to focus on his amorous relationship and, more specifically, on an absence within it that he cannot yet define. After Cédric has an accident and ends up in the hospital, Mathieu accidentally meets his father, who very congenially expresses a sincere interest in getting to know him as his son's boyfriend. When Mathieu recounts this familial encounter over dinner, Cédric raises his glass in jest and toasts 'A notre mariage alors' ('Well, then, to our marriage'). The ironic nature of the comment suggests the possibility of union in a cultural context in which it could become legal at the same time as it emphasizes the impossibility that Cédric the individual has an interest in a stable partnership. Not understanding the force of the irony nor the lack of commitment it could imply,

---

9 The film is decidedly not a simple coming-out narrative since it positions itself as beyond homosexuality per se. Lifshitz himself states that he did not approach the film as a gay film. See his interview with Claire Vassé (Lifshitz, n.d.; also 'Michael', 2006).

Mathieu experiences first-hand the type of domestic arrangement that he cannot accept and begins to understand that the transformations related to love, desire, and adulthood that he is going through are not yet complete. His suicide attempt, which is never directly shown on screen, provokes an intense depression, but it also effects a rupture with his boyhood. Parallels are thus established between his mother who is depressed because she lost a child to cancer and Mathieu who has given birth to a metaphorical sick child, his relationship with Cédric. His depression is indicative of a mourning process in which the lost object is not heterosexuality, as may be the case in coming out, but rather the impossibility of living with the kind of insufficiently stable lifestyle that Cédric represents. Mathieu's suicide attempt allegorizes a larger cultural breakaway from a less stable, perhaps non-monogamous, partnership towards one of greater solidity, even as the loss of the former relationship mode is mourned.

The psychological absence that Mathieu feels is mirrored in the narrative technique of the film in which key elements of the time that the two young men spent together in Nantes are literally missing. Although the periods before and after their cohabitation are recounted in detail, the entire period of time in which Mathieu lived with Cédric (presumably a year and a half) remains outside the narrative, and the actual reasons for the rupture are only vaguely alluded to. Instead, most of the film is structured around a recurring alternation between two temporal frames: the summer when the two boys met and Mathieu's release from the hospital in the winter. When the film opens with his transition out of the hospital and the trip to his family's beach house, it is unclear what has happened, and only gradually do the long flashbacks to the summer during which he met Cédric come together with the winter narrative in present time. The absence of the domestic relationship as temporal centre of the chronology disappears only when Mathieu decides to move away from psychological emptiness towards the idea of the type of relationship that he needs.

Mathieu's transition to a new physical and psychological space, represented by the beach in winter, is one where he can begin to locate stable domesticity. As he begins to understand the failure of his relationship with Cédric, Mathieu moves by himself into the family's vacation home, representative of domestic space in transition. Not having the keys to the house, he must break in and in effect create a new space for himself, without familial or societal 'keys' as models in how to do so. Lacking stable, happy couples around him, he lacks models of domesticity in his life, be they heterosexual or homosexual. At the same time as he begins to reconstruct an identity for himself related to coupledom, he bars Cédric from entering the new space. Though his former partner follows him to the house and demands to be let in, Mathieu will literally not let him enter as he attempts to build a psychological sphere based on a firm domestic element that cannot include what Cédric has come to represent.

In the final sequence of the film, Mathieu locates the home of Cédric's former lover Pierre (Nils Öhlund), whom he has already met. First watching him and his mother through their dining room window as they clean up after dinner, Mathieu is led by this scene to return the next afternoon to visit Pierre. His mother answers the door, explaining that her son is at work but that he is welcome to wait for him in the house. Mathieu accepts and sits at the dining room table with the coffee that Pierre's mother offers him as she continues her ironing. This invitation into the domestic space, first represented by the warm interaction with the mother in opposition to the cold outside, is followed by Pierre's return home and his invitation to go for a walk on the beach (plate 9).

This preliminary integration of homosexuality and familial life transitions into the boys' walk on the beach, the final scene of the film, which encapsulates the possibility of a gay male identity based on solidity. Pierre's name ('*pierre*' meaning 'rock') is particularly appropriate in this context, suggesting the distinct possibility of firmness. Mathieu tells Pierre's mother that he is studying architecture in university, and the viewer learns that Pierre is a mason. Mathieu incarnates a theoretical domestic 'architecture' seeking its missing practical half while Pierre embodies the reality of the construction of a domesticity symbolized by building. These 'hard' references refer back to an earlier scene in which Mathieu and Cédric break into a ruined château. As Mathieu reads from a guidebook, Cédric shows no interest in the architecture, preferring to have sex in the isolated locale, but when Mathieu refuses and tells him to take an interest in the architecture, he responds that they are nothing but 'a bunch of rocks', setting up a marked contrast between his ex-boyfriend, Pierre, and himself as sign of a relationship based on affection and eroticism. The contrast also suggests a difference in the role of signification as part of a relationship: whereas Cédric does not serve as sign in the film, Pierre's potential as partner is suggested by his very ability to signify beyond the actual relationship, to function both as himself and as metaphor. The incorporation of a semiotic 'outside' into the relationship helps inscribe it as something beyond homosexuality per se, as more able to operate within the larger symbolic order in which homosexual relationships require symbolic capital in order to function in any stable way. Pierre is the architect of a new form of sexual representation.

The beach in winter incarnates a hybrid space where Mathieu's sexuality can be simultaneously visible and invisible. The beach had already come to symbolize the public forum for exploration of Mathieu's visible sexuality, in opposition to the domestic sphere. This public/private opposition is destabilized here, however, as the winter walk on the beach is not sexual, but discursive in nature as the two boys explore each other's lives interactively and hint at the potential for an intimate and reciprocal relationship. While walking along, they notice a young boy with a dog, and Pierre wonders where the boy's father is. Although they think that they locate the father in the distance, the child's father is never seen on screen; instead, Pierre takes on the symbolic role of the father, playing soccer with the boy on the beach. While possibilities of domesticity for the two characters and, by extension, for gay couples are central at the end of the film, this final scene also gestures to contemporaneous debates relating to gay parenting (*homoparentalité*) taking place around the domestic partnerships or PACS, which stopped short of providing adoption and medically assisted procreation for gay couples.[10] As temporal scrambling no longer operates as an organizational framework in this final section of the film, the temporal focus shifts from the relation between past and present to the simple future, that of the two adolescents as well as of gay couples and families.[11]

On one level, Mathieu's transition in the film from gay individual to a possible member of a certain kind of couple is a projection of the adult filmmaker and of adult gay culture

---

10 Because of its noted absence in the PACS, '*homoparentalité*' was considered by many the next major gay political issue and the major remaining issue. The cover story of *L'Evevement du jeudi* in June 1998, for instance, is entitled 'Familles Homo: Le Dernier Tabou' ('Gay Families: The Final Taboo'). On the PACS and its (non-)relation to parenting, see for instance Nye (2003).

11 In the same way that the film ends with a gesture towards the future of gay families, the final pages of *L'Homosexualité à l'adolescence* (*Homosexuality in Adolescence*) are devoted to the future of gay parenting: 'On peut imaginer que, dans les années à venir, quand vous serez adulte, la France assouplira sa position et accordera aux homos le droit d'adopter des enfants ... L'avenir tranchera' (Vaisman and Maja, 2011: 106–7). ('Perhaps in the years to come, when you are an adult, France will adopt a more accommodating position and homosexuals will be accorded the right to adopt children ... The future will decide'). The implication of the example is that gay adolescents will become the gay parents of tomorrow, a cultural horizon of the time.

onto the idealized adolescent, a transfer that is itself represented in the film. Under the advice of his therapist, Mathieu tape-records his feelings and actions as he returns to the beach. His therapist first asks him to keep a journal, but he responds that he does not like to write, insisting on recording a vision of homosexuality beyond its written inscription. This recording of a gay self attempting to understand itself, what it wants and where it is moving, is also the self mourning for something that it has lost. Mathieu's oral record is a signifier for the late 1990s queer filmmaker, attempting to record and thereby construct the model of a developing gay male self in the context of gay stability.[12]

It is, thus, a question of a kind of coming of age for both Mathieu and gay male culture. As Cédric is attempting to seduce Mathieu at the beginning of the film, he remarks that Mathieu looks more grown up than he had the summer before. The ensuing scenes reveal that this physical coming of age parallels his sexual coming out. During the final scene of the film, Pierre also remarks that Mathieu has changed since he last saw him, that he is 'less boyish' ('moins gamin') than he was before. In his realization about himself, Mathieu has come of age a second time, but this second step in his double initiatory rite requires the gay adolescent to 'come out' and then to 'come in'. It also has required Mathieu to go back in time, to work through the past to emerge as a future-oriented subject. The final scenes suggest that in a new French cultural context, sexuality no longer has to be the central element of a coming-out process: rather, an assumption of domesticity can be the telos of a process that is individual in nature. What will happen is only sketched out, not delineated, for the idea of futurity ultimately defines the characters and the film's telos.

---

12 Lifshitz discusses the film as the inscription of the director's self, which he considers a first step to move on to depicting something beyond the filming self. See Claire Vassé's interview with Lifshitz (Lifshitz, n.d.).

Transing time: *Wild Side*

Lifshitz's most sophisticated film, *Wild Side* – with the same title in English and French, taken from Lou Reed's song 'Walk on the Wild Side' (1972) – moves away from the gay male subject matter of much of his previous work, particularly *Les Corps ouverts* and *Presque rien*. This shift is conveyed by the opening moments of the film, which depict not a gay male body, but a body in fragments, including shots of body parts traditionally considered either male or female. At the same time as the viewer sees these pieces of what looks to be a transgender body, the first scene appears to take place in a male-to-female transgender space where an angelic person sings in English about falling in love 'with a dead boy', concluding with the line 'Are you a boy or are you a girl?' As a response to the song, the trans character's tears suggest that her corporeal in-betweenness, her location somewhere between 'boy' and 'girl' is problematic. The queer singer (played by the singer Anohni, at the time the lead singer of the group Antony and the Johnsons) might be voicing restrictive cultural attitudes towards transgender as sexually ambiguous and as supposedly lacking a coherent or complete identity, including the French nation-state's historical resistance to legal sexual ambiguity on identity papers and to the legal change of sexual civil status (see Chiland, 2005; Gromb *et al.*, 1997; Reeser, 2013).[13] Transgender fell outside the French cultural context in which same-sex marriage and *homoparentalité* were the high-profile queer issues of the day. This striking musical prelude, which exists outside the narrative movement of the film, establishes an attitude towards transgender to which the rest of the film will respond. Whereas a trans woman who passes might disrupt the supposedly natural sexual binary only when it is discovered that she has transitioned from one gender to

---

13 On the film's relation to the political context, see Rees-Roberts (2007).

another, in this case the main character Stéphanie (Stéphanie Michelini) is introduced as a character who can only disrupt the binary oppositions of sex and gender.

The notion of disruption pertains not simply to sex in the film, however, for it is closely connected to the narrative as well. The rest of *Wild Side* tells the story of Stéphanie's relationship with her childhood and with her two cisgender male lovers Djamel (Yasmine Belmadi) and Mikhail (Edouard Nikitine), but it is narrative itself that forms the main content of the film. The sophisticated story is recounted in three main interspliced but distinct narrative levels: a central narrative in which Stéphanie returns to her childhood home to nurse her dying mother, a reverse chronological narrative of her childhood as the young Pierre, assigned male at birth, and a second backwards narrative recounting the origin and development of her relationships with her two lovers. For Stéphanie, who rejected her past when she moved away from home and her mother as an adolescent and now lives in Paris, the backwards thrust of the childhood narrative has the effect of moving her psychologically backwards to a time of her life that she does not wish to inhabit. Though she makes a journey home to the North of France, the trip is represented as moving her in time more than in space. In particular, the temporal movement repeatedly disrupts a forwardness towards a more complete cultural recognition of her gender subjectivity presented as lacking in the first scene of the film, as Stéphanie is confronted with the cultural assumption of her maleness and with her transphobic mother. The film's temporality thus destroys the possibility of representing narrative teleology as a journey (actual or metaphorical) from point A (man) to point B (woman) – a key representation of gender change in the life and autobiography of trans superstars Bambi and Coccinelle, and in French films such as Gaveau's ground-breaking *Adam est … Eve* (1954), Jérôme Foulon's *Une autre femme* (*Another*

Woman) (2000), or Meier's *Thelma* (2001).[14] On the contrary, here the various narrative levels together create a flow that is anything but linear or teleological, forcing the viewer to work constantly to make meaning out of the film. Transgender, then, disrupts not only a binarized sex/gender system, but also an imagined temporal binary in which a gendered past turns into a differently gendered present.

With this disruptive relation to narrative time, Stéphanie functions on one level as a sign of the end of time and of linear temporality, reiterating gender and cultural theorists' ideas about transgender. Transgender has served as a privileged sign of postmodernity for a number of theorists, as the fluidity of sex has been taken as metonymic for the fluidity of other aspects of postmodernity. For Jean Baudrillard, '[w]e are all transsexuals' because we are composed of the hybrid proliferation of signs and images (2002: 10). Because of postmodern subjects' symbolic transsexuality and their inability to remain whole in the fragmented world of media and signs, we lack 'time to seek out an identity in the historical record, in memory, in a past, [or] indeed in a project or a future' (11). Baudrillard's 'transsexual' is located outside linear or discrete temporality, unable to use time to create subjectivity.[15] Felski studies how transgender, as an incarnation of the end

---

14 On trans journeys in autobiographies, see Cotten (2011); Prosser (1999). Another defining element of trans films' linearity is the (problematic) journey of cisgender characters from transphobia to tolerance. On the issue of 'cisgender tolerance' in French trans films, see Reeser (2021).

15 It is important to note that there are substantive issues with Baudrillard's transphobic essay, including the fact he does not imagine trans* subjectivity not predicated on this kind of signifying movement, and is thinking of the 'transsexuality' of cisgender people. On this issue, see for instance Stryker (1999).

of sex, embodies the end of time: 'The destabilization of the male/female divide is seen to bring with it a waning of temporality, teleology, and grand narrative; the end of sex echoes and affirms the end of history, defined as the pathological legacy and symptom of the trajectory of Western modernity' (2006: 566). Halberstam argues that Western constructs of time revolve around normative assumptions based on the progression of a reproductive life cycle or of a heterosexually defined daily routine: 'Reproductive time and family time are, above all, heteronormative time/space constructs' (2005: 10). It becomes possible, then, to consider how trans subjects may fall outside these normative temporal constructs; for instance, how the boy does not turn into a man and then a father, then a grandfather, etc. Rather, the boy becomes a woman and definitions of the life cycle have to be reconceived retroactively, as alteration takes over the role of the 'natural' process of growing up and aging. With these ideas about disruption in mind, I would like to examine here more specifically how temporal disruption in the film functions narratively vis-à-vis Stéphanie's transidentity. It is my contention that the two disruptions cannot be separated, even as the way in which transgender time is defined morphs over the course of the film. In fact, the film ends up being about what I might call the disruption of disruption, a move from transgender as disruptive to transgender as recreating time and temporality as open-ended. It is in this sense that *Wild Side* produces a new form of queer being as time and transidentity are reconceived as future-oriented.

Disruption of sex, disruption of time

The scene just after the prelude introduces Stéphanie as a character functioning outside the normative cycle of daily life. The viewer sees her at work at night as a sex worker, revealing her breasts and the contours of her penis to potential customers and then having sex with various men. One point of these scenes is to establish immediately that she functions outside heteroquotidian time, including both heterosexual sex work and the constraints of 9-to-5 work time. Later in the film, Stéphanie returns home from work in the early hours of the morning to her two male lovers who are asleep in bed together. The subsequent acts of tenderness oppose Stéphanie's temporal frame to Mikhail's (he works as a dishwasher) and to Djamel's (though a male sex worker, he is shown working during the day).

But even more than the day-to-dayness of time, it is the heteronormative life cycle outside of which she falls and, conversely, which intrudes on her adult life. While the first scene reveals the melodic mechanism by which cultural constraints attempt to establish sexual binarism, a scene soon following represents this process from within a symbolic family structure. Stéphanie appears in a domestic space with the two men that we later learn are her lovers, but the scene creates a sense of family as the two men are playing soccer inside (one younger, one older; one shorter, one taller), and as the 'mother' is making herself up in front of a mirror in preparation for going out. This gesture towards familial heteronormativity, however, only turns into its impossibility as the threesome is shown to be anything but a traditional three-part family. If, as suggested by the song in the opening, one imagines that the film will be about a linear narrative movement towards becoming a girl by killing the boy within, subsequent events disrupt the possibility of a movement forward and reassert the sex assigned at birth, moving her backwards in psychological and narrative progression. First, a flash of a young child in a flat field interrupts her making herself up and presages the major disruption about to come. Then, the phone rings, and we learn that it is a call for Pierre, the young person that Stéphanie had been and that just appeared. After Djamel unknowingly tells the caller that Pierre is not there, she is forced to respond to the phone in a male voice, learning that her mother has fallen ill. The deep voice which disrupts the family-like scene and her gendering process in the mirror codes her former life as disruptive. The hard 'rock' (*pierre*) of boyhood stands in direct opposition to her as a woman, juxtaposing a static notion of boyhood with a trans notion of adulthood.[16] As the viewer will learn through the mouthpiece of her mother, her 'boyhood' was predicated on the assumption of sexual and temporal teleology, the assumed inevitability that Pierre would become a man, while her current sexual subjectivity can be seen as predicated on a move to womanness defined on her terms. These two narrative teleologies stand in direct opposition to each other, creating a tension between past and present that becomes in itself the central motor of the film's progress.

Throughout much of the film, Pierre's childhood continues to function as disruptive memory to Stéphanie, and the entire return home could be taken as a disruptive moment in her own temporality. Like her former home that was and is no longer a home, her former life is not a 'home' for her past memories as her new body has become a new home for a new selfhood. Her past does not map onto her present in a linear fashion; rather, it is a backwards past in opposition to her present, a temporal crash resembling the opposition of her sexual subjectivity and the sex that she 'should' be. In one scene, for instance, she stands in front of what we assume is her old elementary school and we hear the voiceover of her teacher calling the names of the children who each respond '*présent*' or '*présente*' (the masculine or the feminine form of the adjective). When the instructor calls out 'Caumon, Pierre', the voice of Pierre responds 'présent', the silent '–t' in the masculine adjective form reminding Stéphanie that she was forced to be male in this narrative space.

---

16 This Pierre contrasts strikingly with the Pierre character at the end of *Presque rien*, who is the solidity that Mathieu seeks, whereas here Pierre incarnates the sex assigned at birth that Stéphanie wants to work out of her life.

While taking care of her mother, Stéphanie goes to see her former love interest Nicolas (Christophe Sermet), who embodies the heteronormative time she effectively rejected when she left home as a teenager. He has married, had two children, and left their hometown to spend time in Brussels, but he has returned to live at home. When Stéphanie inquires as to his boys' names, he responds 'Pierre and Daniel', suggesting the heteronormative rock that his life has become through paternity. In this scene, Nicolas is closely related to temporality: he wants to know how long it has been since they have seen each other, and he talks about his time in Brussels as duration (five years). More specifically, he embodies permanence of time or lack of change: he cannot recall how long it has been since the two of them have seen each other, his time in Brussels is presented as an aberration from his time in his hometown, and he remarks that Stéphanie is still very much like Pierre: 'It's strange, but you haven't changed. It still seems like you.' Stéphanie concludes the scene by asking him: 'Did you think I'd love you forever?' Her life choices are not predicated on heteronormativity, to be sure, but perhaps more importantly, they are not predicated on the temporality of permanence that Nicolas embodies (even as he sees her inner self as static). On another level, Stéphanie's remark suggests the distinct possibility of Nicolas's bi- or homosexuality or his queerness, and thus his repression of another type of life in his current childrearing moment. In this scenario, Stéphanie is saying adieu to the possibility of a gay or queer life with Nicolas, one that while perhaps not by definition hetero-temporal, would imply a temporality different from the transgender choices she has made. 'Queer time' might start later than heterosexual time (only after the coming-out process), might require one to 'make up for lost time', might disrupt one's previous sexual identity and might be less likely to include a reproductive clock than hetero-time, but it still implies a kind of disruption very different from transgender time here. So while Nicolas himself has not disrupted time, while his life has remained a coherent trajectory of hetero-time uninterrupted by sex or by sexuality, Stéphanie in effect rejects the heteronormative and the gay male time that she could have lived if she had identified with the sex assigned to her at birth.

Stéphanie has a relation to trans-temporality by opposition with other characters as well; she is framed by her two lovers, and particularly Mikhail, who has a much closer relation to space than to time. Having come from Russia, perhaps to escape war trauma or military service (possibly in Chechnya), he crosses the physical borders of the nation clandestinely in the hopes of finding his uncle living in Paris, and his movement via train is one of the minor narrative levels of the film. He makes a phone call back to his mother in Russia, during which we hear only her voice speaking Russian, with the effect of reinforcing the linguistic, cultural, and spatial distance that he is experiencing. It makes metonymic sense, then, that Stéphanie is his lover: each crosses a kind of border (the borders of sex and the body; the borders of the nation). Mikhail's unbordered desire for Stéphanie as trans also makes this link: in one scene late in the film (but early chronologically), he asks her to wear male clothes, which she does begrudgingly. Even as her breasts are exposed, he asks her to use her 'male voice', the one she had when she was a boy, and he removes her earrings. His sexual desire and orientation cannot be located inside or outside hetero- or homosexuality, but are about sexual crossings, an idea further complicated by his simultaneous sexual relations with Djamel. In fact, the initial encounter between Stéphanie and Mikhail defines their sexual relation as a crossing from the very beginning. After a handsome man hires the two of them to watch them have sex, Mikhail makes it clear from the start and until the end of the scene that it is not just a question of money, but of genuine sexual and emotional desire. As a *beur* character, Djamel suggests a crossing of cultural borders from within the nation because he is estranged from his mother, presumably because of their difference in cultural views. In one scene, for instance, he finds himself in an apartment building facing his mother's building, as he gazes upon her from across a vertical space that serves to mark the cultural barrier. For both men, the lack of a mother is delineated spatially, in opposition to Stéphanie's estrangement from her mother, which is defined by its temporal duration.

Despite their spatial orientation, however, past time is not actually irrelevant to the two men; it is just that they refuse to enter into a productive and sustained dialogue with the past. Mikhail appears as temporally static, for though he has suffered from some kind of war trauma, he does not move backwards in time to face it. Similarly, Djamel refuses to go and see his mother, even as his brother asks him to do so, although while watching her he remembers a series of childhood images that are revealed as nostalgic photographs. So while Djamel might evoke movement across cultures within the French nation, Mikhail suggests a physical move across nations, and taken together the two men can be taken to signify the concept of the French nation in movement. For the imagined community to be in transit, people must come from elsewhere (in this case, from the extreme east of Europe), but they must also problematize traditional ideas of France as white and as culturally homogenous from within. If Stéphanie embodies the end of narrative because she disrupts time, then the two men embody the end of the fictional narrative of the impermeable nation because they destabilize the cultural space of France.

It is as signifiers of larger cultural formulations that the three characters are metonymically similar, that their three-way relationship makes signifying sense. The two characters representing the porous nation love Stéphanie in part because they signify her journey from the sex assigned at birth and point out the permeability of sex by analogy. Transsexual narratives, Prosser points out, have tended to use journeys as one of their prime metaphors of sexual crossing, but 'a more appropriate analogical frame for the transsexual's writing of transition as journey may be that of immigration: the subject conceives of transsexuality as a move to a new life in a new land, allowing the making of home, precisely an act of translation' (1999: 92). The metaphor of transnation, however, is suggested here in a somewhat different permutation, by a combination of Stéphanie's journey in time and of her intimate relationship with the two cultural journeymen. In the same way that the nation is disrupted internally as well as externally, Stéphanie's move is an intra- and inter-phenomenon: the 'other' sex has always been within her (as we will see, since childhood), and she is now in the process of movement (which, as we will also see, she comes to realize).

Revising past time

In the last scene of the backwards childhood narrative (the first chronologically), the young, naked Pierre stands in front of a mirror, moving their long hair up and down as if to decide how their hair would look the best.[17] With this image, one reason for the film's juxtaposition of the past and present narratives becomes clear: Stéphanie's move backwards in time, her re-examination of the boy that she was expected to be, and her vision of herself looking at herself (all past events) now appear in proximate time next to her return home and the death of her transphobic mother (present events). As a result, these various events turn into a single series of catalytic conditions for the evocation of previously hidden aspects of her childhood that invert the sex that Pierre was assigned. The mirror scene makes reference to an early scene of the film (mentioned above) in which Stephanie looks in the mirror and makes a movement with her hair very similar to the one Pierre makes here. This intratextual link suggests that, if one looks

---

17 I use they/them pronouns to refer to the young Stéphanie, to reflect the complication of gender.

properly, one can see that Pierre was always already the gendered subject that Stéphanie is now. Prosser points out how in a number of transsexual autobiographies that he studies, the writing subject reflects back on the past to find the trans subject that is already there, a process that creates a coherent narrative movement from the past to the present by locating the transsexual within the former self. As Prosser writes: 'The retrospective structure of autobiography allows the transsexual to appear to have been there all along' (1998: 103). The memory of the child that Stéphanie was serves a function similar to the narrative function Prosser describes; over the course of the film, the narrative with Pierre takes on greater and greater importance as the importance of retro-spection plays a more central role in the narrative. Prosser views this use of the former self as one technique of 'the production of transsexuality both in and through autobiographical narrative' (103) or as one of the techniques by which narrative becomes part of the transition process itself. In this case, transgender is produced not textually through autobiography or discursively through language but rather visually through a series of images mediated by memory.

As one manifestation of memory, Stéphanie remembers more and more her father before his death as the nurturer of the young Pierre and as inexplicably and deeply connected to his child. In one scene, Pierre and their father are standing in a field near the house watching birds fly around in harmonious movement, then sitting on the couch while the father strokes the hair of his sleeping child. This representation of paternity as accepting, loving and natural (or 'in nature') gradually emerges over the course of the film. As the father is increasingly un-died or brought back to life in the backwards motion of the narrative, the trans child can emerge in memory as loved by the father and as accepted outside binary sexual narratives, in the same way that the father becomes increasingly located outside traditional narratives of non-nurturing masculinity, and that the relation between father and son falls outside the grand Oedipal narrative (itself heavily dependent on binary notions of sex). Along with the father is reborn Pierre's sister Caroline (who died with her father) as a second self to her sibling, a cinematic rebirth of the girl that Pierre was. It is never fully clear whether Caroline is a character at all or whether she simply represents Pierre's gendered self. The sister appears increasingly with Pierre in several playful scenes, including a traditional scene of courtly love between knight and lady. Much as the emergence of the father disrupts the mother's imagined narrative of sexual binaries, Caroline's rebirth in memory evokes the playfulness – and thus the artificiality – of childhood binary sex narratives, helping to pave the way for the final scene of Pierre in front of the mirror.

If Pierre's sister stands in for Stéphanie's other half, it is not simply because she signifies the gender that they will become as an adult. For the point of the mirror scene is not exactly that Pierre was always a girl, but that, taken as a boy, she was already 'in transit' between genders. It is the very notion of transit itself that gets remembered in this scene and that helps produce not so much adult transsexuality or adult transidentity, but sexual movement as a trans-age phenomenon. After all, Pierre is not simply trying to make their hair girl-like (it is already long), but to experiment with hair as transition. Whereas the adult mirror scene to which this one refers implies the engendering of the self – putting on makeup in order to continue the process of becoming woman – this scene signifies the process of engendering the childhood self as in sexual movement. This rediscovery of the child in transit is conveyed by contrast with the static image of the photographed child. In the scene immediately preceding the final mirror scene, Stéphanie is emptying the house of all of her mother's possessions and particularly of her childhood photos. As she rips up these photos, Mikhail tells her that he wants to keep one of the photos, a request that she adamantly refuses. Stéphanie will not allow for the possibility that the medium of photography represent her childhood, as she attempts to remain in the gendered present. The mirror scene, on the other hand, suggests that it is the moving images of memory (and by extension of film, the medium reflecting memory and rescripting the past) – not photography – that is best able to depict the trans subject in transit.

The narrative tension is resolved here at the end of the film as the past and present narratives merge, as the past becomes part of the present, and the present part of the past. But this temporal fusion does not imply that the trans child is unearthed in the past like a photo, rather that they may actually be created through memory and retrospection. The issue of the veracity of Stéphanie's memory is put into question in a conversation with her mother about whether her father would have liked to see her as trans. The mother points out that he was so happy to have had a boy and that he would not have liked to see her as a woman. That Stéphanie does not really argue with her mother but remembers her father very differently (though she was quite young when he died) implies the subjective nature of (their) memory and raises the question of whether Stéphanie or her mother remembers correctly, a question that is never resolved in any objective way. It is the undecidability of memory, the inability to determine whether it is constructed or simply remembered which emerges most clearly as the apparatus that views the child in transit. Memory is not used to reconstruct a future ('Because I now imagine that I was always a trans, I was'), nor to simply recollect the past ('I remember that I was always trans'), rather the narrative reflects the inability to determine precisely how the trans child is remembered.

If the past child must be imported into the present to help create trans subjectivity, the adult of the present must also be read back onto the child of the past. This dialogic relation between present and past results from the difficulty of knowing to what extent the trans child is invented or remembered. In this case, the child is born in the present as a reconstituted vision of the past and as one part of the trans present in movement. On her return home to Paris after her mother's death at the very end of the film, Stéphanie sees a young boy named Lucas with his father in the hallway of the moving train. The boy is acting naughty, but the father disciplines him, and then caresses his hair as the two males together watch the moving countryside out the window. Instead of seeing the outside in movement, Stéphanie sees a boy in movement, a boy who evokes memory itself in movement. The apparition of the boy refers back to the earlier scene in the childhood narrative in which Pierre's own father was caressing their hair. Through this image of memory in the present, Pierre and their relation with his father are both revealed as no longer dead: a suppressed part of the past is no longer hidden, rather it has moved symbolically into the present. Father/child intimacy thus signifies the forward migration of memory, the movement of a past form of safe intimacy into the present.

In his study of transsexual narrative, Prosser suggests, through a reading of Leslie Feinberg's seminal trans text *Stone Butch Blues*, that one approach to narrative transition is that transition itself can be its own trans subjectivity, as a movement from one gender to another is not viewed as beginning and end: 'No longer typically ending transition, transsexuals are overtly rewriting the narrative of trans-sexuality – and transsexual narratives – as open-ended' (1998: 11). I read Lifshitz's film as following Prosser's model of 'transsexual' narrative. It does so not so much by rewriting open-endedness per se, but by representing a move from open-endedness as disruptive to a state of open-endedness as harmonious. Or, I might say that the trans subject moves from a state of 'becoming' to a state of 'be-becoming'. From the perspective of Deleuze and Guattari, for whom 'becoming' is without beginning or end, Stéphanie might literalize the necessary connection between becoming and 'becoming-woman' (1987: 277). If so, Stéphanie evokes this kind of becoming here not because she transitioned from one gender to another, but because she is now represented as in a constant process of becoming a woman.

One aspect of this new open-endedness is the permeability of memory that I have discussed, the inability to place past and present in two distinct camps and keep them separate. But it is the final scene of the film that reveals the finality of non-finality. While Stéphanie lies asleep in a train compartment with Djamel and Mikhail on her way back to Paris, the camera positions the three characters together, all asleep, in a pose of contentment and intimacy as the window behind them shows the movement of the train against the landscape (plate 10). As the train continues on, the light from the window moves across the three characters, the train goes through a tunnel, and the film ends. This optimistic scene suggests not an endpoint to Stéphanie's temporal journey but another way of conceiving of sex: not as a move to an endpoint of a stable notion of sex but as open-endedness itself. As a part of the narrative movement, the last scene travels implicitly back to the first scene in the cabaret, rendering the entire question of whether Stéphanie 'is a boy or a girl' irrelevant as the sexual stasis of that scene has now been transformed into ontological movement. If the endpoint of the film is transition itself, the transit zone is not a transitional phase but the very place she is going in this film, which is ultimately about the transition to transition or the becoming of 'becoming'.

The representation of spatiality as movement means that temporality itself has been put in transit for Stéphanie. Because the past has been integrated into the present (and vice versa), time is no longer disruptive for her as she is released from the previously oppressive aspects of temporality. She no longer disrupts time, and time no longer disrupts her. If the dominant final metaphor for her Deleuzian becoming is now spatial movement or 'deterritorialization' (Deleuze and Guattari, 1987: 291–2), Stéphanie has moved into another metaphoric framework, the one her two male lovers had inhabited all along, and the optimistic intimacy of the final scene suggests a group movement that can now be in unison because everyone is metaphorically aboard.

The movement of light across the three characters in the scene refers back to the movement of light in several previous scenes, and particularly ones in the childhood narrative. In the very first glimpse that we get of the young Pierre, the child is in a field flying around like an airplane as light comes across the field. With the hindsight from the end of the film, the point of this imagistic connection would be that movement as movement, transition as definitional is far from a new phenomenon in the life of Stéphanie and that her transidentity has always been part of her selfhood. The visual reference to light, along with its association with transit, invites us as viewers of the cinematic light to move back in time to revaluate the previous scenes of the film, to reconsider what at the time seemed to be disruptive narrative moments and to review them as already containing the enlightened movement we now see as the endpoint. In this sense, the viewer assumes the role of the subject forced to revaluate the past to comprehend the present – a process not unlike the one Stéphanie has already gone through to arrive where she is now located. This invitation to the viewer to re-reflect on the film to (re)construct the narrative can be viewed as a larger strategy to illuminate the viewer through destabilization. For although most of the narrative can be reconstructed coherently and assigned a chronology, other parts resist clear temporality and leave the viewer forced to locate narrative teleology in transit between past and present, between coherence and instability. This temporally centred narrative creates an epistemological fantasy by reeling the viewer into temporality on its own terms and by placing the viewer face-to-face with temporal disruption.

Queering the road movie? *Plein sud*

Following on *Presque rien* and *Wild Side*, Lifshitz's road movie *Plein sud* is structured around the physical movement of the gay male character Sam (Yannick Renier), along with three travel companions: the pregnant Léa (Léa Seydoux), her gay brother Mathieu (Théo Frilet), and her lover Jérémie (Pierre Perrier). The trip begins with Sam alone in northern France, and he picks up Léa and Mathieu who are hitchhiking together. Heading south, Jérémie later joins them in Sam's car, and the four of them arrive at an unidentified beach where much of the narrative takes place. In the final section of the film, Sam abandons them and heads alone to Spain, where his mother currently lives. He had been planning from the start to head there though the others do not know this, and his interactions with the other three characters look to be accidental. The film is in some ways the mirror image of *Wild Side* as the homosexuality of the main character is seemingly irrelevant in relation to his move back in time to recover and understand the source of boyhood trauma. Unlike Stéphanie who recovers her transgender childhood by heading back in time, Sam has a series of memories from his youth not directly related to gender or sexuality. The physical movement through space provokes the movements back in time. Early on, one such scene shows Sam as an eight-year-old boy witnessing his father's death by suicide with a gun, which takes place in his car with his wife (Sam's mother) in the passenger seat. His mother has serious mental health problems, and we learn in a later scene that the adolescent Sam lives in a foster family with a mother and a sister. In a separate scene, his birth mother comes to visit him, and a scene between the two of them in a café concludes with Sam noting that she has not come to take him home with her but for no reason ('C'est juste comme ça'). The focus of the flashback scenes is that the Sam of the present sees his past self watching. With a fixed gaze, he watches his alcoholic mother, he watches his father die by suicide, he watches his mother react to the suicide, and he watches his father on the Normandy beach during cold weather. In other words, Sam unearths his traumatic past, or, more precisely, he witnesses his childhood self witnessing difficult events or moments. He is an adult dealing not only with childhood trauma, but with the very act of watching trauma. Mathieu is very attracted to Sam who does not notice him sexually and whose reasons for not desiring the handsome Mathieu are not really clear. At one moment, the shirtless Sam washes himself with a hose and Mathieu, also shirtless, appears and takes the hose. Instead of being aroused by Mathieu, Sam takes leave without seeing his fit body. He cannot 'see' an erotic male body because his gaze is directed back in time to his childhood. Sam has to learn to re-vision his past as less traumatic before he can focus his present gaze on erotic bodies.

A key moment of the film takes place during a song titled 'Love Song', sung in the film by the writer of the lyrics Leslie Duncan even though the song was written for Elton John whose version of the song is much more famous (as part of his album *Tumbleweed Connection*).[18] A relation between Sam and Mathieu is not yet possible, but the song sets in motion the question of whether 'love' can set Sam free from his trauma. The two men on the beach go swimming together, leading to the first moment of unfettered erotic attraction. The song is juxtaposed with the previous scene in the café with Sam's mother, asking whether her seeming lack of interest for her son in the past can be offset or remedied by another kind of love in the present. A random young boy sits on the beach watching the two men swim since boyhood is observing or affecting Sam more than Sam is watching or seeing his boyhood, for now at least. The lyrics comment on the scene: 'Love

18 The film may reference Elton John's 'My Father's Gun' on the same album. The song is about a confederate man whose father has died and who pledges to carry his gun to the North to fight for the Confederacy but instead he says: 'I'd like to know where the riverboat sails tonight / To New Orleans well that's just fine alright'. The narrator of the song resembles Sam who has what is likely his father's gun, and heads south to take revenge by possibly killing his mother or himself.

is the opening door / Love is what we came here for.' The question being asked via the song is whether loving Mathieu could open a door to healing. That night, the two of them at last have sex on the beach, passionately, and the next day, they have an intimate talk during which Sam tells Mathieu for the first time about witnessing his father's death. The scene would seem to respond that love can open the door to intimacy between them. Yet, Sam later leaves abruptly and unexpectedly in his car (abandoning the three characters on the beach), as he heads south to see his mother in Spain.

Love in the present cannot open the door of love that did not exist in the past. At least not yet. What Sam needs to do is to revision – literally and non-literally – how he sees what happened during his childhood. He has to resee his father from an adult vantage point, just as he has now seen Mathieu's body as erotic. In a flashback as he is about to reveal his past to Mathieu, Sam the boy looks intently at his mother sitting in the passenger seat in the car after his father has shot himself. She looks fixedly at him, and vice versa. Part of his present trauma is based on the way in which the event related to seeing. He shares with Mathieu that there had been something 'bizarre' in his father's eyes, 'as if he wanted to make me understand'. He is not quite sure what this ocular relation is or what it meant, but it becomes clear that Sam's journey aims to excavate and understand this ocular relation from the perspective of the present. As Sam drives alone in Spain, the camera shoots the car's rear-view mirror and we see him indirectly. Other shots are what one would see from the inside perspective of the car and Sam looking out the window of the car while driving, the point being that seeing is the dominant issue circulating in Sam's mind. Two key childhood scenes related to looking return in his mind. First, he sees himself and his father in his bedroom putting on a heavy coat to go out in the cold. The scene has no noise and no words are spoken, but his father conveys paternal affection in subtle ways by looking at him. Second, he and his father walk on the chilly beach, with Sam on his father's shoulders, the two both looking out to sea. In a second shot, we see Sam alone from behind as he looks out to sea on the waves crashing down, and then his father watching him look. Significantly, his father turns his gaze and moves away, no longer looking at his son. Despite his suicide and the absence of verbal affection, the adult Sam is remembering that he had visual connections with his father, even as those connections were cut off – much as his father walks away and leaves him alone on the beach. Sam discovers the presence of love in the non-discursive look, beginning the process of coming to terms with his father's suicide and his sense that his father abandoned him because he did not love him and perhaps because he did not talk to him about his suicide or his love for him. Sam begins to answer yes to Duncan's question in 'Love Song': 'Have your eyes really seen?' Love is the 'opening door', opening in order to see not some essence of another person or to join with their inner being as a kind of romanticized version of love as a joining of two souls, but to see ways of seeing as love itself. This unearthing of looking as love allows Sam in the final scene, after he leaves his mother, to abandon his gun, take off his clothes, and jump in the water to swim. Clearly he is freed up, liberated, since as Duncan's lyrics suggest, 'freedom [is] the lesson we must learn'. Gott and Schilt take this scene as 'the first indication of a possible future for our character' (2015: 281). Sam has a future because he is freed up by the idea that his supposedly indifferent father expressed love visually. It is unclear what precisely will happen to Sam, whether he will go back and find Mathieu, but what is sure is that he will love in new ways as he goes forward and dives into a future.

What is queer about this rebirth then? After all, his discovery about his father and his boyhood do not relate to his sexuality in any obvious manner. It is not that Sam is a queer or gay character that matters, but rather that this human form of relationality defined through seeing is queer. The final scene refers back to the second scene at the start of the film, where Léa performs erotically in front of Sam who watches her intently. It is not entirely clear to what extent she is aware of, or believes, his homosexuality (she asks him if he 'still' feels nothing), but his expression is definitely defined by erotic disinterest. He looks but without being erotically affected by this very attractive and scantily clad woman. Gott and Schilt write of this early scene: 'Sam's (non)reaction ... immediately establishes the film as queer' (2015: 278).[19] His lack of desire parallels the perceived lack of desire on his father's part, both being forms of disconnection. He sees and he looks, but that gaze will not lead to sex. It is a kind of surface-looking, but a looking that denotes a visual relation that functions non-normatively. There is by analogy something queer about the paternal gaze uncovered by Sam: it may not be a normal way to express love – 'un truc bizarre dans ses yeux' ('a bizarre thing in his eyes') as Sam puts it, or something queer. But it was still an expression of relationality that requires an adult thinking back on his boyhood to understand, something that the boy could not understand at the time. *Plein sud* opens with a non-normative male gaze and closes with a gay man recognizing his father's non-normative gaze of love. The film's conclusion resembles Stéphanie's relocating the trans child's gaze in *Wild Side*. She unearths a new way of looking, and her futurity is linked to an understanding that there had been a type of look in her past that she did not recognize as a transgender

19 Gott and Schilt's analysis of the film focuses on Lifshitz's play with the genres of the American western and road movie: '*Plein sud* fully assumes the fact that it is referential, that it is an exercise in or experimentation with genre rather than a bone fide genre film' (2015: 280). The opening scene, then, could be taken as a sign of introductory indifference, or a sign that these American genres will be queered in the film and seen in another way. Sam's homosexuality could be not about his character so much as about the queering of generic conventions.

look. Sam digs into his past, too, to locate a gaze opaque to him at the time. Sam and Stéphanie can both move forward in relationships now that they can answer 'yes' to Duncan's question 'Have your eyes really seen?', or more precisely 'Have your eyes really seen seeing?'

Queer documenting: *La Traversée*

With fictional narratives no longer his focus, Lifshitz's documentary production may be said to begin with the 2001 biographical film *La Traversée*. Extending the road movie into the non-fictional realm, the documentary covers a trip from France to the US, and especially to Tennessee, where Lifshitz's French friend and collaborator Stéphane Bouquet seeks to locate the American father that he never knew. After the father briefly met and loved his mother while a twenty-one-year-old soldier in France, he had no contact with the baby boy born from the encounter. As a result, Bouquet arrives in the US with only minimal information about the man, and many questions about who he is and what he is like. The film resembles, in some ways, *Les Terres froides* since both main characters are trying to locate a father whom they never knew but whom they know exists, as well as *Plein sud* since a gay man's psychological relation to his past is changed by means of a road trip. Bouquet in fact wrote all these scripts (as well as those for *Wild Side*, *Presque rien*, and *Les Corps ouverts*), so the connection between them is not surprising. In fact, this documentary is hybrid, neither fully documentary nor fictional, a kind of transitional point in Lifshitz's career explained in part by Bouquet as scriptwriter. While *Corps ouverts* has an interracial element and while it ends – at least in my reading – in potentiality or in the possibility of potentiality, *Traversée* ends in what looks to be impossibility or failure, the inability to find the father and to reconnect with him meaningfully. This failure does not mean that Bouquet does not actually meet his father – in fact he does – but rather the narrative explicitly avoids being or becoming a narrative about finding and locating, about reuniting with one's biological and long-lost father with a happy or tragic ending. Rees-Roberts notes that *Traversée* works to resist sensationalist video stories of finding long-lost parents: 'The film was conceived in reaction to voyeuristic televisual accounts of parental estrangement and reunion, the camerawork designed to accompany the film's subject rather than to track or capture it' (2015: 447). The search-for-the-father narrative might invite a teleological approach by which father and son are reunited in a teary scene of male reconciliation that then allows for the two to be together and develop a relationship henceforth, or a scene of violent rejection that allows for the son to feel hate for the father that de facto abandoned him before birth. But neither is the case here. The failure is not a failure of the actual meeting, but a failure to represent a certain type of story. Instead, a new narrative is invented in its stead. While the father–son meeting comes about an hour into the film, after much preparation, the encounter itself is not shown on screen. Instead, Bouquet recounts the meeting to Lifshitz in a parking lot in the dark evening light. The setting indicates this is not a momentous event per se, but part of a larger journey for which this is not the endpoint but simply a temporary stop. In fact, it may not be part of the journey at all. Bouquet is simply parked for the short term as he goes to do other business. He expresses emotion when he narrates, but not in any kind of sensationalized sense. He starts to describe his father but adds that he doesn't really know how to describe him ('c'est difficile à décrire quelqu'un'). The details from a later visit to his father's house remain vague and hard for the viewer to picture. Later on, Bouquet calls his father on a payphone to find a time to meet him again, and we hear his voice and his southern accent. Still, the focus remains on one side of the conversation and not on who this man is or what he looks like. Finally, when two men part ways for the last time in the film, the camera shoots the brief conversation from afar, followed by a hug before the father gets in his car and drives off. Taking the directorial position, the viewer is permitted to catch a glimpse of the man, but the scene is really only composed of a slow shot of Bouquet walking in the parking lot silently, still aware of the camera. We follow him walking, as if this – and not the father himself or the encounter between them – is the sight to see. This is not a story of an actual meeting, but an autobiographical narrative of what it means to go through a search journey.

The film replaces the long-lost father narrative with a new one in both psychological and visual terms. While in New York City before going to Tennessee, Bouquet goes to visit a tarot card reader because he desires to know the future. After a typical discussion about what will happen in his life, the scene concludes with a final reading about what is to happen with his father. The tarot reader turns over a sword card, implying some kind of battle. The implication may be that he and his father will have an acrimonious meeting, that a father–son clash will ensue. In hindsight, that fight can be seen to take place in Bouquet's head as he fights with himself. He is not sure he wants to find his father. But more profoundly, he struggles with the question of his own presuppositions about his own narrative in his own head and their relation to the reality of the meeting itself. There is a struggle over the role of the idea of a lost father – the exaggerated reality of the flesh and blood man. On the one hand, Bouquet has imagined his father for decades, wondered about him and created his own narratives about him. In the earlier part of the film, Bouquet recounts some possible narratives. Did he die in Vietnam for instance? Bouquet goes to the archives in Washington DC to locate more information but is unable to. The representational swordfight in his mind ends in a sense once the reality of the father is presented, leading to the loss of his representational force and of the proliferation of invented narratives.

But there is another representational struggle too: because the story of the long-lost father is disbanded as such, the narrative arc struggles, fights with that one to create a new story. The film is a struggle between two ways to tell a story, but one in which new ways of representing in the present reality of things and images triumphs. As the struggle implies, the story is not in Bouquet's control. At one point on his trip, his rented car's steering wheel breaks and he has to have it repaired. A still photo of the wheel-less driver's seat conveys his inability to drive the narrative in the direction that he may want or that he has been driving in, at least temporarily. In other words, what he has been imagining about his father – the narratives that he has himself constructed over time, his own mental journey about the man that he never knew – is not one that he can steer any longer as he comes face-to-face with the actual man. As a giant in his mind, his father is reduced in size now, thus outside his mental control.

That replacement of past narrative with the reality of the present is represented not only by the absence of the diegesis of the father–son scene, but also by the visual replacement of past photos with present ones. Bouquet presents a long series of photos of his mother and of himself as a baby, child, or adolescent by himself or with his mother. He explains in a voiceover that the photos reveal to him and only him the absence of his father ('mon père qui n'est plus là'). Another manifestation of paternal absence is the fact that his father did not take the photos, that there is no watchful eye of the father in his past nor in his present. Like Lifshitz's books of photos with which I began this chapter, absence of information leads to the production of narratives and stories about this man in Bouquet's mind. Yet, the documentary, through the eye of the director, in a sense replaces those childhood photos with ones from the trip. Bouquet mentions to Lifshitz that he has a photo of his father, but we never see it nor hear a description of it. Nor do we hear about it again. It is a photo that represents nothing, unlike those seen on screen. At first, then, these two forms of photographic representation are in a representational struggle (fatherless photos vs. photo of the father), but the present wins out, effectively effacing the father's image. In one sequence, as the spiritual 'Sometimes I Feel like a Motherless Child' sung by Odetta plays, we see still shots of Tennessee, including roadkill, dilapidated houses, and businesses that could be anywhere. This present is not beautiful, or unique even, but shows the dead past, the fallen-down or dilapidated houses paralleling a fallen-down past representational structure of the father that cannot stand up any longer to a real present. It is not just that new, present images replace old ones on this journey, but that the new images reveal a fallen representational structure, one that like the dead raccoon is visible but still dead. It may be dead, but its death is the reason for its visibility. The juxtaposition with music conveys meaning here: Bouquet may lack a parent (as a 'fatherless child'), but the very emphasis on being or feeling fatherless, or the uncertainty of being fatherless, is what is going to crumble, like the buildings shown.

This photographic replacement of past with present takes place in Bouquet's head. Before he arrives in Tennessee, he visits New York City where he checks in to a cheap hotel. The camera follows him down a dark hallway along which we see his silhouette, referencing the silhouette of his father in his psyche. The present journey evokes the spectre of the past that haunts him. Yet, as he enters his room, the door closes and we see still photos of New York and the hotel room. The screen becomes Bouquet's mind, what he sees in the mind's eye, and the silhouette of his father in his mind turns into the photographic image of his present, before our very eyes.

Even if past becomes present and even if father absence becomes photographic presence, Bouquet is still not in control of representation. Lifshitz is. Bouquet lacks the representational steering wheel. If the childhood photos reveal absence because the father did not take them, here Lifshitz in a sense replaces the father because he captures Bouquet on film. In fact, the entire documentary can be viewed as a replacement of the childhood photos and of the absent photographing father with the present that is Lifshitz's film. The closing scene suggests just this: that the ultimate presence is friendship in the current moment. Lifshitz himself emerges in the documentary, as Bouquet begins to have qualms about making the film. The director's voice appears to ask questions, as if to comfort him that he is not alone, that their friendship constitutes the present. The whole film began with Bouquet narrating that there had been no 'game of seduction' (erotic attraction) between them, but that their candid relation had been defined as 'friendship'. Lifshitz appears as a friend or a second self, and Bouquet notes that in fact Lifshitz is seeking his own father by making the film, that this is his own film. Bouquet's past may be replaced not only by the present, but also by a present intimate commonality with another man. The film concludes with this presence, abandoning the idea of the father altogether. In the final scene, as the two friends drive back to Washington DC and Bouquet is shot from the side, Sébastien asks him if he is ok (plate 11). They continue their conversation as Van Morrison's song 'Beside You' plays very loudly (not as background music), to the point that the music takes over from the dialogue. Over the music, Lifshitz asks if he is happy that he found his father, but we cannot really hear the response because it does not matter and it is decidedly not the film's telos. The story, the narrative, and the film end in the co-presence of the song, which could be taken as words of a supportive father speaking to his grown 'child'. The final presence is the present of co-being, paternal co-being having become the co-being of friendship. The sensationalized lost father narrative becomes a sedate narrative of friendship, of two friends in conversation and in movement together. The camera angle is important: we see Bouquet from the side. We never see Lifshitz's side, for we too may be with him, or beside him in the passenger seat of the car. If the narrative can become the director's, can it not become ours too? It is not Lifshitz's exact story, to be sure, but a replacement narrative for his own narrative to which we do not have access. For a viewer with an absent father, this story may become theirs too. Our own specific stories have the potential to be Bouquet's – the ultimate 'crossing' of the title, representational crossing that can pertain to anyone.

The film ends by bringing the past to the present. The final scene begins with shots of the mountains and falling leaves. Old representations have fallen too, but now the narrative allows Bouquet to see the present as it is, because it is now open to new representational forms as well as to new forms of being 'beside you'. I take the narrative arc as queer not simply because Bouquet is gay. It is a story of two gay men whose relation comes to replace the father–son relation, a queer mode that emblematizes co-presence. Male homosexuality is not insignificant or external to the family structure, as it is sometimes thought to be in homophobic contexts, but the notion of kinship itself is reorganized here as gay friendship defines human relationality. Biological familial kinship, then, is queered as it is opened up to alternate relational forms through the medium of non-erotic male homosexuality. We return in a sense to the final scene of *Wild Side* where one could imagine Van Morrison's 'Beside You' as an apt song to play as well because there too kinship is redefined in queer terms, albeit more complicated ones.

Documenting queer: *Les Invisibles*

After *La Traversée*, Lifshitz moved to a documentary format focused on archiving and documenting LGBTQ lives. In each case, the films unearth subjectivities not frequently represented on film or not necessarily imagined as part of a queer canon. Winning the César for best documentary, *Les Invisibles* creates a record of those who fought for lesbian, gay, and women's rights and are now seniors. *Bambi* documents the work of the famous trans pioneer and performer Marie-Pierre Pruvot, known as Bambi. Awarded the Queer Palm at the Cannes Film

Festival, *Les Vies de Thérèse* (*The Lives of Thérèse*) (2016) expands on the life of one of the subjects from *Les Invisibles*, a queer feminist activist at the tail end of her life. Thérèse had asked Lifshitz to film her in her final days, essentially documenting her death while putting it into dialogue with elements of her life relating to gender and sexuality. These three documentaries could be seen as inflected with Lifshitz's photographing impulse since each one, even though they focus on people living in the present, offer snapshots – whether in discourse, in actual photos, or in videoclips – of LGBTQ history. While the recovery of lost or untold narratives parallels the characters' recoveries in the fictional films (e.g., Sam in *Plein sud*, Stéphanie in *Wild Side*), these documentaries are not simply recovery narratives that unearth a hidden past, for they reflect on the very act of recounting the queer past.

Les Invisibles includes ten senior men and women recounting anecdotes from their past along with photos or videos. The documentary is mostly set in rural parts of France and in the case of most of the subjects, shots of nature (landscape, animals) help tell the queer stories. Queer subjectivity, these shots suggest, is constituted not only by an individual's psychic experience of gender and sexuality and their imbrication in social movements or groups, but also by the natural environment. In an interview, Lifshitz stated that he wanted to interview anonymous people and to avoid the cliché that gay people live only in artistic milieux in urban areas (Entrée libre, 2015). The documentary in a sense inserts nature into queer subjectivity, making visible people not normally seen on screen as well as relations between queerness and nature not often seen either. Like Rémi whose story is told in part by means of his relation to the land in *Les Terres froides*, these people's subjectivities, defined in part by their location in nature far away from urbanism, has been invisible in cinematic history. The gay male couple who open the film, Yann and Pierre, live in a rural location near mountains, and they raise exotic birds from eggs. The two of them very gingerly pull pieces of shell off an egg as a baby bird emerges: the hatching bird serves as an apt metaphor for the documentary as it opens. Lifshitz is hatching a new animal, as it were, a new narrative that has not yet been told. The two men later check their video screen to see their birds and know that everything is fine with them. They resemble the director of the film who is watching though his lens those that he is taking care of by representing them, knowing that they too are fine. The hatching of a new narrative, however, is also a look back in time: Pierre narrates how the two men first met. He was driving in his car and saw Yann's eyes in his rear-view mirror. They got out of their vehicles and then began a relationship that has lasted a very long time. Looking in the directorial rear-view mirror on Lifshitz's part and viewing the queer past is also the birth of a new representational relationality. One element of such a birth is the resistance to 'metronormativity', the assumption that coming out and migration to the city cannot be disassociated. In this way, the documentary parallels a courant in later French films that highlight queer characters in rural settings, such as Catherine Corsini's *La Belle Saison* (*Summertime*) (2015) and André Téchiné's *Quand on a 17 ans* (*Being 17*) (2016).

Lifshitz's *Bambi*, too, is structured as a move back in time as Bambi herself narrates in the present of the film, with sections about her childhood, her adolescence, her years working at the Carrousel cabaret in Paris, and finally her time teaching at a public school in Normandy. As in the other documentaries, video footage and photos from the past allow for contrasts and continuities between the present and the past.[20] The documentary does not, however, serve as a way for Bambi to go back in time and talk about her gender confirmation surgery as the centre of her life narrative. The second scene of the

---

20 On the use of photos as 'animation' in the documentary, see Devine (2021).

film is important for this reason, as the Bambi of the present heads by boat to what looks to be a North African country. As it is well-known that Casablanca in Morocco was a capital of gender confirmation surgery, a viewer might assume that Bambi is going back to the place where her surgery took place. But in fact, the viewer learns, she is not going to Morocco but to Algeria, where she grew up and went to grade school. Her stories and thus the narrative of the film will focus in the first portion of the documentary on her life in Algeria, displacing medical intervention as focus and queering any 'transsexual' linearity that might be assumed. After this section is a narrative about her life at the famous Parisian cabaret Le Carrousel where she lived very happily. Her presumably transphobic mother's visit to see her in Paris – and her anxiety around the visit – takes up about as much screen time as Bambi's trip to Casablanca for surgery. There is a brief shot from inside an airplane, but there is no more discussion of the trip. Bambi's boyfriend did not want her to have surgery, which may have led to their breakup (though that is not totally clear). What may seem to be significant life transitions are evoked so as to be subsequently ignored: the journeys in time and in space are not focused on corporeality and medical treatment, but on other life events.[21] The documentary does not conclude with Bambi becoming a 'real woman' or a 'full woman' or some other teleology – unlike the narrative about European trans women (including Bambi) in Michiel van Erp's documentary *I am a Woman Now* (2011). Instead, she passes the French national exam to become a schoolteacher, and her story ends with her teaching young students and living 'anonymously'. Her ability to pass as a cisgender woman and to leave her past behind is a precondition for normativity, but the narrative

---

21 In this sense, the film resembles Bambi's autobiography, *Marie parce que c'est joli*, where the trip to Casablanca takes up less than half a page of the book (Pruvot, 2007: 201).

focus is on teaching and learning what she is 'in the inner core of the self' ('au fin fond de soi'), as she puts it.

This conclusion suggests a future narrative of Bambi's life centred on the self, not on surgery, hormones (which play almost no role in the narrative), or transphobia. In the final video footage, Bambi hikes near the shore, presumably in Normandy, with a big smile on her face, as she looks to be on a life path that will allow her to move forward in time happily. The documentary's move from Le Carrousel – a space largely defined by gender and sexuality towards a nationalized space where gender is (theoretically) overshadowed by universalism – means that a trans woman who wishes to pass can be left alone to, as Bambi puts it, 'live my life'. The juxtapositions between past and present in the earlier parts of the film are left behind such that past and present merge into a single temporality that looks forward to other journeys. What is ultimately queered is not trans subjectivity per se, but how to tell a trans story in a way not centred on 'sex change'.

Distorting gender representation: *Petite Fille*

Lifshitz's *Petite Fille*, which played first on the television channel Arte and garnered a very large viewership,[22] extends the work done on transgender representation with *Bambi* into the realm of the transgender child. Lifshitz's idea for the documentary arose because Bambi had herself talked about how, when she was three or four, the idea of a transgender child was impossible to articulate publicly, even as she knew then that she was not a boy (Teddy Award, 2020). In 2020, however,

---

22 The film had the largest audience of the year for a documentary shown during prime time (5.7 per cent of the audience). See Vandeginste (2020).

there was cultural interest in a documentary about a child who was assigned one gender at birth but knows unequivocally that that gender is incorrect – as is the case with Sasha, the seven-year-old subject of the film. The subject is not only Sasha, nor is it only Sasha's mother whose love and fight for her daughter (her 'role to play' in life, as she says) are documented at length. It is also responses and reactions to what is never shown – the cisnormativity and gender binarism that necessitates the mother's and Sasha's fight and, by extension, the documentary in the first place.

During the family's summer vacation at the beach, Sasha and her siblings stand in front of a funhouse mirror which distorts their bodies and reflects back to them a body that is not theirs. The mirror might recall the mirror through which the adult Stéphanie locates her transgender childhood at the end of *Wild Side*. In this case, however, the mirror does not reflect back a trans child, but stands in for normative culture's gender binarism that distorts the image that the child has of her own self and her own body. It better resembles the mirror in which Stéphanie looks early on in *Wild Side* as her life is interrupted by her past with a phone call for 'Pierre' and her auto-reflection is distorted as she is forced to speak in a male voice and to act masculine. Sasha looks in the mirror, but what she sees is very different from the body that she sees herself having. Her phenomenological vision is distorted by the provincial culture surrounding her and representing her gender on her behalf. Sasha takes dance lessons and is subjected to a very negative reaction from a transphobic dance instructor who does not accept her as a girl, sends her out of the room, and pushes the door closed on her with a smile on her face. The incident, not shown but recounted by her mother, essentially tells Sasha that she is not allowed to move her body except as a boy. Above all, her school will not let her attend dressed in girls' clothes or use girls' facilities. Unlike Bambi for whom the *éduction nationale* was a homecoming, for Sasha the school system is a constraining normative gender system that refuses to allow her to be herself, and much of Sasha and her mother's pain results directly from this refusal, in marked contrast to the loving family (three siblings, mother, and father) and a very supportive and knowledgeable doctor in Paris who is part of the French medical system. No teacher or principal is ever shown, interviewed, or cited, but the absent presence of the system is ubiquitous and part of what Sasha and her family discuss. The flow of the documentary over time corresponds to the movement towards being able to go to school as a little girl, not to gender change within Sasha. In a key scene, after winning the battle with the school, Sasha dresses as a girl for the first time and heads to school as such, with a close-up of her girlie shoes, but this victory over the normative school system is, however, not the ultimate telos of the film.

If there is a telos in *Petite Fille*, it is the replacement of the transphobic corporeal image with representations that displace or reject the cisnormative image of the trans child. Most visibly, Sasha's affective reactions to the off-screen incidents and to her loving mother offer a counter-narrative that makes it clear that sex assigned at birth and experience do not correspond and that it is the cultural reaction to her that manipulates the image of corporality. In particular, Lifshitz aestheticizes Sasha's transidentity, portraying it as sublime instead of physically distorted. Classical music figures prominently in the documentary, commenting on the incidents. Julian Bream's guitar rendition of Ravel's processional 'Pavane for a Dead Princess' accompanies Sasha's first trip to school dressed as a girl, affirming the walk to school as a ceremonial procession of great importance, but also affirming that part of the child has died, not a young princess but the young boy that no longer has to be presented to the public. Debussy's 'The Girl with the Flaxen Hair' plays during the final shots as Sasha dances with butterfly wings by herself, moving to her own tune. The documentary shows videos and photos of

Sasha before her external transition, forced to present as a boy and as boy-like. It might seem as though the videos and photos – like the boyhood photos in *Wild Side* that Stéphanie wants to destroy – have the potential to distort the gender subjectivity of Sasha, and to reveal her as 'really' a boy or a 'he', but in fact the photos are reread to transform the past of the child. Baby videos are shown but only after Sasha's mother explains how 'it was written' that Sasha was trans and that it was destiny that she was given a unisex name, retroactively coding the videos as false representations, as having distorted gender – much like the funhouse mirror.

Near the end of the film, Sasha addresses the camera for the first time in her room, showing Lifshitz a photo of herself when she was younger (three, four, or five) and presented as a boy. It is only then that a series of photos of Sasha as a boy is shown to the camera, revealing that those images are in a sense distorted and do not reflect back the image that Sasha has of herself and presumably did not have of herself at the time, even if she did not or could not articulate it. Sasha unearths a past that reveals not hidden images, but false representations in the first place. She interprets those photos of herself from her own present vantage point – embodying much of Lifshitz's film career in which characters and people re-examine the past and in so doing transform or queer it. Sasha too resembles the director himself who collects photos – as I discussed at the opening of this chapter – but then rethinks the queer past through them to offer new narratives around gender.

References

Amir-Moezzi, Mohammed Ali, ed. (2007), *Dictionnaire du Coran*, Paris, Laffont.

Baudrillard, Jean (2002), 'We Are all Transsexuals Now', in *Screened Out*, trans. Chris Turner, London, Verso, pp. 9–14.

Chiland, Colette (2005), *Exploring Transsexualism*, trans. David Alcorn, London, H. Karnac.

Corrigan, Timothy (2011), *The Essay Film: From Montaigne, after Marker*, New York, Oxford University Press.

Cotten Trystan, ed. (2011), *Transgender Migrations: The Bodies, Borders, and Politics of Transition*, Florence, Taylor & Francis.

Dasgupta, Sudeep (2005), 'Suspending the Body: Biopower and the Contradictions of Family Values', in Patricia Pisters, Wim Staat, and Sudeep Dasgupta, eds, *Shooting the Family*, Amsterdam, Amsterdam University Press, pp. 165–80.

Deleuze, Gilles and Félix Guattari (1987), *A Thousand Plateaus: Capitalism and Schizophrenia*, trans. Brian Massumi, Minneapolis, University of Minnesota Press.

Devine, Jonathan (2021), 'Documenting the Trans* and Animating the Still in Sébastien Lifshitz's *Bambi*', *French Screen Studies*, www.tandfonline.com/doi/full/10.1080/26438941.2020.1870851 (accessed 20 August 2021).

Dinshaw, Carolyn, Lee Edleman, Roderick A. Ferguson, Carla Freccero, Elizabeth Freeman, Jack Halberstam, Annamarie Jagose, Christopher Nealon, and Nguyen Tan Hoang (2007), 'Theorizing Queer Temporalities: A Roundtable Discussion', *GLQ: A Journal of Lesbian and Gay Studies*, 13, 2, 177–95.

Entrée libre (2015), 'Sébastien Lifshitz: Docu *Les Invisibles*', www.youtube.com/watch?v=d_i_th2oT2I (accessed 11 August 2020).

Felski, Rita (2006), 'Fin de siècle, Fin du sexe: Transsexuality, Postmodernism, and the Death of History', in Susan Stryker and Stephen Whittle, eds, *The Transgender Studies Reader*, New York, Routledge, pp. 565–73.

Garnier, Philippe (1999), 'Cinéma. Sébastien Lifshitz, Claire Denis et Jane Campion', *Libération*, next.liberation.fr/culture/1999/09/06/cinema-sebastien-lifshitz-claire-denis-et-jane-campion-trois-reussites-qui-ont-marque-la-mostra-ce-w_282988 (accessed 11 August 2021).

Gott, Michael and Thibaut Schilt (2015), 'Crossing Borders and Queering Identities in French-Language European Road Cinema', *Studies in European Cinema*, 12, 3, 275–91.

Gromb, Sophie, B. Chanseau, and H. J. Lazarini (1997), 'Judicial Problems Related to Transsexualism in France', *Medicine, Science, and the Law*, 37, 1, 27–31.

Halberstam, Jack (2005), *In a Queer Time and Place: Transgender Bodies, Subcultural Lives*, New York, New York University Press.

Hardwick, Joe (2004), 'Bodies That Loiter: Genre, Generation and Subjectivity in *Les Corps ouverts*', *Australian Journal of French Studies*, 41, 3, 75–87.

Laronde, Michel (1993), *Autour du roman beur: Immigration et identité*, Paris, L'Harmattan.

Lifshitz, Sébastien (2010), Interview with Lifshitz, *Plein sud*, mk2 et Ad Vitam, DVD.

Lifshitz, Sébastien (2013), *Les Invisibles*, Paris, Hoëbeke.

Lifshitz, Sébastien (2014), *The Invisibles: Vintage Portraits of Love and Pride*, New York, Rizzoli.

Lifshitz, Sébastien (2016a), *Amateur*, 4 vols, Göttingen, Steidl.

Lifshitz, Sébastien (2016b), *Mauvais genre: Les Travestis à travers un siècle de photographie amateur*, Paris, Textuel.

Lifshitz, Sébastien (n.d.), 'Interview with Claire Vassé', chez.com/filmolifshitz/99PresqueClaire.htm (accessed 24 August 2020).

Mack, Mehammed Amadeus (2017), *Sexagon: Muslims, France, and the Sexualization of National Culture*, New York, Fordham University Press.

'Michael' (2006), 'Sebastien Lifshitz', forum.criterionforum.org/forum/viewtopic.php?p=54706&sid=aa45726ba1e860fb7be864b901d6ae9a#p54706 (accessed 24 August 2020).

Nye, Robert A. (2003), 'The *Pacte Civil de Solidarité* and the History of Sexuality', *French Politics, Culture and Society*, 21, 1, 87–100.

Péron, Didier (1998), 'La Queue d'une idée. *Les Corps ouverts* renouvelle le récit d'initiation sentimentale', *Libération*, www.liberation.fr/culture/1998/06/24/la-queue-d-une-idee-les-corps-ouverts-renouvelle-le-recit-d-initiation-sentimentale-les-corps-ouvert_239492 (accessed 10 July 2021).

Prosser, Jay (1998), *Second Skins: The Body Narratives of Transsexuality*, New York, Columbia University Press.

Prosser, Jay (1999), 'Exceptional Locations: Transsexual Travelogues', in Kate More and Stephen Whittle, eds, *Reclaiming Genders: Transsexual Grammars at the Fin de Siècle*, London, Cassell, pp. 83–114.

Provencher, Denis M. (2017), *Queer Maghrebi French: Language, Temporalities, Transfiliations*, Liverpool, Liverpool University Press.

Pruvot, Marie-Pierre (2007), *Marie parce que c'est joli*, Paris, Bonobo.
Quran: Sahih International [29:41–51] (n.d.), quran.com/29/41-51 (accessed 24 August 2021).
Rees-Roberts, Nick (2007), 'Down and Out: Immigrant Poverty and Queer Sexuality in Sébastien Lifshitz's *Wild Side* (2004)', *Studies in French Cinema*, 7, 2, 143–55.
Rees-Roberts, Nick (2008), *French Queer Cinema*, Edinburgh, Edinburgh University Press.
Rees-Roberts, Nick (2015), 'Hors milieu: Queer and Beyond', in Raphaëlle Moine, Hilary Radner, Alistair Fox, and Michel Marie, eds, *A Companion to Contemporary French Cinema*, Malden, MA, Wiley-Blackwell, pp. 439–60.
Reeser, Todd W. (2008), 'Representing Gay Male Domesticity in French Film of the Late 1990s', in Robin Griffiths, ed., *Queer Cinema in Europe*, Bristol and Chicago, Intellect, pp. 35–48.
Reeser, Todd W. (2013), '*Trans*France', *Esprit créateur*, 53, 1, 4–15.
Reeser, Todd W. (2016), 'On Gender', in Philippe Desan, ed., *The Oxford Handbook of Montaigne*, Oxford, Oxford University Press, pp. 562–80.
Reeser, Todd W. (2021), 'Transing Dynamics: Ozon's *Une Nouvelle amie* (2014)', in Loïc Bourdeau, ed., *ReFocus: The Films of François Ozon*, Edinburgh, Edinburgh University Press, pp. 143–61.
Stryker, Susan (1999), 'Christine Jorgensen's Atom Bomb: Transsexuality and the Emergence of Postmodernity', in E. Ann Kaplan and Susan Squier, eds, *Playing Dolly: Technocultural Formations, Fantasies, and Fictions of Assisted Reproduction*, New Brunswick, Rutgers University Press, pp. 157–171.
Teddy Award (2020), 'Zsombor Bobák in conversation with Sébastien Lifshitz on *Petite fille*', www.youtube.com/watch?v=zUqUHZ5Ut34 (accessed 4 January 2021).
Vaisman, Anne and Daniel Maja (2011), *L'Homosexualité à l'adolescence*, Paris, De la Martinière Jeunesse.
Vandeginste, Louise (2020), 'Record d'Audience pour *Petite fille* de Sébastien Lifshitz sur Arte', *Les Inrockuptibles*, www.lesinrocks.com/cinema/record-daudience-pour-petite-fille-de-sebastien-lifshitz-sur-arte-190805–03-12-2020 (accessed 16 September 2021).

4

Céline Sciamma: the look of queer representation

The opening scenes of Céline Sciamma's four full-length films to date all tell the viewer how to watch what is to come, and especially how to consider relations between visuality and gender. Her first film, *Naissance des pieuvres* (*Water Lilies*) (2007), opens with the main character Marie coming to an indoor pool to watch a synchronized swimming performance by young women, which she does with great attention. Before her arrival, we see a variety of young women of various ages making themselves up to perform, applying heavy makeup. The surface of the female body, we are being told, will be an object of visual consideration, and Marie will be looking at the make-up of female sexuality over the course of the film. In the opening scene of *Tomboy* (2011), Sciamma's second film, the main character stands looking out from a sun window atop the car that their father is driving down the street. First, we see their neck from behind and it is not clear that the neck belongs to a person assigned female at birth, as is the case. A viewer might take the neck as belonging to a young boy, and such an assumption might bring the viewer in to a world in which gender is not based on the medical declaration of sex at birth. We then see the world from their perspective as they ride down the street standing in the car, and that perspective will be presented and will be challenged by society in the film to come. *Bande de filles* (*Girlhood*) (2014) begins with an American football match in process, but as the scene goes on, the male bodies that viewers might assume are under the helmets and uniforms, turn out to be not male, but female. Our gendered assumptions about cultural practices might be wrong, and this opening fantasy scene tips us off that looks may be deceiving. This paratextual scene – not part of the main narrative of the film – may not however actually happen, only revealing that gendered fantasies or dreams can dismantle normative gender constructs. Sciamma's first film about adults, *Portrait de la jeune fille en feu* (*Portrait of a Lady on Fire*) (2019) opens as the main character Marianne is giving students an art lesson, sitting in front of them as the model that they are to paint, while simultaneously instructing them on how to look at her. She tells the young women to look at the details of her position (of her hands, of her arms), to take their time to really see and observe those details. Sciamma, too, is telling the viewer to look closely at the film to come, and more specifically to observe how the positioning of the body will be a key element of the narrative. We should look at hands, at arms, but also at eyes. This will be a film about the very act of looking. As viewers, we are invited to look attentively at looking.

Each of these opening scenes functions as a prologue that tells the viewer something about watching gender. The four films focus on female transformation, related to same-sex desire, transgender, coming of age, queerness, and blackness. This chapter will consider all four films in terms of movement-centred states of transformation – what Sophie Belot in a study of *Naissance des pieuvres* calls 'be-coming', which 'rather than becoming … emphasize[s] the idea of movement and process as opposed to the idea of a universal and natural state' (2012: 172). It is not a question of a linear move from identitarian point A to B (e.g., from heterosexuality to homosexuality, from femininity to masculinity, male to female), but rather of showing subjectivities existing in motion. That motion itself may well 'be' a kind of state of being, but it is closely linked to 'becoming' something new. With synchronized swimming as the organizing element of her first film, *Naissance des pieuvres* (literally translated, 'Birth of the Octopuses', but rendered into English as *Water Lilies*) tells the story of adolescent eroticism and sexuality, but as a fluid or water-like form of desire and subjectivity. Carrying the same title in English and in French, *Tomboy* focuses on sex and gender ambiguity around what might be called transgender, female masculinity, butch, or lesbianism, as well as on cisgender relations to transgender, as non-trans characters are connected to the main character whose given name is 'Laure' but goes by 'Mickäel'. *Bande de filles* (translated as *Girlhood*, but literally 'Girl Gang' or 'Group of Girls'), is ostensibly about black female (post)adolescence in the Parisian *banlieue*, but late in the film queerness comes to allegorize the creation of new racialized subjectivities, inviting the question of what the intersections of race and queerness are doing. These three films, all focused on gender in pre-adulthood, can be taken together as a 'trilogy on adolescence', as Sciamma herself has noted in interviews (Tremblay, 2020; see also Fennessey and Dobbins, 2020). As a film with adult characters, *Portrait de la jeune fille en feu* recasts traditional relations between gender and looking through a historical story of same-sex female love and desire while also queering traditional Western narratives of love and looking.

Shorts and scripts

Like these four feature-length films to be discussed in this chapter, Sciamma's short film and the scripts she wrote for or with other directors invite the viewer to see in a certain way. *Pauline* (2010), part of a collection of five short films made by young directors 'against homophobia', positions the titular young woman (Anaïs Demoustier) talking about homophobia and coming out, seemingly sad and alone, but late in her monologue a woman partner who was just off frame the whole time (Adèle Haenel) appears, transforming the short from a seemingly sad, isolated narrative to one about discursive intimacy. Homophobic experience may well be turned into a positive moment when the viewer sees who is listening to – or who could be listening to – homophobic narrative.

Though Sciamma is known today as a director, she began her career as a scriptwriter, having studied in the 'Département Scénario' at La Fémis,[1] and she wrote the scripts for all her own films. Consequently, the focus on the look of gender in her oeuvre as a whole resides both in the script and in the visual field. *Quand on a 17 ans* (*Being 17*) (2016), co-written with gay director André Téchiné, opens with images of the landscape in the Pyrenees Mountains in southwestern France, as viewed from a moving car. The images change because the seasons change as well, offering two forms of movement that parallel the changes to come with respect to sexuality. After these images, one of the two main characters, Thomas (Corentin Fila), appears trekking to high school through the heavy snow. This film will treat the movement of Thomas's unexpressed sexuality as he slowly develops feelings for his classmate Damien (Kacey Mottet Klein) whom he hates at first, as well as normative meanings accorded to family and to nature. Damien will negotiate his sexual subjectivity through the natural and the cultural meanings given to the concept. The film concludes in an open-ended way as there looks to be a future for Thomas and Damien as a couple, though how precisely is not entirely clear. Instead of images of nature seen from a moving car, in the final scene Thomas moves through nature towards Damien as he has control over his sexual 'nature' and is no longer constrained by constructs of same-sex love as unnatural.

---

1 La Fémis' website lists her as an alumna, having completed her studies in 2005 (La Fémis). Sciamma also co-wrote the script for Jacques Audiard's *Les Olympiades* (2021).

Sciamma's script for the stop-motion (clay figure) animated feature *Ma vie de courgette* (*My Life as a Courgette*) (2016), directed by Claude Barras, begins with the main character Courgette flying a kite with an image of what we later learn is his absent father on the front side. The kite metaphor returns at the end of the film, this time with an image of Courgette's non-biological family to whom he has become attached in the orphanage where he has lived. Meaning of family – or more precisely, how family is represented – is in literal and symbolic movement. This final movement of Sciamma's script transforms the end of the book on which the film is based (Gilles Paris's *Autobiographie d'une courgette*, or 'Autobiography of a Courgette'), which concludes with an imaginary photo of the group of children that Courgette is leaving behind at the orphanage. Courgette notes 'cette photo-là, c'est sûr, on va l'emporter pour toujours avec nous' ('that photo, we will definitely carry it with us forever') (Paris, 2002: 255). The film puts the idea of a static photo 'with us forever' into flying motion, casting the image of family as movement itself not necessarily defined by the supposed stability of genetics or biology.

Eyes wide open: gazing in *Naissance des pieuvres*

The final scene of *Naissance des pieuvres* suggests a queer baptism. Having finally kissed her love interest Floriane in the locker room, Marie (Pauline Acquart) wipes off the lipstick from the kiss with the water of the swimming pool and then she dives in the water. Is this, as the conclusion of the film, the moment of initiation into lesbianism? A moment representing that she has come of age as a lesbian? Is Marie in a sense diving into queer sexual subjectivity?

Such a symbolic baptism would correspond to the film broadly. The third main character, Floriane (Adèle Haenel) technically has sex for the first time – if defined as breaking the hymen – when Marie penetrates her with her fingers. In the opening scene, Marie attends a synchronized swimming competition that she watches with great attention, and when the captain of the team (Floriane) appears out of the water as the star of the performance, she watches with even greater interest. Floriane (from *florens* in Latin, meaning flowering or blooming) sprouts up like a flower (or 'water lily') whose beauty is very visible to Marie. Erotic interest presented in the opening scene transforms into desire to be with Floriane one-on-one and to experience her erotically or sexually. The two kiss later in a dance club, and then again in the locker room scene which takes place right before the baptism scene described above. While the relation does not lead to lesbian sex involving a number of body parts, it does lead to an erotic attachment on a given individual of the same gender, opening the question of whether the film is Marie's story of erotic – if not sexual – awakening.

That awakening cannot be separated from how Marie learns to see. The opening scene offers a detail about watching and establishes that the film will comment on erotic looking. After Marie notices the synchronized swimming team and decides that she wants to watch them more closely, she moves towards the bleachers to take a seat. But before she sits down, she stands at an open seat staring at the competition. In so doing, she blocks the person sitting behind her. That anonymous person taps her on the shoulder and asks her to sit down so she can see. A presumably heterosexual woman with a camera in hand, she stands in for the idea of normative watching, the very kind of watching that Marie will not do in the film. Marie blocks her view because she looks in a way in which others do not. Even if they are trying to record what they see with their camera, or their own eyes, they are not able to see what Marie will be able to see by the film's end. Had the character who cannot see been male, the message conveyed might be that Marie is blocking the male gaze, or male heterosexual scopophilia by virtue of being neither heterosexual nor male. This is not what is emphasized: she is blocking the normative gaze on female bodies, the gaze that belongs not simply to heterosexual masculinity but rather to heterosexuality more broadly. She sees something here that will later allow her to be baptized into another world based on synchronicity and a group-oriented formation in which she will play a role, albeit metaphorically. Whatever she does not yet have in view in the opening scene is what she will come to see in the final scene. Indeed, in the very last shot of the film Marie floats on the water's surface with her eyes closed, but then opens up her eyes to look up at the camera filming from above (plate 12). The film then concludes in this way because the narrative is an eye-opening experience. What then are her eyes opened to? Are they really opened to lesbianism? Is there synchronicity between her and same-sex sexuality? Is she in formation with lesbianism? What precisely does she learn to see?

On one level, the film is about a 'birth' – as per the French title – of same-sex desire. A viewer might take the final scene as Marie's diving into her sexuality, her readiness to head out into the world as a lesbian and assume that in ten years she will be living as a grown 'lesbian', perhaps with a female partner or wife. But her eye-opening is not predicated on her seeing homosexuality or same-sex desire per se, but signifies something else. While one could not really say that she is not awakened to lesbian desire over the course of the film nor that the film does not represent her first experience of same-sex desire, on the other hand the film is not centred on her becoming lesbian in any kind of linear way. This is not a film about coming out of the closet, nor is it about a heterosexual becoming a homosexual. Nor is it even about a 'girl' who becomes a 'woman' through the medium of lesbianism. Marie does not simply 'grow up' nor does she leave behind straightness. As Jean-Louis Douin in a review in *Le Monde* put it, the film 'refus[es] the stereotypical scene of coming out' (2014).[2] Stéphane Delorme in a review in *Cahiers du cinéma* notes that the originality of the film resides in avoiding the familiar territory of 'the discovery of homosexuality' (2007: 32).[3]

Naissance des pieuvres does not resemble traditional coming-out films that include a coming-out scene or process and that conclude with the triumph of lesbian love, such as Philippe Faucon's *Muriel fait le désespoir à ses parents* (*Muriel's Parents are Desperate*) (1995), Sylvie Verheyde's *Un amour de femme* (*A Woman's Love*) (2004), and Patrick Grandperret's *Clara cet été là* (*Clara's Summer*) (2004). This last film concludes as the teenage main character Clara recounts to her friend Zoé how she will come out to her family, with a staged coming out playing the role of the telos of the film itself, as the place where the narrative leads. What I would like to ask here, then, is what movement without commonly used motifs consists of and how non-linear movement breaks out of lesbian narrative convention, while still telling a story about same-sex desire and attraction, or how – as Bradbury-Rance puts it – the film lies 'in the conceptual space between lesbianism and queerness' (2019: 81).

One way to move towards a response to this question is to re-examine the final scene, for it comments on the very idea of movement, positioning the two young women not as growing up, but as growing horizontally. Jonet notes that the film 'align[s] with what Kathryn Bond Stockton calls "sideways growth"' in *The Queer Child*, and 'creates opportunities for alternative desires between the young women in a way the characters can never themselves categorically communicate to one another or articulate to themselves' (Jonet, 2017: 1130;

---

2 Raphaël Lefèvre's review on the site Critikat (2007) also comments on the film as not about coming out.
3 Delorme writes: 'L'originalité de Céline Sciamma est de se placer sur ce terrain en fait peu balisé' (2007: 32).

see also 1131). The film thus 'complicates the narrative expectations of the coming-of-age and refuses entirely the trajectory of a coming-out story' (1130). Or, for Bradbury-Rance: 'Not only do we see a refusal of the singular moment of identity enunciation, but also a refusal to predict it' (2019: 85). Indeed, *Naissance des pieuvres* rejects discursively defined categories of identity in favour of other ways to be, to act, and to see. It is not linear but sideways movement – both literally and metaphorically in this case – that defines the trajectory of Marie. In the final scene, Marie and her best friend Anne (Louise Blachère) float horizontally on the surface of the pool, floating sideways together. Anne has appeared in the swimming pool after Marie dived in and then she jumps into the pool to be with her friend. There is something especially queer about this moment and about their positioning, following Stockton, something that resists standard or predictable linear movements in terms of narrative and characterization and that refused to allow Marie and Anne to 'grow up' into normative heterosexuals. As Stockton puts it, 'The child who by reigning cultural definitions can't "grow up" grows to the side of cultural ideas' (2009: 13).

Replacing the synchronized swimmers of the opening scene, Marie and Anne float to the side of teleological normativity. Looking upwards refers back to an earlier scene during which Marie and Floriane lie on the bed in Floriane's bedroom looking together at the ceiling. Marie notes that 'the ceiling is probably the last thing most people see', and that since the last thing a dying person sees stays imprinted in the eye, most dead people must have a ceiling imprinted in their eye. Marie is commenting not so much on death as on their relation, which is doomed to die. Their relationship has a ceiling, as it were, and the gaze of imagined near-death prefigures their doomed relation since Floriane does not, and will not, fully give herself over to same-sex love. Their relation may remain imprinted in Marie's eye once it ends, but end it will. In the final scene, on the contrary, Marie alone looks up at the ceiling, but not because of any kind of death or finality. Here, the ceiling serves to open up, not close down. She sees the camera, and she is aware of the fact that she is being filmed. She is conscious of her cinematic trajectory, as well as of how the visual field functions. The ceiling is not being imprinted on her eye as the end of a relation approaches, for Marie opens up the narrative trajectory. Her story enters into visual and cinematic culture in a way unlike other stories, where there is a ceiling to how their representation can be fielded, a limit to how the story can be told because of the culturally legible or molar terms of coming-out narratives. The static image of a ceiling imprinted on a dying person's eye transforms into a final image of Marie in narrative movement, imprinted in the viewer's eye. As Marie dives into the pool, Sciamma's static camera focuses on the wall of the pool where a light built into the pool shines and remains the focal point of the dive. Marie swims down with the light behind her and disappears from the visual field, and then the viewer has to wait until Marie swims back up in front of the light. The scene calls attention to the camera seeing her, shining its metaphorical light on her. She is a cinematic subject as much as a gendered one. Since her story is also about the eye, the light of the camera shines on her, and she in turn sheds light on same-sex sexuality. The light in the pool is also her own eye, and the telos of the film is her ability to see. The pool scene is juxtaposed with shots of Floriane nearby dancing through a blue filter. Light is shined on her as well, but it is a coloured light that renders images opaque and dream-like. The spotlight is on Marie as the star of the show because she learns to see something represented by Floriane. What she comes to see, as I will discuss in the next section, is how lesbianism is represented in dominant culture and how she can revision it.

Looking is not the only way Marie comes to know: other senses have the potential to create a deeper connection between herself and Floriane. Marie steals a bag of trash from Floriane's trashcan as she heads home after staying at her house.

She takes out the various pieces of trash, and she touches and smells cotton pads that she has presumably used for makeup removal, and she tastes part of an apple that remains in the sack. I agree with Jonet that this scene alludes to 'the intensity of Marie's desire' and is 'an expression of sexual energy' (2017: 1137), but the scene also alludes to the fact that Marie does not only 'know' via sight. She functions in a world of epistemologies that are not only visual in nature, even if the focus in the film is the sense of sight. Bradbury-Rance notes that her 'desire for Floriane holds within it both appreciation and disgust, experienced here on a multi-sensory level' (2019: 78). When she blocked a spectator with a camera from seeing the synchronized swimming performance in the opening scene, Marie was the only one who could see Floriane's inside or see beyond the external, and here too she can experience Floriane in ways beyond scopophilia. These other senses point to alternate epistemologies of knowing a female body that Marie experiences, but they also point to alternate ways of knowing in a broader sense.[4] Unlike the character François (Warren Jacquin) who desires Floriane for her body, Marie is not limited to looking at the surface of Floriane and simply seeing her: she sees beyond the external surface and she can experience her multi-sensorially.

Turning lesbianism

Seeing in *Naissance des pieuvres* cannot be uncoupled from the question of lesbian representation in a larger sense. Annamarie

---

4 Music, too, offers a non-visual epistemology that transcends the normative. Gemma Edney studies how electronic music in the film 'offer[s] the girls a space in which they can express themselves freely without pre-existing signification or stereotypes' (2020: 285). See also Handyside (2016).

Jagose asks a key question at the start of *Inconsequence*: 'why is the problem of lesbianism so frequently a problem of representation?' (2002: 1). One response is that lesbian representation in mainstream culture can often be difficult to extricate from the hold of male heterosexual desire, which creates an image of lesbianism for its own erotic fantasies or titillation. Lesbianism may be far from a mimetic or realistic depiction, and more a trope or figure that does not correspond to the actual experience of women who identify as lesbian or to the way in which they would want to represent themselves. It may be a way for heterosexual masculinity to flirt with the idea of same-sex sexuality, while safely distanced from the threat of male–male sexuality (see Reeser, 2010: 127–9). Or, lesbianism may exist but not be seen as such, ignored and collapsed into the category of 'woman'. French culture has a long history of male representation of lesbianism. Gretchen Schultz in her book on French nineteenth-century lesbianism, *Sapphic Fathers*, studies 'discursive practices and constructs having little or no correlation with historic persons or lived reality' (2014: 5), including canonical male writers like Balzac, Baudelaire, Verlaine, and Zola. In *The Apparitional Lesbian*, Terry Castle begins by noting that 'when it comes to lesbians ... many people have trouble seeing what's in front of them. The lesbian remains a kind of "ghost effect" in the cinema world of modern life: elusive, vaporous, difficult to spot – even when she is there, in plain view, mortal and magnificent, at the center of the screen' (1993: 2).[5] Castle lists many French writers who write the lesbian as such (including Balzac, Flaubert, Zola, Maupassant, Colette, Proust, and Sartre), names specific French texts such as Diderot's *The Nun* and Laclos's *Dangerous Liaisons*, and includes a chapter of her book on Marie Antoinette's supposed lesbianism. The lesbian may be

---

5 Patricia White extends Castle's argument into the realm of Hollywood film (1999: especially chap. 3).

made to disappear because she threatens the hegemony of masculinity or of heterosexuality and the need for the male body or the penis to be involved in love or sex. Or, as Jagose discusses, lesbianism may be represented as lesbian for a limited time, but then be made to disappear as 'inconsequential' or to become heterosexual for normative purposes. In such a way, the lesbian can be shown as 'derivative' (2002: 35), following from heterosexuality, and any threat that she might pose to heteronormativity can be contained through a release-valve function that does not simply ignore or ghost her but evokes her to 'secure the originality and primacy of a heterosexual culture from whose entitlements the former is debarred' (35). She is depicted in order to be rejected and eradicated. Jagose's approach is especially relevant for lesbian adolescent films as same-sex desire and acts might be assumed to be temporary for young women, a passing phase that will necessarily end in heterosexual womanhood.

In light of these representational issues, then, how does *Naissance des pieuvres* represent lesbian desire or affect in a non-normative manner? How does it remedy the 'problem of lesbianism'? One the one hand, as is obvious, same-sex desire – if not the label of 'lesbian' – is fully present in the character of Marie from the opening scene and continues in her sexual and erotic relation with Floriane. Same-sex desire is not simply an ambiguous tension between young women that dissipates in time. Her same-sex desire is clearly not a passing phase. No one 'sees' Marie and decides what she should look like or how she should desire. She is never ghosted nor is her same-sex desire made to disappear. She is not a trope. Heterosexual masculinity does not represent her on her behalf, or even have much relation to her at all, and in fact there are very few young men in the film to begin with. Even adults who might try to determine her desire on her behalf are entirely absent. Presented as a character who can see from the opening scene, Marie – I am suggesting here – does not exist representationally in the service of heterosexual masculinity, but over the course of the film gains insight into how same-sex desire functions in the realm of representation. What she sees in the final shot is seeing itself. It is no accident that the first exchange between Marie and Floriane takes place with the latter in front of a mirror, with only the latter looking at herself. Marie is not interested in the mirror because her sexual subjectivity is not mediated by heterosexual masculinity. She does not need to look into an object to see her reflection as a sexual subject.

On the other hand, however, some of these representational problems around lesbianism pertain to the character of Floriane. Ultimately, lesbianism – if the two young women taken together constitute lesbian representation in the film – oscillates between experiential desire in the form of Marie and the coming and going of figuration in the form of Floriane. The latter herself oscillates between heterosexual and lesbian desire and acts, at times seeking out François or other men and at other times wanting Marie. Or so it seems. It is never fully clear what her desire is or how she imagines herself and her erotic desire, but asking the question of what her orientation is misses the main point.[6] For the film comments through her on the 'problem' of lesbian representation (to return to Jagose's important question) and presents her as a character not so much ghosted as much as caught between ghosting on the one hand and experiential representation on the other.

Taken together, three key scenes in *Naissance des pieuvres* tell a story not so much about coming out, but about sexual representation. The first begins in the middle of the film in a club, as Floriane faces the camera through a red filter, with Marie in the background out of focus. From a recent confession, it is clear that Floriane wants to lose her virginity with a

---

6 Sciamma herself has noted that she avoided giving 'any answers as to the sexual identity [of the two main] characters, so the viewers can decide', even as she adds that for her Marie 'is going to like women forever' (Oumano, 2011: 214).

man and has brought Marie into the club so that she can help her find a man older than she is for this purpose. But the scene is less about the potential for heterosexual sex and more about portraying Floriane as in sexual movement. Is she heterosexual or lesbian, the scene might seem to be asking. Floriane turns to Marie sitting at the bar with her drink and heads towards her, mimicking the pickup scene that she wants to take place with a man. She takes her friend out on the dance floor and slowly, erotically begins to kiss her, and it may appear that their love affair is beginning. Marie stands with her eyes closed as if inside an erotic dream. The dream-like ambiance, conveyed in part by the red lens, ends however when Floriane disappears, Marie opens her eyes, and she sees her friend on the dance floor with an older man. Floriane's status as erotic object of male heterosexual desire has been re-established. We know from a scene just before this one that she ran away from François when things got hot and heavy, after ten minutes. While it is not entirely clear whether she wants to have sex to prove that she is heterosexual or that she is not lesbian, it is clear that she oscillates as to the object of desire that she wants (Marie and heterosexual men). It is certainly possible that she desires primarily or entirely other women, but her status as object of desire changes unexpectedly here, seamlessly and without transition. The dream or the unreality in the bar might suggest that she desires men or that she desires Marie. Marie may be fantasizing or dreaming on her own, or Floriane might be dreaming that she can be heterosexual. But whatever the dream is, it is related to Floriane's status as sexual subject.

A key detail in this scene comments on the idea of the representation of sexual subjectivity: as Marie sits bored at the bar on a stool, she turns herself around twice while Floriane is out of view. This circular move suggests a 'turn', what in Ancient Greek is a 'trope' or a form of figuration. Marie signals that in this scene in particular, Floriane will function as a form of signification that can be 'turned' in the direction of lesbianism or in the direction of heterosexuality. When Floriane literally turns away from Marie, towards a man, she turns into a trope or a signifier of male desire that positions her outside her own subjectivity, leaving her figurative.[7]

But if Floriane turns towards heterosexuality, she can also be turned back to same-sex desire. If she is a trope, Marie has the potential to do the turning as well. Once Floriane and the older man are in his car making out, Marie finds them and taps on the window and tells him that he is a pervert, using figurative language ('vieux porc'), and that Floriane's dad is looking for her. Floriane greatly appreciates the performance and leaves the man behind and heads off happily with Marie. She has been turned back, and once they arrive in the morning light back at Floriane's house, she asks Marie to penetrate her with her fingers, displacing what could have happened in the car. Her request suggests that Floriane is operating in a heterosexist framework (she has to be penetrated to have sex for the first time), but by virtue of same-sex penetration, is operating in a lesbian framework too, again leaving her positioning as a sexual subject unclear. Is the goal to have sex so she can have penetrative heterosexual sex? Or is it to dispose of the concept of heterosexual virginity altogether so she can be physically with women in another sexual way?

A similar representational dynamic occurs in the important penultimate scene as Marie and Floriane kiss in the locker room of the swimming pool. After the kiss, Floriane begins looking in the mirror, primping herself so as to 'return' to the party and find a man. While looking, she invites Marie to come and save her if the guy she finds is a 'jerk', as she did in the club scene. She will 'make a sign' to Marie ('je te fais signe', she says), but in fact she is a sign, one that changes.

---

7 In his review, Delorme critiques the party scenes ('scènes de soirée') as too abstract and script-focused (2007: 33), but for me this scene is about abstraction itself in the way I have described here. For me, Floriane becomes abstract, entering the status of trope.

The mirror of the earlier scene in which they meet and this mirror frame the narrative, or more precisely they frame Floriane as in need of representational mediation. She cannot look at herself without a mediator that turns her representation backwards or that reverses her. In both of these scenes, Marie is disengaged from the mirror, not part of it, she is her own representational medium with no need of a mirror and with no need of heteronormative representational systems. In the locker room, she approaches the mirror but it remains out of focus, as she turns a blind eye to representational mediation and highlights Floriane's need for this device.

More directly than any other scene, the final scene in the swimming pool (which directly follows this one) comments on lesbian representation. Floriane dances in her blue sleeveless shirt directly in front of the camera with her eyes closed. She cannot see, look, or desire through visual means. She is outside the young collective seen behind her. For Belot, Floriane's dancing stands in for her 'be-coming' as her 'budding subjectivit[y]' is revealed and she comes into subjectivity 'in [her] own terms' (2012: 181). She may be dancing alone, to her own beat, moving towards sexual self-definition, whatever that definition might be. Taking a different route, Jonet notes that Floriane does not change here, but returns 'to maintaining her façade of normative desirability' and that she does not progress but regresses (2017: 1139). For me, however, these ethereal shots of Floriane reveal that she remains a visual signifier for heteronormativity. She cannot see because she remains seen as a signifier, albeit as an unstable signifier whose sexuality is unclear. She dances, as she did in the club scene with Marie where she 'became' a trope, but this time she does not turn into a trope since she is a trope. On one level, she remains queer in the sense that her sexuality is not fixed in terms of object choice, but that lack of fixity is related to seeing, or more precisely to her not seeing. She is an object of desire for the person who looks, to be sure, but more importantly for me, she is rendered as a form of representation that is unstable and undefined. Her sexuality here has less to do with her actual desire, and more to do with her being a trope in a normative world that fixes her as unfixable. The camera shoots her in medium shot, but the eye of the beholder remains unclear: is Marie imagining her dancing as a queer fantasy that cannot ultimately exist? Or is she being 'seen' by heterosexual masculinity's eye in the form of the young men positioned behind her or of the men who desired her for her looks? With the light filter connecting the scene back to the club scene, Floriane is ghost-like in this scene and she is real, neither fully present nor fully absent. Her eyes seem to begin to open in the final second of the scene as if she has the potential to be a seeing subject, but even that is unclear. Is this perhaps the moment when she leaves behinds the male heterosexual desire that she has so desired? Does she begin to see that she is objectified and is made into a heterosexual woman? She is in the end, for me, located somewhere between Belot's 'budding subjectivity' and Jonet's 'façade of normative desirability', between representing herself and being represented.

As she dances in this scene, behind her are located young men and women acting out desires and sexuality in ways that appear highly normative. One young woman appears to be crying next to a young man her age as though he has done something to hurt her feelings or done violence to her. But juxtaposed with this image of gender hegemony is an image of fluidity. A group of young male swimmers from the polo team are dancing shirtless with swimming suits over their heads, for reasons that are not immediately clear. The camera focuses on their hairless toned bodies playing and celebrating, with their heads not visible. They are in a sense only bodies, fully corporeal, represented in a way that suggests that they cannot see but can only be seen. The swimsuits on their heads reveal their inability to look or gaze, as if they too had their eyes closed. The dancing bodies resemble Floriane in a sense:

there is sexual ambiguity in these shots, there is a homosociality that verges on – or perhaps becomes – homoeroticism. This image of male homosociality/homoeroticism parallels the representation of Floriane's fluidity. Sciamma allows (or perhaps forces) male group relations to be viewed as fluid, as caught between heteronormativity and queerness, constructing them as tropes or signs in support of female representation and not in control of lesbian representation. Normative masculinity might here be a 'problem' of its own, neither visible as heterosexual nor as queer, when seen not by normative cultural constructs but with a queer gaze. Male heterosexuality is a fluid sign, taking on the same representational place as the lesbian, ghosted in a way and made inconsequential to the representational story.

Synchronicity

If there is a synchronicity between Floriane and the male swimmers in terms of sexual representation, there is a different synchronicity between Marie and Anne – relating to consciousness of representation, not loss of representational agency. As Marie swims to the side of the pool and Anne comes to the pool's edge, it may seem that Anne is going to help Marie get out of the pool and dry off, that her baptism into adulthood or lesbianism might be complete now, at least symbolically, and that she can leave the pool and the film can conclude with its telos reached. But that is not what happens: Anne jumps in with her and the two of them construct their own representation of synchronicity. The queerness of the narrative includes Anne, as there is something queer about her, her fatness, and her own narrative, even as there is no tangible erotic desire between Anne and Marie. Their names reference the Christian mother and daughter Anne and Mary, a non-erotic, familial relation without sex. What is queer is the close link between their non-linear narratives, one defined through same-sex sexuality and the other through heterosexual coming of age.

This idea of relationality and synchronicity refers to a film that Sciamma has referenced, namely Eric Rohmer's *L'Ami de mon amie* (*Boyfriends and Girlfriends*) (1987) (Dawson, 2008). Like Sciamma's film, this one takes place in the Parisian suburb on the far northwest side of the city called Cergy-Pontoise, where Sciamma is from. Rohmer's film contains a short swimming scene in which the two female heterosexual characters Blanche and Lea (the *amie*, or female friend of the title) go swimming together. The plot of the film revolves around Lea who is in the process of breaking up with her boyfriend named Fabien, whom she likes but has trouble being with. Things in the end work out and the two women find male partners, Blanche ending up with Lea's boyfriend Fabien and Lea with the man Blanche fancies. The plot is rather banal and contrived, but that narrative sterility is the film's actual content. It reveals the emptiness around heterosexual partnering, an emptiness reflected by the sterility of the fabricated white, bourgeois suburb and its soulless architecture. In fact, it is unclear whether the film's sterility is a sterility of relationships or a sterility of space. Any chance of female–female desire is erased from the moment the two young women meet, and non-normative gender relations are never possible. There is, however, perfect symmetry in the final shot of the film as the two couples appear in outfits that reflect an extreme – almost absurd – parallelism in terms of colour. They are perfectly parallel, normative couples, fabricated like the modern architecture of the suburban space, and one of them is exchangeable for the other in the era of commodified capitalism and suburban life without soul. With Rohmer's film as reference point, Sciamma plays off this cold, ludic parallelism of female bodies, but moves it in a radically new direction that renders heterosexual teleological parallelism a queer becoming – a new way for Anne and Marie to be and to co-be in Cergy-Pontoise.

Naissance des pieuvres ends in a form of parallelism between Marie and Anne in the swimming pool as they lie on the surface of the pool in the same position, touching. The sideways parallelism is not a ludically normative endpoint, as it is in Rohmer, but a non-normative ending that opens up new relational forms related to gender and desire. The two of them are swimming in a synchronized way, as it were, referencing the synchronized swimming of the opening scene. The film does not end as it began since here the form of synchronicity is one in which the two are horizontally proximate instead of in a standard synchronized swimming move. Floriane rose up in the opening scene from the water like a flower, but here Marie and Anne spread out horizontally, side by side. They illustrate Stockton's definition of 'sideways growth': 'something that locates energy, pleasure, vitality, and (e)motion in the back-and-forth of connections and extensions that are not reproductive … moving suspensions and shadows of growth' (2009: 13).

Their synchronicity, their connection with their arms extended, is much of what the narrative ends up being about: Anne's story is not unlike Marie's. Her object of desire for the film is François (Warren Jacquin), the young man with whom Floriane flirts just enough to keep him interested, though she does not have sex with him. Anne's desire for François is unrequited, at least at first. One evening after Floriane has led him on but not had sex with him, he comes to Anne's house in a frenzy and has sex with her as a replacement for Floriane. But she cannot really have him as it is Floriane that he desires and follows, thinking he can have what he wants, much as Marie wants Floriane but cannot have her. Both Anne and Marie come to see lack of erotic fixity as what they do not want. What might have been a love story, a coming-out narrative, or coming-of-age narrative ends up as not that at all. Anne rejects François in the end by spitting in his mouth after he seems to want her and tells her that 'in fact' he 'likes' her. Heterosexual affect or sexual act is decidedly not her telos and her spit renders that form of sexuality abject for herself as well as for her coming-of-age narrative. Instead of coming of age because she has sex with a young man, she has a narrative of synchronicity, a 'moving suspension' on the surface of the water, gesturing forward to other synchronicities that might happen in future years. Anne's overweight body connects her to Marie's queerness, as the element of her corporality that throws her sideways out of growing up.[8] Their non-reproductive sideways '(e)motion' and 'suspension' is a queer way to be that goes well beyond orientation. It is not a parallelism in which Marie's same-sex desire parallels Anne's heterosexual desire, with two orientations connected, but an assemblage on its own terms.

The final scene refers to the French title of the film (literally, 'The Birth of the Octopuses'). The two girls together float like a single octopus. Delorme in his review of the film takes the image as pertaining to 'seduction', or 'alternating between approaching affectionately and retreating', like the tentacles of the octopus.[9] Sciamma has pointed out that the octopus in the 'common imaginary' refers to simultaneity of desire and of jealousy the first time one falls in love (British Film Institute, 2019).[10] As she puts it, 'it feels like there's this octopus in your belly with this black ink'. The ink might confuse the one desiring. Sciamma cites Proust who refers to the octopus as desire and jealousy. Proust describes Swann's jealousy in *Swann's Way*: 'Sa jalousie, comme une pieuvre qui jette une première,

---

8   Stockton takes fatness as a sample metaphor of sideways growth (2009: 19–22). Bradbury-Rance sees a return to childhood in the final scene: 'The star shapes that Marie and Anne make in the water are like propulsions back to childhood' (2019: 95); 'Marie ends up more childish than she began' (96). I see her movement as sideways, not regressive.
9   'la séduction, ce mouvement successif d'approche cajoleuse et de retrait rétracté' (2007: 32).
10 Sciamma notes that she had the title before she made the film and also that at one point the film was titled 'The Octopuses'.

puis une seconde, puis une troisième amarre, s'attacha solidement à ce moment de cinq heures du soir, puis à un autre, puis à un autre encore' (1919: 92) ('His jealousy, like an octopus which throws out a first, then a second, and finally a third tentacle, fastened itself firmly to that particular moment, five o'clock in the afternoon, then to another, then to another again' (1982: 309)).[11] The black ink may have kept Anne and Marie from seeing as they were confused by the octopus of jealousy. Here, however, the tentacles do not clutch the object of desire, for they have released them. Anne has let François go, and Marie has let Floriane go. The two women are 'born', but as symbolic octopuses beyond the metaphor of jealousy. Jealousy's tentacles has unattached itself from temporal moments. Their tentacles do not grasp objects of desire and close the individual off to what they cannot have, but instead they are opened up and shared, the two together resignifying the Proustian image as synchronized or as Stockton's 'back-and-forth of connections and extension that are not reproductive'. They had an octopus inside them before, but now they *are* the body of the octopus. Anne is in formation with Marie because they both reject jealousy (Marie for Floriane, Anne for François) in favour of a co-being and non-normative relationality.

Marie's eye-opening experience is to become animal, not to have a metaphorical animal within, to take over the metaphoric ability to squirt ink, or to have control over the visual field. She is 'born' as an animal in control of the visual.[12]

---

11 In the same interview, Sciamma mentions writer Violette Leduc for whom youthful lesbian desire is figured as an octopus (but not jealousy). In *Thérèse and Isabelle*, during an erotic encounter for instance, the narrator Thérèse notes '[s]omething is crawling in my belly' (2015: 24) and later '[t]he octopus in my guts was quivering' (2015: 87; see also 89, 186).
12 Anne, too, takes control over the visual field through her own naked body. François had walked in on her naked in the locker room and upset her because of body image issues. But in a later scene in the

She is not Floriane in the opening scene, viewed by a large audience as forming quasi-metaphorical forms. She is now the one seeing: if her gaze on Floriane set the narrative in motion, her gaze on the gaze or her ability to understand how the optical field functions closes it. Now a seeing queer subject, Marie has changed. She sees how lesbianism is represented. It is not so much that she sees that lesbianism is invisible, ghosted, unknowable, or inconsequential, nor does she come to see that lesbianism is visible, out, knowable, or consequential. Rather, she sees that lesbianism is a dynamic of absence and presence, an oscillation between visual poles. Floriane's sexual movements, she knows now, are the movements of lesbian representation itself. Marie comes to understand what Valerie Traub articulates about lesbian representation: 'Inhering with the figure of "the lesbian" … is a dynamic conjunction, whereby fathomability, intelligibility, and comprehensibility are always fastened … to their negation' (2016: 287). The lesbian does not equal or become ontological certainty, nor does she equal absence. Marie sees that her own life and her own relation to lesbian representation will be based in this complicated dynamic as she enters a symbolic order of sorts. With her Proustian tentacles, Marie cannot simply unfasten negative representation from presence, but she can see it as an element of a representational dynamic. It is for this reason that she becomes part of a metaphoric body on the surface of the pool: she sees that she is present as a queer desiring subject but also absent, a metaphorical animal.

By extension, Marie stands in for cinematic representation: she sees that lesbian representation on film, that the camera floating above her will and will not make lesbianism present in the future. Future representation is opened up, will be constituted by a play with these forms of representing. With

> exact same locale, she stands naked, arms out, to welcome him to see her full body. Being an object of the male gaze has become a possibility for her and not simply a source of shame.

this ending, opened up to the future, Sciamma sets the stage for similar approaches to concluding her other films, the rest of which will conclude in an open-ended manner as well. With her first feature film, the complications of queer female seeing are, along with the octopuses, born as a representational feature of her cinema. I take Marie as looking forward to Sciamma's queer representation – an autoreferential cipher for a director who will very acutely see the camera and make problems of gender representation central to the rest of her oeuvre.

Transing the father: *Tomboy*

In *Tomboy*, it is not fully clear whether the central character Mickäel (Zoé Héran) – who was assigned the name 'Laure' at birth – could be categorized as transgender, non-binary, tomboy, or lesbian. Or more precisely, it is not clear what they will grow up to become.[13] What is clear is that they are in a state of movement, a movement that could refer to multiple forms of gender change. From girl to boy, from feminine to masculine, from non-sexual to queer, from cisgender to transgender. This movement-centeredness is, in part, represented by play: Mickäel, their younger sister Jeanne (Malonn Lévana), and their friends are in a near-constant state of play that suggests non-adult worlds in which the pre-pubescent child can function in a state not defined by binarized sex/gender impositions and in which play does not mean leaving behind gender norms since they have not yet been firmly established. Play is its own form of gender performativity. In one of the

13 She/her pronouns are used by other characters to refer to the character named Laure. To recognize the problematic of gender, I will use they/them pronouns here, with the understanding that they are not used in the film (and in French cannot be used in this same way as in English) and that the character does not use them either. My choice is simply for my own text.

most remarkable scenes in the film, Mickäel fashions a play-dough penis and inserts it into their trunks to go swimming with friends, but it is not fully clear whether this prosthetic invention stands in for a desire to be male or masculine, or whether it is a form of fluid gender play and performativity that puts into question the penis as definitional of maleness. The film makes queer desire a central element as well in the form of Lisa (Jeanne Disson), whose attraction to Mickäel is reciprocated. Lisa in fact sets in motion the immediate gender narrative when she first meets the character with the name Laure and addresses them with a masculine adjectival form ('Tu es nouveau?'), suggesting her desire may be for the boy she sees or for gender movement itself. In a sense, Mickäel plays along with Lisa, telling her that their name is 'Mickäel', not Laure, and in so doing, begins the process of passing to other children. Whether Lisa is playing with gender and/or French grammar is not immediately clear.

Play in the film is defined by near-constant physical movement, games, jokes, dancing, corporeal movement, etc. In an early scene, Mickäel poses for a portrait in their family's apartment for Jeanne who is drawing them with magic markers in front of a makeshift hanging sheet serving as background (also the cover image of the American DVD case), and she tells them: 'Stop moving' ('Arrête de bouger'), so that she can draw them. But Mickäel is in movement and cannot sit still, or cannot be captured in static forms of representation like a drawing. The film itself, a kind of portrait, cannot capture them either because they are in transition. Even though Jeanne has not finished the drawing, Mickäel ends up leaving to go hang out with Lisa, with Jeanne left at home, sad to be there without her sibling. It is an unfinished portrait: it cannot be completed. Gender, too, is never completed in the film, never finalized.

This unfinished drawing contrasts with an image in the previous scene taking place in the middle of the night: Mickäel cannot sleep, gets up, goes to look in the closet at clothes, presumably to think about what boy-like clothes they can wear the next day (and the clothes they are wearing for their portrait drawing may be those very clothes). As Mickäel opens the closet, a full-length mirror appears on the inside door, with their profile in the mirror. The scene is decidedly not about self-reflection nor is it a consideration of how the inner sense of gender does not correspond to the corporeal outside, as the mirror in transgender narrative has traditionally signified (see Prosser, 1998: 99–134). Like Marie in *Naissance des pieuvres*, indifference to mediation for the auto-gaze reflects the character's own relation to gender identification as beyond traditional metaphors. The scene concludes as Mickäel goes back to bed, leaving the closet open. In an earlier scene, as Mickäel is washing clothes in which they urinated, they stand in front of the bathroom mirror. The viewer sees them in medium shot through the mirror, but they do not stand and stare in the mirror. The point of both of these mirror images is that the viewer's gaze on Mickäel is mediated, is not direct on the character but necessarily mediated by binarized culture. Mickäel takes a brief look at themself in the mirror, but again the indifferent look is not for self-reflection, instead acknowledging the mirror as mediator for the viewer. This is not a film about self-reflection or self-discovery, nor is the character asking the question 'who am I', as a gaze in the mirror might suggest. It is about portraiture, how a child in gender movement can be captured or represented in dominant culture which attempts to keep gender stable, binary, and unambiguous. There is no real ambiguity about Mickäel's gender: they are not questioning who they are or coming out. The narrative is largely about relationality between Mickäel and the cisgenderism of dominant culture which reflects to them and to us who the character should be and how they should act.

Tomboy is not thus simply a minoritizing film about a single category of the human. As Darren Waldron puts it in his study of the film, '[b]y placing blame squarely on the shoulders of society, *Tomboy* underlines how that society straightjackets gender within two modes' (male/female) (2013: 69). Mickäel's pregnant mother, with her categorical imperatives coming in part from outside herself, stands in for society in this sense, forcing her child to comply. She is especially concerned about the need to match sex assigned at birth with school records when her child goes to school, suggesting that French universalism as mediated through the school system does not permit official gender change. Mickäel – unlike their mother – reveals that gender is performative, or as Waldron writes, reveals 'the conditionality of all gendering by highlighting the performative strategies undertaken by boys to comply with compulsory masculinity' (2013: 60; see also Saunders, 2014). The character 'confirms … that gender does not naturally derive from sex' and that 'disruption of the established binary' is forced out of the screen on to the audience (Waldron, 2013: 68). Waldron considers the intimate camera work from the perspective of a child that positions the viewer as 'an unseen extra child' (65), who might well not conform to gender binarism. The spectator is not expected to identify with Mickäel per se, but to enter the queer visual world of the child is to enter a queer world not predicated on binarism and to open up the possibility of an epistemological fantasy of another gender system via camerawork.

A key purveyor of gender movement in the film is the character of Mickäel's father, a cisgender man who actively participates in the category of gender movement (played by Mathieu Demy, Jacques Demy's son). In the opening scene in which he drives Mickäel in the car, he moves them along in terms of gender. When Mickäel takes over the wheel, he helps them move the car in a forward direction and to manoeuvre it (plate 13). Mickäel asks if they should go straight, and he answers no, that they should go 'to the right'. He tells his child to turn the wheel but then to straighten it out ('Redresse'). He is showing his child assigned female at birth how to manoeuvre in non-linear or 'straight' ways and how to manoeuvre around in the realm of gender which requires both going 'straight' and not going straight. Another element of driving in this scene relates to the turn signal: Mickäel does not know how to operate the signal, nor do they know that to push the signal up signals a coming right turn. It is not simply the parameters of the car's movement that Mickäel is being taught by their father (turn/go straight), it is also the signs of gender, the ways in which gender movement can be signalled to others who are watching. Mickäel does not talk to their sympathetic father about gender, even when he asks what is wrong when they do not seem happy. Mickäel does not know how to discuss the turns of gender in language to their family, but the father figure is there to help manoeuvre turns and to show his child what they are doing in signs. He teaches his child how to show the world how to 'turn' away from gender normativity, prompting in a sense the later scene with the playdough penis that signals boyhood to other children. The father, too, in a sense, is in gender movement: for reasons that are not clear, he has had a series of jobs, and the family has recently had to move into the new apartment in which much of the action takes place. His position as masculine breadwinner for his family is not firm, but his affective attachment to Mickäel is rock solid. What explains the complicity between the two characters might be that there is something non-normative about him, perhaps something queer or trans, similar to his child.[14]

14 As the well-known actor and son of director Jacques Demy who died of AIDS, Mathieu Demy himself brings a queer heterosexual element to the role thanks to previous roles that have a queer element. He played the heterosexual man who dies of AIDS in Ducastel and Martineau's musical *Jeanne et le garçon formidable* and the adult Eric in Philippe Barassat's short *Mon copain Rachide* (*My Friend Rachid*) (1998), whose child self is obsessed with the large penis of the titular character. Demy appears at the end of the short with his nuclear family to show that any queer desire for the sexualized *beur* male body in childhood has been displaced into heteronormativity, opening the question of whether queerness inhabits the normative-looking family.

On the other hand, it may be less the case that Demy's character is queer and more the case that he wants to have a son, even though he loves his daughter Jeanne. In a card-playing scene – the only play scene that an adult participates in – the father and Mickäel play a French game (the Game of the Seven Families) in which a player has to construct a full family of six members (father, mother, son, daughter, grandmother, grandfather) by asking one's opponent if they have a missing family member from a certain family in their hand. The father asks Mickäel if they have the son of a certain family. He needs the son card to complete the family in his hand, but he also wants a son for himself to have a complete family in his life, the card game being a projection of his own paternal desires. Mickäel on the other hand asks for the daughter in a different family. Their father has that card and hands it to Mickäel, asking if they are cheating ('tu triches ou quoi?'). He willingly gives his daughter card away to his actual child who does not have a girl in the family because he has no issue 'giving up' Laure for Mickäel. He then gives Mickäel a sip of his beer in the middle of the game and notes that he cannot wait to see how they play poker later on in life, helping to construct his son as a son. Mickäel may or may not be cheating with respect to gender and may well go on to cheat or to bluff not in poker but in terms of gender. But what is especially important in this scene is that Mickäel's father plays along, as the normative construct of family – with a son and a daughter and presumably two 'opposite-sex' parents (and grandparents) – is a game constructed by an act of volition and negotiation, and not by some natural or God-given force. If the gendered family is constructed, it can be reconstructed, precisely what Mickäel is doing to this family with their father's help and support.

This scene ends with one of the most touching moments of the film as the father holds Mickäel in his arms and rocks him repeatedly like a monkey clinging to him. It is one of the most peaceful moments in the film as the two of them share a special bond, represented by a horizontal circling or a torque around, not unlike the car turn of the opening scene. It is no longer a simple turn of the car on the street of the city, it is a half-circular continuing movement, a kind of perpetual movement machine that bonds father and child here and for the long term. The scene then cuts to Mickäel who is unable to sleep (the closet scene mentioned above): they seek boy's clothes in the closet in part because of the father's movement-centred approach to normativity and gender which puts Mickäel into movement in their bedroom. While it would be going too far to suggest that the father alone causes the gender movement (in part because of Lisa's contribution, noted above), it is clear that he contributes to it.

What of gender movement in the all-important final scene? Here, Mickäel meets their love interest Lisa again, but this time she knows that Mickäel was assigned female at birth. She stages a new introduction very much like the one they had earlier, asking Mickäel the same question she had asked when they met: 'what is your name?' After a pause and confused look, Mickäel responds 'Laure,' their feminine name rejected for Mickäel. This response could be taken as the closing down of gender change, the successful imposition of cultural binarism on the character who now accepts it. Gibson takes this scene in this way, as the manifestation of a 'suddenly idealized conformity' (2016: 225). But significantly, Mickäel smiles or smirks here at the conclusion of the film. We do not really know what this ambiguous smirk means. It could be taken as an opening up, a form of futurity to come in which 'Laure' will pass as a girl but will destabilize that gender construct in other less-obvious ways. The name 'Laure' suggests the laurel, the symbol of victory in competition (*lauré* meaning to be crowned with the laurel). Mickäel achieves a kind of victory now by virtue of being Laure but taking gender non-conformity in a new direction based on negotiation or a new form of play. I agree with Waldron who takes Laure as 'surmount[ing] the challenges of her existence by identifying herself with her given name, without compromising her preferences in terms of appearance, behavior, and attractions' (2013: 71). The scene suggests an erotic relation with Lisa, and points to possible futures – as lesbian, genderqueer, non-binary, or transmasculine with desire for cisgender women. While the precise nature of the identity category in the future is far from clear, what is clear is that there is a form of queer futurity yet to be determined. The film is opened up, much like the end of *Naissance des pieuvres*, to an undetermined future. It will perhaps not be the gender story that has been told in the film, but one that is more movement-centred or more prone to negotiation with cultural constraint. The final scene refers back to the opening scene in the car with the father: 'Laure' will remain in transit, simply in a new way yet to be determined. The father's lessons about turning and straightening out are put into practice here: 'Laure' may bend in terms of gender, may queer gender, but then return to a position of normativity. It will be the negotiation with gender normativity – not gender non-normativity alone – that will ultimately be playful. The father was swinging sideways with Mickäel in the scene discussed above, but also in a broad sense, he can leave his child in a state where they can swivel queerly left and right as they grow sideways, but also go straight when need be. The queer child negotiates growing up and growing sideways in open-ended ways that their father may teach them. Mickäel has learned the lesson given in the opening scene: how to turn as well as how to straighten out.

Producing girlhood: *Bande de filles*

Unlike in her two queer-focused previous films, it is only in the final section of *Bande de filles* that queerness appears. The main character Marieme or Vic (Karidja Touré), short for 'Victoire' meaning victory, transitions to a state of queerness in terms of both desire and gender. Having left home to work as a drug dealer for a local drug kingpin named Abou (Djibril Gueye), Vic attends one of his parties and dances with a woman with whom there is obvious chemistry. The queer moment does not go over well: Abou interrupts the dancing and demands that Vic dance with him, clearly cutting off desire and re-establishing patriarchal heteronormativity. This queer moment for Vic temporarily releases her from the constraints of life in the *banlieue*, including but not limited to patriarchal rule and gender normativity, which she wants to leave behind. This moment, however, also reveals that such constraints cannot be abandoned since Vic is unable to negotiate queerness with her life in situ.

The mirror inverse of the dancing scene takes place when Vic meets with her male love interest Ismaël (Idrissa Diabaté), a sweet and respectful young man to whom she was attracted from the first moment that she saw him. Vic has taken on an increasingly masculine appearance, with shorter hair and more masculine clothes. The two begin to make out, but then Ismaël notices that Vic has bound her breasts. He responds negatively to her, and the scene ends because eros dissipates.[15] Ismaël later apologizes and tells her he was an idiot ('j'étais con'), but it is clear that queerness cannot enter into their heterosexual relation. Vic attempts to negotiate gender with him by showing up transed, but his unwillingness to work with her suggests that, although he is not a violent or aggressive man like her brother Djibril, she cannot function in a queer relation with him that exists both inside and outside the constraints of heteronormativity. He suggests that if she moves in with him and they get married, there will be no longer be a 'problem' ('il n'y a plus de problème si on se marie'), ostensibly the problem

---

15 In the DVD commentary of the French version of the film, Sciamma notes that the binding resembles a bandage (Sciamma, 2015). Wilson (2017: 17–18) compares the binding to Brandon's in Peirce's film *Boys Don't Cry*. On this scene, see also Smith (2020: 86–7).

of her bad reputation for having had sex with him, but really the problem of her queerness which normative marriage can solve or cover up. With him, she can be 'a good girl' ('une fille bien'). Female masculinity or proto-trans masculinity are problems to be solved in the gender scheme that surrounds her, Ismaël's comment only expressing much broader cultural constraints around her.

Momentary queerness is transformed into a state of queerness in the last segment of *Bande de filles*. The question that arises in light of the earlier scenes is: in what ways does queerness pertain not so much to being queer (as butch, bisexual, lesbian, non-binary, or transgender), but to negotiating the broad constraints of the French *banlieue*? The opening football scene, mentioned at the start of my chapter, had already tipped off the viewer that the film would be about queerness in the end. In fact, the first scene takes place in slow motion, suggesting that it is replayed action that happens in real time, as if this prologue to the film is the second time that queerness is presented. It is a prologue that gestures to what comes after it in the film itself – the actual play – and resees what will happen later on. In a sense, the film ends where it began: the football players function in a highly codified game with strict rules, but by virtue of their gender are also overturning other rules, including especially those that govern a viewer's assumption that the players must be men. The gap between rules and subversion in the opening scene is defined as queer. Noting that 'black, lesbian musician, [Sharon] Funchess's presence on the soundtrack enables an alternative identity position to resonate within the film from the start', McNeill writes that the scene 'sets up the film's queer disorientation' (2018: 331) as it begins with a seemingly solid gender orientation put into movement. The dream-like scene ends abruptly right before the credits as the lights on the field are turned out quickly, effectively ending the night-time queer vision. The opening scene, then, tells the viewer to juxtapose its temporary 'queer disorientation' and the overarching constraint represented by the sudden ending. The two later attempts to shutdown queer (dancing scene, scene with Ismaël) intimate that the normative world in which Vic functions resembles the football game that the men will turn the queer lights out on. Things do not fully end as they began however. Vic's dream will lie elsewhere, or more precisely her dream will lie in a theoretical mode different than in her life with Ismaël or her life with Abou. The lights will not go out to end her queer dream but relocate it in an elsewhere beyond the constraints of the metaphorical playing field. Vic will take her game elsewhere.

The final scene of *Bande de filles* serves as the culmination of the aborted queer dream of the prologue. Vic buzzes the interphone so as to go talk to her family from whom she is estranged, but when she is buzzed in the door, she changes her mind and lets the door close. Returning home to her family will be more of the same life that she wants to reject and leave behind. She moves away from the door and begins crying. But as she does, she moves out of the screen as the camera focuses on the environment behind her. The shot becomes fuzzy, Vic re-enters the field of vision, but then darts off in some other direction. The environment in which she is embedded and located cannot be escaped so easily, it is part of the normative constraints under which she lives. It has to be focused on. At the same time, it is fuzzy and allows for wiggle room or room for manoeuvre in which Vic can operate. The big question of the film is where Vic heads as she leaves (plate 14). She is not heading towards any fixed point, and certainly not in a straight line. She is zig-zagging, moving between two positions, the position of cultural constraint and the position of individual subjectivity beyond constraint. Like Mickäel in the opening sequence of *Tomboy*, she is turning away as well as going straight. Her visible queerness does not overturn normativity, but integrates the two poles and allows for a new structure to emerge. Her flight is a line of flight towards queer cultural manoeuvring. Vic is heading neither out of the *banlieue* nor into the *banlieue*, but in a third direction. She is heading to a situation in which she could be a drug-dealer and dance erotically with a woman, or in which she could be with a man with her breasts bound. She is, as Wilson puts it, 'about to run, or dive, into her future', even as 'Marieme's future [is] unknown, radically unscripted' (2017: 18).[16] The unknowing with respect to futurity goes hand in hand with the inability to code her as a gendered subject: she cannot be called a 'lesbian' nor 'butch', nor 'transgender', nor does 'female masculinity' necessarily capture her gender here. It is not clear that she desires women or that she wants to become a man. Her queerness is beyond any single identitarian category as she is not limited to any one morphology.[17]

This queer possibility is born in a remarkable scene filmed with blue filter in which the four girls rent a hotel room for

---

16 Smith has a similar but somewhat different reading of this key scene: she takes it as expressing freedom: 'Now fully rid of any social role, she is free to adopt the identity she chooses and move wherever she pleases' (2020: 89). Smith calls this 'queer': I agree that it is queer but in the sense outlined above, as a movement between structure and constraint – much like the end of Sciamma's three other films, as I read them.

17 This is one reason that critics are undecided about what her identity is, because if she has an identity, it is one that is non-identitarian. Wilson for instance notes that the scene with the bound breasts 'references trans identity, though this suggestion is not explored' (2017: 18). This futurity might be represented via queerness, but it exists in the film as part of Vic's age category: as Frances Smith notes, 'Sciamma works to undercut the possibility of pursuing the normative life course and instead orients her protagonist towards the present and the absence of futurity' (2020: 80). Using Ahmed's ideas on temporal linearity as heteronormative, Smith links the absence of traditional trajectories of the young woman's life course to the queerness of the film. It is a question of a 'queer temporality of adolescence' (85). *Bande de filles* is queer, then, because of the lack of rigidly imposed constraints based on age.

the night and lip sync and sing along to Rihanna's 2012 hit song 'Diamonds'. The three other members of the *bande* begin by dancing to the song together, with Vic sitting on the bed intently watching them as the camera slowly approaches her. The viewer watches her watching first as she is established as the point-of-view character in the sequence. On one level, the scene is the moment when Vic decides to join the '*bande de filles*' and becomes one with them, singing and dancing along with them. They are all four 'diamonds in the sky', they all 'shine bright like a diamond', and they all see 'eye to eye'. Or at least they imagine that they do for now. Being together becomes precious in this scene, like diamonds, ending disunity in the *bande*. The scene suggests a group-oriented fantasy of becoming a famous, successful black woman like Rihanna, a shared dream of being in another world radically different from the one in which they live.

But underneath the shiny exterior lies a fracture. McNeill's close reading of the scene (and of music more broadly in the film) highlights its queerness, influenced by the complexity of Rihanna's music video and personal life. What is conveyed in the film is a 'problematic luminosity' (2018: 338) that does orient all the characters in the same communal direction at the same time as it disorients. As McNeill writes: 'the gloss of image and the appeal of music are relentlessly recuperated by normative, neoliberal ideologies' while the scene also conveys 'the shared, evanescent and infinite possibilities of music as a formative experience' (338). Yet despite this homogeneity, the music displaces 'any fixed gaze upon or rigid apprehension of the characters' embodied subjectivities' (338). This is a scene of freedom for the four characters as it 'expose[s] the frightening extent of the forces that act upon them, but also ... present[s] an unknowable subjectivity that just as forcefully asserts its continual reinvention' (338). The blue filter references the dancing character of Floriane in the penultimate scene of *Naissance des pieuvres* (also filmed in blue) since she too was a bifurcated subject, caught between male representational fantasy and a subjectivity that cannot be fully pinned down.[18] The four young black women here are simultaneously constrained by their current lives and their unrealized dream of being diamonds in the sky, as they are also freed from stable identities shaped by the *banlieue*. Their performance is both a fictional, wishful theatrical performance imitating Rihanna – reinforced by the closed curtains that recall a stage – and a performance that opens up the possibility of other identitarian performances and reveals the arbitrariness of the identitarian constraints imposed upon them.[19]

While the scene might be commenting on all four of the young women, there is nonetheless something different about Vic. She is a diamond in the rough as her true value will emerge only once she becomes a queer subject later on. Rihanna's reference to twoness ('You and I / We're beautiful like diamonds in the sky / Eye to eye') refers not only to Vic and the other young women as a foursome, but also to Vic's gendered self that is on the verge of splitting into a stable self and a queer self that will see 'eye to eye' as two distinct subjectivities that function in tandem. Similarly, Rihanna's music video is very focused on the singer herself and her body, only containing brief moments that show two humans in the form of two hands touching.

---

18 McNeill reads the blue of the scene as melancholy, the underbelly of the communal fantasy. To me, the blue links the film back to *Naissance des pieuvres* and Floriane's representational status, split between normativity and queerness. Sciamma has noted that Kieslowski's film *Blue* (1993) was deeply influential on her as a budding filmmaker. The film makes blueness a key element of liberty, leaving open the question of whether the blue filter here has a referential or autobiographical element. See Sciamma (2020a).

19 Central to McNeill's argument is also the queering of the boundaries between viewer and Sciamma's film: 'By destabilising diegetic space, the film's disorienting qualities resist containment within the film's fictional world' (2018: 328).

In *Bande de filles*, a mirror appears in the lead up to the song, and while the three young women use it to look at themselves before the song, Vic herself does not. We see her not seeing herself as a unified subject or as a single totality. Like Marie in *Naissance des pieuvres* and Mickäel in *Tomboy*, she is indifferent to the mirror's mediation: she will find her own mediation and not rely ultimately on her friends or the form of black female subjectivity established in this scene. She, above all, will embody, as per McNeill, the 'unknowable subjectivity that just as forcefully asserts its continual reinvention' as she becomes queer and does not reject her community.

Claire Mouflard (2016: 113) takes another scene as central to the film as well, one in which the four young women play mini golf with miniature structures or buildings built into each putting green. After putting around the Eiffel Tower, the four of them end up at a hole in which there are two options: to try to putt 'straight' through a classical building or to go around the buildings to the left through a tunnel. An argument ensues between two of them (but not Vic) about which way is proper since 'there are rules', as one of them notes. They can attempt the hazard of aggressively going straight through, risking being put off course by the building, or they can take the detour and avoid the classical structure. The point is that the girls themselves in the *banlieue* have the option of ploughing straight through, with the risk of being put off course by classical, white French culture, or of attempting to go around it and taking a detour where they would get stuck and would not have access to classical French cultural privileges. During this animated and emotional debate, Vic stays out of the discussion, for she – the remainder of the film will show us – will take a third option. Or more accurately, she will take both options: she will remain straight but also take the detour on the left. She will remain in place and move forward with the unavoidable socio-economic constraints in place, part of the classical or traditional structures of French culture, but she will also go around them, trying to navigate through and bending around. She takes a third way. In so doing, she is simultaneously queer and straight, simultaneously bent and straight. It is an approach that the other three friends will not take, but is the same bi-directional approach that Marie in *Naissance des pieuvres* and Mickäel in *Tomboy* take. All three of these queer characters plough through normativity while growing up sideways. Sciamma's fourth film also focuses on negotiating straightness with bending, albeit in a very different way. The two women characters will head straight into their love affair and in so doing will bend cultural narratives of gender and sexuality in new directions.

'Inventing something': the queer artist on fire

While conducting her art lesson in the opening scene of *Portrait de la jeune fille en feu*, Marianne expresses an emotional reaction to something coming from behind the camera. One of the students has taken a painting out of storage and put it up in the back of the studio, provoking the reaction from Marianne (Noémie Merlant) who was unaware of the painting until this moment. She is thrown off guard. Her control over the artistic gaze is lost as her affective reaction lies beyond her control. She no longer controls what the students look at or see. When the student asks what the title of the painting is, Marianne offers the title of the film. The narrative or 'portrait' from the past that we are about to see may disrupt our act of looking as much as it will open a narrative about looking. It will make us look at something that we do not expect to see, something that has been brought out of storage or out of the historical past into our present. The call of the film will, in part, be a proposition to look at history in new ways. As we will learn later, the '*jeune fille*' or young woman in the painting – literally on fire – is a lover that Marianne had in the past, and the film's central narrative will be composed of their story, looking back on what happened from the vantage point of the present in the art school. The film will disrupt the twenty-first-century present with a story of same-sex love between two women in the eighteenth century, and the articulation of representational questions will be closely linked to what we now call lesbian love, opening up new sexual possibilities or new ways of looking. In a sense, then, the film returns to the questions about same-sex love and looking posed in *Naissance des pieuvres*, this time with artistic representation itself the explicit content of the film.

On one level, although Marianne is caught very much off guard, gender normativity has not been majorly disrupted in the story that the painting evokes. Marianne has been invited by Héloïse's Italian mother to come paint her portrait to be sent to a possible suitor in Milan, but she is to paint her without her knowing what she is doing because she refused to pose for the previous (male) painter. As an artist, she is hired to create a painting that will participate in a patriarchal, heterosexist system predicated on marriage, what Michel Foucault calls a '*deployment of alliance*' in *The History of Sexuality*: 'a system of marriage, of fixation and development of kinship ties, of transmission of names and possessions' (1978: 106, italics in original). The painting will serve as an object of exchange between this moderately wealthy family in the western province of Brittany and a presumably wealthier, and presumably unattractive man for reasons that are not clear. The portrait itself needs to be created so that the suitor can determine whether Héloïse (Adèle Haenel) is attractive enough to marry this man and provide him children (or, more likely, sons) to carry on his name. If acceptable, the portrait will participate in Foucault's system by fixing and developing kinship ties between the two families and transmitting names and possessions to a next generation. The lack of precise information about the suitor and the families suggests the presence of the deployment of alliance, defined as a system more than as individuals' stories.

Although she is the one enforcing this normative system, Héloïse's mother (Valeria Golino) in fact tells the story of suffering herself from this same system. While in her native Italy, her portrait was sent to Brittany to the man to whom she is now married (whom we never see or meet or hear talked of), and that portrait is visible hanging on the wall in one of the rooms of the chateau. As she narrates, the painting arrived at the chateau before her and, when she arrived, it was already there. Her presence in a sense was already determined by the patriarchal system that captured or fixed women in painting and used the art form to determine marriage alliance.[20] As a woman, she was a victim of, but now actively propagates, that system.

The deployment is, of course, successful as Héloïse is in the end married off to the suitor, thanks to the painting, and the love affair ends when the painting is completed. In a striking all-woman outdoor choral scene, the singers clap in unison and sing 'Fugere non possum' ('I cannot flee' in Latin), reflecting the inability of women broadly to be liberated from sexist constraints even as they locate an all-woman space in which to express themselves (as suggested by the song's line later 'Nos resurgemus' ('we will rise up')). Being trapped by external constraints is suggested, too, by the implied reference of Héloïse's name to the title character of one of the most popular novels of the century, Rousseau's *Julie, ou la Nouvelle Héloïse* (1761). This Héloïse falls passionately in love with a humble man named Saint-Preux whom she meets

---

20 This marriage system also has a relation to the film's use of the Orpheus myth (to be discussed later in this chapter). One of the stories that Orpheus sings after he loses his beloved Eurydice is the story of Pygmalion who invented the perfect woman in art and then brought her to life. The story of Héloïse's mother parallels that story as in a certain sense, her artistic rendition is brought to life when she arrives in the flesh. The song of Pygmalion is being sung as a side-story in the film.

early in life but cannot be with because of class difference. She then goes on to marry an older man named Wolmar with whom she spends her life and becomes a mother. If Rousseau's Héloïse is barred from true or authentic love because of class, Sciamma's Héloïse is constrained by the heterosexual marriage system. The novel's main character refers in turn to the medieval Héloïse, the famous lover of Abelard with whom she exchanged a series of letters critical of marriage. The medieval Héloïse writes in her first letter: 'I preferred love to wedlock, freedom to a bond' (*Letters of Abelard and Héloïse*, 1925), a statement that Sciamma's Héloïse could have made as well.

Clearly a love story about two women taking place in eighteenth-century Brittany is a new narrative. But a narrative about what? About lesbianism? The film does not code the relation between then in any morphological way: twentieth-century descriptors such as 'lesbian' and contemporaneous words in linguistic circulation like 'sapphic' or 'tribade' are never used.[21] It is never fully clear whether Héloïse in particular would be described in today's terms as 'lesbian', 'pansexual', or 'bisexual', or whether in fact she simply falls for Marianne as an individual. The film's take on lesbian love is not driven by questions of identity per se, but centred on manoeuvring through pre-existing power relations set by the gendered and sexual order of things. Foucault contrasts the 'deployment of alliance' with 'the deployment of sexuality' that begins to manifest itself in the eighteenth century. The latter deployment is not about 'the link between partners and definite statutes' and 'the economy', but about 'sensations of the body, the quality of pleasures, and the nature of impressions' (1978: 106). If this deployment and exertion of power is beginning in the period, the two women's corporeal pleasures still go unchecked until the alliance system forces an

---

21 See Wahl (1999: 17–42), on contemporary manifestations of same-sex female sexuality.

end to their pleasure and affective links through the family structure. It is also possible that Héloïse's desire arises precisely because of the constraints imposed upon her by the alliance system, corresponding to late-eighteenth-century ideas of 'sapphic love' as – in the words of Jacques Peuchet in his *Methodological Encyclopedia* (1789) – 'caused by constraint, subjection, effervescence of the senses, rather than an actual disorder' (Merrick, 2019: 191).

Despite the ultimate domination of the alliance system, the film corresponds to lesser-known representations of same-sex love in the period that do not involve male representational domination and are not subject to the deployment of sexuality. As Lanser sums it up about the texts that she studies from the century: 'Sapphism has become feminist separatism' (2002: 108).[22] And indeed the film expels men from the narrative: a group of men row Marianne to the island where the family's home is located even as they appear entirely indifferent to her and to her journey. When her blank canvas falls in the water accidentally and she jumps in to save it, the men are uninterested in the problem and unwilling to help. Marianne is diving into an all-female space. Late in the film, after the painting is completed, a messenger appears in the kitchen to take Marianne's painting and deliver it to her suitor in Italy. He leaves with great disinterest in the women. In the penultimate scene at an art opening, a crowd of men walk around the room where Héloïse is displaying her painting as the lone woman in a crowded room of men. This man-framing highlights the woman-only centre in the middle, a narration of feminist separatism that cannot be uncoupled from Enlightenment sapphism.

Also important to feminist separatism is the island setting off the coast in Brittany. The two women are far from places where normative and sexist discourses are being produced, but

---

22 See also Bonnet (2001); Wahl (1999: 75–129), for 'idealized' female–female bonds.

the island setting, established in the second scene as a locus where men are not interested in visiting, evokes the Island of Lesbos where the girl-loving ancient Greek poet Sappho famously lived. The 'mysteries of Lesbos' were indeed a substantial element of eighteenth-century discourses on same-sex love.[23] The two women's relation in the film is expressed in part via visual art, like the Sapphic lyre which put same-sex love into music and poetry, coming into existence apart from hetero-patriarchal constraints in an imagined elsewhere. Sappho's poetry, like the painting in the opening scene, mirrors the dominant image of being on fire: in one of the best known poems, number 31, the poetess sings 'a subtle fire has stolen underneath my flesh' (Campbell, 1982: 81), or in a late seventeenth-century translation: 'Un feu subtile, un feu dangereux, consumant, / S'allume dans mon corps' ('A subtle fire, a fire dangerous and consuming, / Is lit in my body') (Anacreon and Sappho, 1692: 381). Discussing Sapphic love, Peuchet includes that she 'burned' 'with the fire of this love' (Merrick, 2019: 190). The presence of Lesbos in the period was for Bonnet a sign that French royal absolutism was in crisis (2001: 141–2), or that the French Revolution is coming. Sexual non-conformity was less and less something to scorn and more and more what Bonnet calls a 'subject of admiration' (2001: 142), presaging a desirable new social order on the horizon in a French province known to be conservative and royalist. Evoking the now-famous figure of democracy, Marianne's name itself suggests the coming Revolution and its attendant principles of liberty, equality, fraternity (or in this case, sorority).[24]

Still, despite the Sapphic separation and the futurity it may have stood for, the film does not simply liberate same-sex love

23 See the chapter with this title in Bonnet (2001: 139–215).
24 Her name might also be related to Marivaux's unfinished novel *La Vie de Marianne* (1742), about the adventures of an independent woman.

from the constraints under which it would have operated in the period. It is not simply freed up, but remains caught between societal constraints of alliance and free expression. Contextually, the early modern period, Lanser notes in her book on the sapphic, 'witnessed an intensified interest in lesbians' (2014: 1) and at least textually in cases such as the sapphic picaresque, there is in the end 'some kind of sapphic possibility' (163) which may or may not be a happy ending per se. In fact, picaresque texts do not judge the women harshly, but 'turn their judgment against the system' (164) and 'reject both gender and sexuality as social constraints' (165), even as high social standing remained a necessity for this resistance. In the film, Marianne resembles a sapphic picaresque character as she journeys to Brittany to paint her future lover's portrait and is critical of the alliance system, herself resisting marriage but also suggesting that her lover should resist marriage as well. Héloïse's potential rise in social class through marriage means that although she may see the system's injustice, she also enters back into it once the painting is completed. In this way, the film is more akin to texts like Diderot's well-known *La Religieuse (The Nun)* (1796) in which sapphic possibility is opened but then foreclosed or evicted. For the normative social order to continue, Lanser notes, 'the sapphic [must remain] a force of disorder that is resistant to resolution' (2014: 174), which is the case in the film. The painting as object, in particular, inscribes Marianne's desire and, though it is shipped off to a man, is an object inscribed with the disorder of eroticism.

Sciamma's key final scene at the symphony reveals 'a force of disorder' that is neither constrained nor free. Héloïse may be married and the mother of a little girl, and the fact that she does not see Marianne in the symphony hall suggests that she is in another world, one of order that Marianne gazes upon as she gazes upon her former lover who does not see her. Yet, Héloïse has a very strong affective reaction to the memory of their love when she hears Vivaldi's music that takes her back to an earlier scene where her lover had played the same music for her. The long-take affect, without discourse, reveals the permeability of the order that cannot stamp out same-sex affect. The very striking representation of affect reveals queer anti-normativity that does not disband or eradicate heteronormativity but opens it up by resisting resolution and closure. In the end, the film is not simply a story of two women in love that has to end because of cultural constraints. Affective openness – far beyond the realm of language – reveals that discursive conventions of gender and marriage have holes. As she walks towards her seat at the far end of a row of chairs, Héloïse moves along the balcony edge in a way reminiscent of a moment early in the film when she ran to the edge of a cliff, overlooking the sea with a worried Marianne behind her. After stopping cold, she noted that she had wanted for years 'to run', or to be free, even as it seemed to Marianne that she might be heading towards suicide (with the suggestion that she might be following her sister, who may have killed herself, or Sappho, who in in the tradition of Ovid's *Heroides*, jumped off a cliff because of unrequited love for a man). In the final scene, too, Héloïse may not look free, but affective representation suggests freedom from constraint. The final scene resists reading their relation as inconsequential, leaving their love story quite consequential, subject to return at any moment in the form of affect, a stand-in for the fire that consumed her in the painting in the opening scene. Lanser writes about the historical context: 'an erotic intimacy between female confidantes disrupts narrative closure and, in so doing, calls into question the security of heteronormative social order' (2014: 177). Héloïse's affective reaction represents eighteenth-century erotic intimacy, disrupting the cinematic narrative – much as Marianne was disrupted in the opening scene by the woman on fire. The film ends where it began, in a sense, by refusing to allow the heteronormative social order to be fully determinative.

Such a refusal of social order pertains to the viewing present of the film as well as the historical context. The narrative from the past might surprise the viewer for a number of reasons. For one, we do not have, or do not remember, many coherent narratives of same-sex female love from early modern France. Wahl studies the 'rich' presence of such love, even though it is 'fragmentary' (1999: 19). Terry Castle's *The Apparitional Lesbian* documents the ways in which same-sex female sexuality, not yet called lesbianism, are represented beginning in the eighteenth century as ghosts or as phantoms. Marianne and Héloïse here are anything but ghosts: their love affair is unambiguous, erotic, carnal, and deeply emotional. Many narratives of same-sex female love describe or take for granted the figure of the 'tribade', a woman defined as man-like in terms of sexual act and desire. In the sexist logic of early modern France, she is imagined as having an enlarged, penile clitoris and as taking over the man's supposedly natural role with another woman.[25] The 1778 edition of the dictionary of the *Académie Française* defines the tribade as: 'Woman who abuses another woman' ('Femme qui abuse d'une autre femme') (1778: 630).[26] But there is no such tribade here: there is no man-woman who penetrates or 'abuses' the other. In the film's main sex scene, Marianne penetrates Héloïse's armpit, not her vagina, as a sign that this is not a film about a woman with an enlarged clitoris penetrating the vagina of another woman. Neither woman even comes close to being portrayed as the penetrator of the other one, rejecting the very morphology of the tribade. After they kiss for the second time, Héloïse asks Marianne: 'Do [you think] all lovers feel they're inventing something?' Historically speaking, the answer is that these two lovers are inventing a

---

25 A good collection in English of primary sources on Enlightenment tribades is Merrick (2019). See also Creed (1995); Park (1997); Traub (2002).
26 The Enlightenment *Encyclopedia* includes an entry for tribade as 'femme qui a de la passion pour une autre femme' ('woman who experiences passion for another woman'), but adds that it is as inexplicable as a man's love for another man (ARTFL Encyclopédie Project, 2017: 617).

way to be lovers not based in sexist, pathological morphologies such as the tribade, and that they are indeed 'inventing something' – a story and a non-morphology for the twenty-first-century spectator.

Wahl documents the ways in which marriage and love are so disconnected in the period that a space for 'friendship' or other relations while being married was nonetheless a possibility (1999: 75–129). The deployment of alliance represented by the marriage portrait does in fact create the possibility for their relation since the painter needs to come to the island. The very idea of a new form of erotic representation (painting) points to contemporary concerns about being able to locate, as Wahl puts it, 'a language of intimacy that would allow women to speak as autonomous, desiring subjects and not remain within the confines of silence and passivity dictated by their conventional role as objects of desire' (1999: 102). The final show of affect at the concert is its own modern 'language of intimacy' – along with the paintings produced – that does not involve language at all, reconstructing speaking women of the period in affective and visual terms outside the linguistic parameters used to think about the period. Above all, the Sapphic metaphor of fire is rendered in visual, not linguistic, terms both in the painting in the opening scene and in the choral scene where Héloïse's dress actually catches on fire – a precursor to their first kiss. These are new languages of intimacy, expressed in the visual and affective terms facilitated by the medium of film.

While the two women share intimacy without words, they are in a way 'cheating' the patriarchal system, temporarily cheating on deployment of alliance. Interrupting the scenes in which Marianne paints Héloïse is a seemingly random scene that comments on the women's working around these cultural systems. The two women along with the household maid Sophie (Luàna Bajrami) play a fast-moving card game in which each player puts down a card and if a card played is the same as a previous card, the first person to slap the pile of cards picks up all the cards played and keeps them in their own pile. The winner of the game is the one who ends up with all the cards in their pile. At one point, Marianne tells Héloïse that she is cheating. She may well be cheating, but not at cards. Mickäel, in a similar card scene with their dad in *Tomboy*, is also metaphorically cheating in terms of gender, but here Héloïse is cheating not in terms of gender per se, but in terms of living out her desire and resisting marriage. She cheats on her future husband by not remaining the passive object of the patriarchal system. But her response is that she is not cheating, that she is 'playing fast' ('Je joue vite'). In other words, she is moving faster than her cultural context allows. She is, in a sense, ahead of her time – a kind of twenty-first-century character in an eighteenth-century body. Still, she does not win the game that they are playing, she cannot win the game (*fugere non possum*), and she ends up losing out to Marianne who takes the pile of cards. Marianne refuses heterosexuality and marriage outright, has a career as an artist, and in so doing wins at the game that her lover can only temporarily cheat at before she loses out to the deployment of alliance. Héloïse's cheating is temporary because she refuses, despite her lover's wishes, to resist her situation – the entire hetero-patriarchal cultural game that her lover ignores, but she also cheats by virtue of the cinematic narrative, offering up a new way to play the game of gender on screen.

Queering the Orphic gaze

Integral to the ways in which *Portrait* recasts the pre-modern sexual and gender past is the recasting of the ancient myth of the poet Orpheus and his wife Eurydice in the version of the Roman poet Ovid.[27] In a scene at the dining room table after

27 Virgil, too, has an influential version of the myth in *The Georgics* (Book 4).

the halfway point of the film, Marianne, Héloïse, and Sophie sit drinking in the evening in front of the fire as Héloïse reads aloud the myth of Orpheus and Eurydice from a French translation of Book 10 of Ovid's *Metamorphoses*. Orpheus sings to Hades and his wife Persephone to convince them that he be allowed to bring his wife back up to Earth. They consent but tell the poet that he cannot look back on her as they head back to Earth with him in front. But Orpheus 'eager to see her' ('impatient de la voir') 'turns his eyes back' ('tourne les yeux') and looks at her as she falls back to the underworld. The original line in Ovid's Latin notes that Eurydice says nothing but 'good-bye' ('vale') and that she falls back into the place from where she had emerged (1984: 68).[28] The story provokes a lively discussion among the three women about why Orpheus turns his eyes back. Héloïse notes that he is so in love that he cannot resist (and the French translation describes him as 'amoureux époux', 'the husband in love'), but Marianne disagrees, noting that 'the reasons are not serious'. It is not that he is being loving or is eager to see her, but that he makes a choice to look back, that he chooses the 'memory of Eurydice' over the actual Eurydice, or that he 'makes the choice not of the lover but of the poet'. Héloïse counters in the final comment of the scene that perhaps Eurydice tells him to look back on her, in other words that she does not want to be with Orpheus.[29] This queer or feminist rethinking of the myth in some ways resembles Ducastel and Martineau's *Théo et Hugo dans le même bateau* which, as discussed in chapter 1, queers the myth

---

28 The French translation used in the film is not contemporaneous with the period, even though Enlightenment translations were available, but a twentieth-century translation by Latinist Georges Lafaye. For the text read in the film, see Lafaye's translation (Ovid, 1965: 123–4).

29 This idea is not absent from the period. In Pierre-Louis Moline's play *Orphée et Euridice* (1774), Eurydice tells Orpheus: 'I still prefer / Death which distances me from you' (1776: 28).

by transforming the tropes of looking onto two men in love. In this case, the power dynamics between the male poet and his almost entirely silent female beloved are transfigured in the film. Sciamma herself noted that although the idea of including this myth came relatively late in the film's conception, once it was included it allowed for a 'thread' or framing device for the film and filled a hole that she had felt in the story, allowing for the script to be complete (Sciamma, 2020b).

On one level, the myth is transposed on to the two women in love, recurring at a number of points in the remaining parts of the film as a framing device for understanding their relation. As the visual artist not unlike the poet-singer Orpheus, Marianne parallels the man who gazes on the woman he loves and then loses her. At the opening of the film, Marianne arrives on the Breton island alone and then in the dark, austere chateau during nightfall, as if arriving in the underworld. She looks at her lover throughout the film to paint her, and by virtue of painting her, she will lose her beloved, in this case to the male suitor for whom the portrait is being painted. Héloïse maps onto Eurydice as well: she is looked at as an object and she is lost as she is obliged to marry a man. Eurydice's Hades in a certain sense is heterosexuality, the place Héloïse has to remain without Marianne. At one point during the night, she appears as Marianne walks about the castle with a candle, as a figment of her imagination that will haunt her after her departure. She appears a second time in her wedding dress which her mother has had made for her, as both Eurydice and phantom, at the very moment that Marianne leaves the chateau for good. 'Retourne-toi' ('Turn back'), she says, referring back to the Ovidian scene to suggest that by asking Marianne to turn around she will lose her for good (plate 15). Héloïse follows her own reading of the myth of Eurydice, taking agency over the Orphic gaze that causes loss and forcing Marianne to leave her forever.

The myth becomes their story and their story contributes to queering the myth, but it does more than that: it replaces a long-standing Western myth about the male artist who becomes an artist only after his beloved dies. Art is coded as male, and the muse or absent beloved is coded as female, the lack of woman inspiring masculine art. Not so here. In a scene in bed, Marianne sketches an image of herself on page 28 of the Ovidian book from which they read, as their story glosses over the written patriarchal narrative. Héloïse has asked her to leave her an image of herself and the one she produces overlays the written text, adding a new layer to it. Same-sex love, as was the case in *Paris 05:59*, can dismantle the myth predicated on gender domination and the death of the woman, of course, but unlike in Ducastel and Martineau's film, questions of artistic representation here are linked to the depiction of lesbianism. The male directors are able to sidestep the gender issues in the myth by removing women, but here the position of woman is problematized.

While Héloïse as Eurydice has some agency since she tells the Orphic Marianne to turn around, what is more important is that the very link between absence and gender is dismantled. Here Marianne is not the lone artist in charge of representation whose art depicts or 'brings to life' that which is lost or absent. If she is Orphic in nature, she should in theory create art once she loses her beloved, and loss should lead to the production of artistic narrative. That does not happen. During the art exhibition in the penultimate scene, a man comes up to Marianne to comment on what he thinks is her father's painting of Orpheus and Eurydice. Marianne tells him that she entered it in his name but that she painted it. The random man notes its uniqueness, as a painting that does not depict Orpheus before or after the loss, as tends to be the case with paintings of the poet, but at the moment of loss. Further, the moment of loss is reciprocal: 'on dirait qu'ils se saluent' ('it looks as though they are greeting each other'). They are saying goodbye as well as hello via the painting, and Eurydice does not depart and become present only in absence. It is no accident, then, that there is a second painting at the art opening that Marianne gazes upon, namely a portrait of Héloïse with her young daughter. Significantly, her former lover holds a book open to page 28, the very same page on which Marianne had sketched her image. The partially open book, which does not show the image sketched, suggests Marianne's presence in the painting, as someone represented via art (albeit by some other unknown artist) but not as an artist. In a sense, we return to the opening scene where Marianne is both being painted and directing the painting. She is now at the end of the film both artist and represented lost lover. She is, in a sense, Orpheus the poet as well as the dead Eurydice.

But it is in the very final scene that the dismantling of the Orphic myth appears most forcefully. Sciamma has noted in interviews that this scene was the first that she had in mind and that the rest of the film was written and made to lead to this scene.[30] During the performance of Vivaldi's 'Summer', Marianne sees Héloïse from afar, but the latter does not see her. The Vivaldi piece, because Marianne had it played for her on the harpsicord during their love affair, brings back memories like an affective flood, and she begins to sob at the music. Quite simply, Héloïse is not fully absent now, rather she incarnates – to a certain extent at least – Ovid's Orpheus: for tears belong to the poet in the myth. After he loses Eurydice and tries unsuccessfully to return again to Hades, he remains unable to move and 'care, anguish of soul, and tears were his nourishment' (Ovid, 1984: 69). She is the one to feel loss and anguish deeply, and though she does not go on to become an artist and sing poetry as Orpheus does in loss, her depth of feeling is an element of art traditionally belonging to the male poet. Like the musical elements of summer in Vivaldi's music, the affect gestures towards external representation without words.

---

30 See for instance Sciamma's interview with IndieWire (Erbland, 2019).

In Ovid, Eurydice's loss becomes Orpheus's poetic presence and the source of the narrative poetry that he sings at great length, including the songs of Ganymede, Pygmalion, and Adonis – what he describes as songs 'of boys beloved by gods, and maidens inflamed by unnatural love and paying the penalty of their lust' (1984: 75). But that poetic presence in Ovid is based on Eurydice's death or absence. For Héloïse, the poetic functions quite differently. Marianne paints her first version of her portrait and finally shows it to Héloïse, who is not at all happy with it: 'There is no presence', she proclaims. Marianne destroys the painting by disfiguring her head and painting a bar across it, rendering it unusable for the purposes for which it was meant. And she begins again. This time, however, Héloïse will not pose as a passive model, the subject of art, rather she takes agency over the painter gazing at her and helps create presence this time around. Héloïse's presence, including her erotic presence, is transformed into the presence of the painting itself. Art becomes predicated on presence of the beloved, not absence. Such is the case as well with the titular tableau in the opening scene, which disturbs Marianne: as the lady on fire refers to the scene in which Héloïse's dress actually catches on fire. It is not clear however where reality stops and the artistic rendition begins. Is Marianne in the opening scene remembering this past image artistically from the perspective of the present? Or is Héloïse in a sense creating the artistic image from her own vantage point in the narrative? Does the fire, as it were, radiate from her? She may well be artistically agential in this fluid representational mode. Her own experience of eros (fire) invents at least part of the artistic oeuvre. Instead of post-mortem stories of 'maidens inflamed by unnatural love' told by a male poet, the two 'maidens' both have a hand in the narrative's telling.

This transformation of the mythic poetry/object opposition is a narrative about cinematic modernity and part of a twenty-first-century cultural move to reconfigure sexist myths. What is the film saying about artistic historicity? What we could know historically about their relation – were there no film – would be lost in ephemeral affective reactions, in ambiguous painting, and even in the sketch in the middle of Héloïse's Ovid. Marianne does not paint or draw the two of them together to create an erotic tableau. Rather, the film points out that contemporary stories of lesbianism are both present and not present, solid and apparitional, consequential and inconsequential, as was the case in *Naissance des pieuvres*. The lesbian character here highlights very well the theoretical approach to what Valerie Traub calls 'the sign of the lesbian': 'In the history of lesbian representation, "the lesbian" is simultaneously known and not known, simultaneously signified and rendered insignificant' (2016: 287). Eurydice might become an apparition as she falls back to Hades, but she is present for Orpheus. Here, she is both signified and insignificant, she is left behind and she remains. The point is not only that Eurydice's voice must be heard and that she has more to say than 'farewell', but that she is not simply present or absent to the poet. The Enlightenment lesbian, likewise, is both present and absent to Sciamma the cinematic artist. Considering lesbianism does not require knowing the past based on what remains of it, or as Traub puts it, ' "the lesbian" [does not] allude or lead to epistemological surety, but rather to the obstacles, difficulties, and recalcitrance of knowledge relations' (2016: 286). No written record remains of the two women's love; the painting with the page open to page 28 is unreadable to anyone except Héloïse, pointing out how this kind of love is not immediately knowable. Traub notes: ' "the lesbian" is what *we have never known* and what has *resisted knowledge* across a remarkable enduring set of cultural coordinates' (2016: 291, italics in original). Sciamma is not simply telling a love story, then, she is also telling the story of same-sex love as what we know in film, but do not know about the actual historical context. The film reveals a gap between knowing lesbianism cinematically and not knowing or not being able to know historically. By representing lesbianism for historical posterity, the film will disrupt future viewers, like the titular tableau in the opening scene, because it is an untold narrative.

Queer dialogues

While my approach to the film centres around its relation to lesbian representation and to the Orphic myth, the film should be considered as well in relation to film history. Sciamma herself has noted that the film is in dialogue with David Lynch's *Mulholland Drive* (2001), Ingmar Bergman's *Persona* (1966) and Hitchcock broadly (Big Picture Podcast, 2020). The film in a sense extends the lesbian representational questions in Lynch's film, reconsidering the erotic heterosexual male cultural fantasy of two attractive women and, on the other hand, of the supposed impossibility of two women to love each other (the tragedy of lesbianism) (see Love, 2004). It is true that *Portrait*'s two women are attractive and also that their affair does not end happily ever after, but the representational questions comment more squarely on the historicity and the Orphic than they do on cultural fantasies.

In the director's narration on the French version of the DVD, Sciamma states that the arrival on the beach in the second scene is a reference to ('une pensée pour') Jane Campion (Sciamma, 2020c). The second scene of her landmark film *The Piano* (1993) shows the main character Ada arriving by boat on the beach in New Zealand – like Marianne arriving in Brittany – where she is to move inland to meet the man that she has not met but is supposed to marry. In both cases, the women are brought by an all-male crew of oarsmen to the beach and then head through rough terrain to the house where they are supposed to be. Each woman arrives with an object embodying potential for female self-expression, Ada with piano and Marianne with canvas. Ada parallels Héloïse, too, as both women have been promised to men for marriage without their consent. We later learn that

Ada's future husband Alisdair has been sent a painting of her in advance, as will be the case with Héloïse.

At the same time as Sciamma's film channels Campion, it also establishes that something new will take place here and will extend and go beyond the older film. For Campion, patriarchy begins as the problem and Ada begins as a pure object of exchange between men. Her arrival on the beach is filmed not as her arrival per se, for a group of men's hands and arms help move her from the boat to the shore. A shot from below the boat is the only one seen as the boat comes in, as Ada is not a visible subject entering the film. She enters the film through the male body, the men's extended arms showing that she is an appendage of male masculinity. The entry of the woman main character in Sciamma is not brought about by men: Marianne has been called by Héloïse's mother, not her father, and the men rowing the boat to bring her to the island where she will paint are shot from the back, the camera focused on the oars that they are rowing, not on their bodies or arms. The man who steers the boat is the one man whose face we do see, and he leads her to the beach and gives directions to the house where she is headed once Marianne asks where it is. He conveys masculine disinterest in the female story: when he returns later to pick up the completed painting, he departs painting in hand, not even saying goodbye, remaining indifferent to the narrative. This opening scene, then, replays Campion's but in a new manner. This will not be a story about patriarchal masculinity's control over women's bodies (or attempts at control) through the regulatory institution of marriage. Men are not part of the story and the story will take place 'behind their backs'. In Campion, the men from the boat urinate in a circle on the beach once they arrive, marking the territory of the beach – but also of the story – as a male space. Sciamma's beach and landscape will be an all-woman space, a no-man's land where another gendered story can and will take place.

Sciamma's opening scene is also a reference to the penultimate scene of *The Piano* in which Ada and George – the man she was not supposed to marry – are leaving in a boat like the one on which Ada arrived early in the film, with her piano on board. Ada insists that the piano be thrown overboard and when it is, her foot gets stuck in a cord attached to the piano and she is thrown into the water to drown. Something very similar happens to Marianne in the rowboat when her blank canvas falls in the water and she jumps in to save it. In each case, the object by which the woman character expresses herself in patriarchal culture goes overboard. For Ada, the entry into water is a rebirth and a renewal, and she is shown playing another piano in the next scene as she now lives with George in a house in town. Her mode of expression is maintained but in a new way, less patriarchal than before. Marianne's mode of expression is about to begin anew as well: the canvas is empty and the loss of the canvas in the water is a baptism, an entry point into a new form of portraiture which will be predicated on representing lesbian desire on the canvas. She jumps in, and we should too. At first, Marianne paints Héloïse in traditional, academic ways, and new ways of painting with 'presence' will come later on. So while Ada's piano overboard looks back and rejects a past, Marianne's canvas overboard looks forward and suggests a representational future to come. What this 'thought' suggests, then, is that Sciamma's scene begins with Ada in the background, extending the character's musical self into the realm of the visual. Sciamma is picking up where Campion ended as much as she is retelling a story of heterosexual feminism in a queer manner.[31]

It would be impossible in French film for the Orphic myth to be evoked without some kind of comparison to the canonical and influential Orphic films of Jean Cocteau, and particularly his most well-known film *Orphée* (*Orpheus*) (1950). Cocteau's take on the ancient myth takes innumerable liberties,

---

31 The feminism of *The Piano* is a complicated topic however. For an overview, see Polan (2001: 44–5).

and only some key elements of the original myth are maintained, even as the film remains a story about Orphic artistry. Cocteau splits the figure of Eurydice into two characters, one being his wife called Eurydice and the other the Princess who is the source of erotic attraction. A third woman character named Aglaonice is also invented. Still, the film by and large maintains the objectification of the women characters. As Rebecca Conolly notes, 'each of the three female characters in *Orphée*, although seemingly vital players in the film's action, are ultimately restricted to the role of dramatic device – serving solely to forward and ensure the completion of Orpheus' heroic quest for artistic immortality' (1999: 146). In the film, Cocteau's mirror repeatedly serves as the portal between the world of the living and the underworld, suggesting a narcissistic masculinity that will achieve poetic greatness. Sciamma's film rejects the women as dramatic devices, as they are the vital players of the narrative. Marianne is far from narcissistic and she is not focused on herself in order to become an artist. When Marianne uses a mirror to see herself so that she can draw herself in Héloïse's book, her goal is not artistic greatness, but the desire to leave a form of visual presence for her lover after she is gone. In this way, Sciamma's film might be seen as a corollary to Jacques Demy's *Parking* (1985), which updates Cocteau's film and the Orpheus myth to the musical world of the 1980s and includes some queer/bisexual elements (see chapter 1).

Finally, the title of Sciamma's film evokes the title of a one-hour made for television film directed by Belgian director Chantal Akerman: *Portrait d'une jeune fille de la fin des années 60 à Bruxelles* (*Portait of a Young Woman in the late 60s in Brussels*) (1994). In interviews, Sciamma has expressed her debt to Akerman, particularly in the area of mise en scène.[32] The scene in which the three women characters

---

32 See for instance Sciamma's interview with Lannoy (2019).

prepare dinner at a long table, all on one side, and then tell and debate the story of Orpheus and Eurydice recalls the framing that Akerman is known for, particularly in her best-known film *Jeanne Dielman, 23, quai du commerce, 1080 Bruxelles* (1975). Akerman's long takes of Jeanne Dielman doing day-to-day chores – especially at the kitchen or dinner table – in juxtaposition with other non-domestic elements – brings attention to women's work in its specificity and thereby, as Margulies argues, 'questions an essentialist view of woman' (1996: 143). Sciamma, too, deessentializes the category of woman, to be sure, but she also performs the representational work necessary to dismantle a male-dominated narrative around Orpheus by retelling the male-centred story of artistry.

References

Anacreon and Sappho (1692), *Les Œuvres d'Anacreon et de Sapho*, Paris, Charles Clouzier.

ARTFL Encyclopédie Project (2017), *Encyclopédie, ou dictionnaire raisonné des sciences, des arts et des métiers, etc.*, Denis Diderot, Jean le Rond d'Alembert, Robert Morrissey, and Glenn Roe, eds, Chicago, University of Chicago, encyclopedie.uchicago.edu.pitt.idm.oclc.org (accessed 3 June 2021).

Belot, Sophie (2012), 'Céline Sciamma's *La Naissance des pieuvres* (2007): Seduction and Be-coming', *Studies in French Cinema*, 12, 2, 169–84.

The Big Picture Podcast (2020), 'Céline Sciamma on The Big Picture Podcast', *YouTube*, www.youtube.com/watch?v=0YuVj6l-sDk (accessed 3 June 2021).

Bonnet, Marie-Joe (2001), *Les Relations amoureuses entre les femmes: XVIe–XXe siècle*, Paris, Odile Jacob.

Bradbury-Rance, Clara (2019), *Lesbian Cinema After Queer Theory*, Edinburgh, Edinburgh University Press.

British Film Institute (2019), 'Screen Talk with Tricia Tuttle', *BFI London Film Festival 2019*, www.youtube.com/watch?v=gzb40RY-E6w (accessed 23 August 2021).

Campbell, David A., ed. and trans. (1982), *Greek Lyric, I, Sappho, Alcaeus*, Cambridge, MA, Harvard University Press.

Castle, Terry (1993), *The Apparitional Lesbian: Female Homosexuality and Modern Culture*, New York, Columbia University Press.

Conolly, Rebecca (1999), 'Servicing Orpheus: Death, Love and Female Subjectivity in the Film *Orphée*', in C. D. E. Tolton, ed., *The Cinema of Jean Cocteau*, Ottawa, Legas, pp. 145–62.

Creed, Barbara (1995), 'Lesbian Bodies: Tribades, Tomboys and Tarts', in Elizabeth Grosz and Elspeth Probyn, eds, *Sexy Bodies: The Strange Carnalities of Feminism*, London and New York, Routledge, pp. 86–103.

Dawson, Tom (2008), 'Interview-Céline Sciamma', *The List*, film.list.co.uk/article/6997-interview-celine-sciamma (accessed 13 October 2020).

Delorme, Stéphane (2007), 'La Grande Séduction', *Cahiers du cinéma*, 626, September, 32–3.

Dictionnaire de l'Académie françoise (1778), II, Nimes, Pierre Beaume.

Douin, Jean-Louis (2014), '*Naissance des pieuvres*', *Le Monde*, www.lemonde.fr/culture/article/2014/03/21/naissance-des-pieuvres_4383281_3246.html (accessed 10 October 2020).

Edney, Gemma (2020), 'Electronica, Gender and French Cinematic Girlhood in Céline Sciamma's Films', *French Screen Studies*, 20, 3–4, 285–97.

Erbland, Kate (2019), '*Portrait of a Lady on Fire*: Filmmaker Céline Sciamma is Trying to Break Your Heart', *IndieWire*, www.indiewire.com/2019/12/portrait-of-a-lady-on-fire-filmmaker-celine-sciamma-interview-1202193537 (accessed 3 June 2021).

La Fémis (n.d.), 'Céline Sciamma, scénariste', www.femis.fr/index.php?page=fiche_ancien&id_ancien=4984 (accessed 3 June 2021).

Fennessey, Sean and Amanda Dobbins (2020), 'Have the Academy Awards Changed for Good? A Post-"Parasite" Oscars Mailbag', *Ringer*, www.theringer.com/2020/2/12/21134465/have-academy-awards-changed-for-good-post-parasite-oscars-mailbag (accessed 4 August 2020).

Foucault, Michel (1978), *The History of Sexuality: An Introduction*, I, trans. Robert Hurley, New York, Pantheon.

Gibson, Brian (2016), 'Falling for Innocence: Transchild Freedom vs. Adult Judgment in *Tomboy* and *Ma vie en rose*', *Children's Literature*, 44, 1, 219–37.

Handyside, Fiona (2016), 'Emotion, Girlhood, and Music in *Naissance des pieuvres* (Céline Sciamma, 2007) and *Un amour de jeunesse* (Mia Hansen-Løve, 2011)', in Fiona Handyside and Kate Taylor-Jones, eds, *International Cinema and the Girl*, New York, Palgrave Macmillan, pp. 121–33.

Jagose, Annamarie (2002), *Inconsequence: Lesbian Representation and the Logic of Sexual Sequence*, Ithaca, Cornell University Press.

Jonet, M. Catherine (2017), 'Desire and Queer Adolescence: Céline Sciamma's *Naissance des Pieuvres*', *The Journal of Popular Culture*, 50, 5, 1127–42.

Lannoy, Stéphanie (2019), '"Je pense plus à Chantal Akerman qu'à Vermeer", Céline Sciamma, *Portrait de la jeune fille en feu*', *Madame fait son Cinéma*, madamefaitsoncinema.be/2019/09/28/je-pense-plus-a-chantal-ackermann-qua-wermer-celine-sciamma-portrait-de-la-jeune-fille-en-feu (accessed 3 June 2021).

Lanser, Susan (2002), '"Au sein de vos pareilles": Sapphic Separatism in Late Eighteenth-Century France', *Journal of Homosexuality*, 41, 3–4, 105–16.

Lanser, Susan S. (2014), *The Sexuality of History: Modernity and the Sapphic, 1565–1830*, Chicago, University of Chicago Press.

Leduc, Violette (2015), *Thérèse and Isabelle*, trans. Sophie Lewis, New York, The Feminist Press.

Lefèvre, Raphaël (2007), 'Glissement progressif du désir', *Critikat*, www.critikat.com/actualite-cine/critique/naissance-des-pieuvres (accessed 2 June 2021).

The Letters of Abelard and Heloise (1925), trans. C. K. Scott Moncrieff, New York, Alfred A. Knopf, webspace.ship.edu/cgboer/heloise.html (accessed 2 June 2021).

Love, Heather K. (2004), 'Spectacular Failure: The Figure of the Lesbian in *Mulholland Drive*', *New Literary History*, 35, 1, 117–32.

McNeill, Isabelle (2018), ' "Shine Bright Like a Diamond": Music, Performance and Digitextuality in Céline Sciamma's *Bande de filles* (2014)', *Studies in French Cinema*, 18, 4, 326–40.

Margulies, Ivone (1996), *Nothing Happens: Chantal Akerman's Hyperrealist Everyday*, Durham, NC, Duke University Press.

Merrick, Jeffrey, ed. (2019), *Sodomites, Pederasts, and Tribades in Eighteenth-Century France: A Documentary History*, State College, Penn State Press.

Moline, Pierre-Louis (1776), *Orphée et Euridice*, Paris, Delormel.

Mouflard, Claire (2016), '"Il y a des règles": Gender, Surveillance, and Circulation in Céline Sciamma's *Bande de filles*', *Women in French Studies*, 24, 1, 113–26.

Oumano, Elena (2011), *Cinema Today: A Conversation with Thirty-nine Filmmakers from around the World*, New Brunswick, Rutgers University Press.

Ovid (1965), *Les Métamorphoses*, II, trans. Georges Lafaye, Paris, Les Belles Lettres.

Ovid (1984), *Metamorphoses: Books IX–XV*, trans. Frank Justus Miller, Cambridge, MA, Harvard University Press.

Paris, Gilles (2002), *Autobiographie d'une courgette*, Paris, Plon.

Park, Katherine (1997), 'The Rediscovery of the Clitoris: French Medicine and the Tribade, 1570–1620', in Carla Mazzio and David Hillman, eds, *The Body in Parts: Fantasies of Corporeality in Early Modern Europe*, New York, Routledge, pp. 171–93.

Polan, Dana (2001), *Jane Campion*, London, British Film Institute.

Prosser, Jay (1998), *Second Skins: The Body Narratives of Transsexuality*, New York, Columbia University Press.

Proust, Marcel (1919), *Du côté de chez Swann, À la recherche du temps perdu*, Paris, Gallimard.

Proust, Marcel (1982), *Swann's Way, Remembrance of Things Past*, I, trans. C. K. Scott Moncrieff and Terence Kilmartin, New York, Vintage Books.

Reeser, Todd W. (2010), *Masculinities in Theory*, Malden, Wiley-Blackwell.

Saunders, Keeley (2014), 'Gender-defined Spaces, Places and Tropes: Contemporary Transgender Representation in *Tomboy* and *Romeos*', *Journal of European Popular Culture*, 5, 2, 181–93.

Schultz, Gretchen (2014), *Sapphic Fathers: Discourses of Same-Sex Desire From Nineteenth-Century France*, Toronto, University of Toronto Press.

Sciamma, Céline (2015), DVD Commentary, *Bande de filles*, Pyramide Video, DVD.

Sciamma, Céline (2020a), 'Céline Sciamma on the Cinema Utopia, the Cinema of Her Teens', British Film Institute, www.bfi.org.uk/sight-and-sound/interviews/dream-palaces/celine-sciamma-on-cinema-utopia (accessed 3 June 2021).

Sciamma, Céline (2020b), Interview with Sciamma, *Portrait of a Lady on Fire*, Criterion Collection, DVD.

Sciamma, Céline (2020c), DVD Commentary, *Portrait de la jeune fille en feu*, Pyramide Vidéo, DVD.

Smith, Frances (2020), Bande de Filles*: Girlhood Identities in Contemporary France*, Abingdon and New York: Routledge.

Stockton, Kathryn Bond (2009), *The Queer Child, or Growing Sideways in the Twentieth Century*, Durham, NC, Duke University Press.

Traub, Valerie (2002), *The Renaissance of Lesbianism in Early Modern England*, Cambridge, Cambridge University Press.

Traub, Valerie (2016), *Thinking Sex with the Early Moderns*, Philadelphia, University of Pennsylvania Press.

Tremblay, Odile (2020), 'Dans la nef des femmes avec Céline Sciamma', *Le Devoir*, www.ledevoir.com/culture/cinema/572448/dans-la-nef-des-femmes-avec-celine-sciamma (accessed 22 September 2021).

Wahl, Elizabeth Susan (1999), *Invisible Relations: Representations of Female Intimacy in the Age of Enlightenment*, Stanford, Stanford University Press.

Waldron, Darren (2013), 'Embodying Gender Nonconformity in "Girls": Céline Sciamma's *Tomboy*', *Esprit créateur*, 53, 1, 30–73.

White, Patricia (1999), *unInvited: Classical Hollywood Cinema and Lesbian Representability*, Bloomington, Indiana University Press.

Wilson, Emma (2017), 'Scenes of Hurt and Rapture: Céline Sciamma's *Girlhood*', *Film Quarterly*, 70, 3, 10–22.

Filmographies

For further information on the films, see www.imdb.com, cboboxoffice.com, and www.unifrance.org.

Filmography: Olivier Duscatel and Jacques Martineau

Le Goût de plaire (1987) (Ducastel only)

10 minutes
Screenplay: Olivier Ducastel
Principal actors: Anne Alvaro (Hélène), Christiane Millet (Cécile), Jacques Bonaffé (Geoffroy)

Jeanne et le garçon formidable (1998)

98 minutes
Screenplay: Olivier Ducastel, Jacques Martineau
Principal actors: Virginie Ledoyen (Jeanne), Mathieu Demy (Olivier), Jacques Bonaffé (François), Frédéric Gorny (Jean-Baptiste)

Drôle de Félix (2000)

95 minutes
Screenplay: Olivier Ducastel, Jacques Martineau

Principal actors: Sami Bouajila (Félix), Patachou (Mathilde), Ariane Ascaride (Isabelle), Pierre-Loup Rajot (Daniel), Charly Sergue (Jules), Maurice Bénichou (fisherman/father figure)

Ma vraie vie à Rouen (2002)

102 minutes
Screenplay: Olivier Ducastel, Jacques Martineau
Principal actors: Jimmy Tavares (Etienne), Ariane Ascaride (Caroline), Jonathan Zaccaï (Laurent), Hélène Surgère (the grandmother), Lucas Bonnifait (Ludovic)

Crustacés et coquillages (2004)

93 minutes
Screenplay: Olivier Ducastel, Jacques Martineau
Principal actors: Valeria Bruni Tedeschi (Béatrix), Gilbert Melki (Marc), Jacques Bonnaffé (Mathieu), Romain Torres (Charly), Edouard Collin (Martin), Jean-Marc Barr (Didier)

Nés en 68 (2008)

173 minutes
Screenplay: Olivier Ducastel, Jacques Martineau, with Catherine Corsini, Guillaume Le Touze, François-Olivier Rousseau
Principal actors: Laetitia Casta (Catherine), Yannick Renier (Yves), Yann Trégouët (Hervé), Christine Citti (Maryse), Marc Citti (Serge), Sabrina Seyvecou (Ludmilla), Théo Frilet (Boris)

L'Arbre et la forêt (2010)

97 minutes
Screenplay: Olivier Ducastel, Jacques Martineau
Principal actors: Guy Marchand (Frédérick), Françoise Fabian (Marianne), Sabrina Seyvecou (Delphine), Yannick Renier (Rémi), François Négret (Guillaume), Catherine Mouchet (Françoise), Sandrine Dumas (Elizabeth), Pierrre-Loup Rajot (Charles)

Juste la fin du monde (2010)

99 minutes
Screenplay (original play): Jean-Luc Lagarce
Principal actors: Pierre Louis-Calixte (Louis), Catherine Ferran (the mother), Elsa Lepoivre (Catherine), Julie Sicard (Suzanne), Laurent Stocker (Antoine)

Théo et Hugo dans le même bateau (2016)

97 minutes
Screenplay: Olivier Ducastel, Jacques Martineau
Principal actors: Geoffrey Couët (Théo), François Nambot (Hugo)

Haut perchés (2019)

90 minutes
Screenplay: Olivier Ducastel, Jacques Martineau
Principal actors: Manika Auxire (Veronika), Geoffrey Couët (Marius), Simon Frenay (Nathan), François Nambot (Louis), Lawrence Valin (Lawrence)

Filmography: Alain Guiraudie

Les Héros sont immortels (1990)

16 minutes
Screenplay: Alain Guiraudie
Principal actors: Alain Guiraudie, Jean-Claude Feugnet

Jours perdus (1993)

25 minutes
Principal actors: Aurore Fagmen, Celine Laprevost, Eric Palssnig, Vanessa Randuineau

Tout droit jusqu'au matin (1994)

10 minutes
Screenplay: Alain Guiraudie
Principal actors: Stéphane Valgalier (young man), Christian Ducasse (the painter)

La Force des choses (1997)

16 minutes
Screenplay: Alain Guiraudie
Principal actors: Morgan Nicolas, Martial Petit, Polo

Du soleil pour les gueux (2000)

55 minutes
Screenplay: Alain Guiraudie
Principal actors: Isabelle Girardet (Nathalie Sanchez), Jean-Paul Jourdaa (Pool Oxanosas Daï), Michel Turquin (Carol Izba), Alain Guiraudie (Djema Gaouda Lon)

Ce vieux rêve qui bouge (2000)

50 minutes
Screenplay: Alain Guiraudie
Principal actors: Pierre Louis-Calixte (Jacques), Jean-Marie Combelles (Donand), Jean Segani (Louis), Yves Dinse (Marc), Serge Ribes (Hubert), Jean-Claude Montheil (José), Rui Fernandes (Pierre), Jérôme Mancet (Robert), Laurent Lunetta (Laurent)

Pas de repos pour les braves (2003)

107 minutes
Screenplay: Alain Guiraudie, Frédéric Videau
Principal actors: Thomas Suire (Basile Matin/Hector), Laurent Soffiati (Johnny Got), Thomas Blanchard (Igor), Vincent Martin II (Bodowski), Pierre-Maurice Nouvei (Sorano), Roger Guidone (Roger)

Voici venu le temps (2005)

93 minutes
Screenplay: Alain Guiraudie, Catherine Ermakoff
Principal actors: Eric Bougnon (Fogo Lompla), Guillaume Viry (Jonas Soforan), Pierre-Louis Calixte (Radovan Remila Stoï), Jacques Buron (Rimamba Stomadis Bron)

On m'a volé mon adolescence (2007)

52 minutes
Principal actors: Chivaun Corney (Evelyne), Pénélope Biessy (Martine), Laure Calamy (the mother), Jessica Goldman (Sylvine), Regis Romele (the father), Luc Guiol (Hervé)

Le Roi de l'évasion (2009)

97 minutes
Screenplay: Alain Guiraudie, Laurent Lunetta
Principal actors: Ludovic Berthillot (Armand Lacourtade), Hafsia Herzi (Curly Durandot), Pascal Aubert (Paul), François Clavier (commissioner), Bruno Valayer (Jean-Jacques), Jean Toscan (Jean)

L'Inconnu du lac (2012)

97 minutes
Screenplay: Alain Guiraudie
Principal actors: Pierre Deladonchamps (Franck), Christophe Paou (Michel), Patrick d'Assumçao (Henri), Jérôme Chappatte (inspector)

Rester vertical (2016)

98 minutes
Screenplay: Alain Guiraudie
Principal actors: Damien Bonnard (Léo), India Hair (Marie), Raphaël Thiéry (Jean-Louis), Christian Bouillette (Marcel), Basile Meilleurat (Yoan), Sébastien Novac (producer)

Filmography: Sébastien Lifshitz

Il faut que je l'aime (1994)

10 minutes
Screenplay: Stéphane Bouquet, Sébastien Lifshitz
Principal actors: Valérie Mréjen (Juliette), Florence Giorgetti (voice), Hélène Foubert (voice), Philippe Demarle (voice)

Claire Denis, la vagabonde (1995)

48 minutes
Principal actors: Claire Denis (self)

Les Corps ouverts (1997)

48 minutes
Screenplay: Stéphane Bouquet, Sébastien Lifshitz
Principal actors: Yasmine Belmadi (Rémi), Pierre-Loup Rajot (Marc), Margot Abascal (girlfriend), Malik Zidi (friend), Mohamed Damraoui (father), Sébastien Lifshitz (trick)

Les Terres Froides (1999)

60 minutes
Screenplay: Stéphane Bouquet, Sébastien Lifshitz
Principal actors: Yasmine Belmadi (Djamel), Bernard Verley (M Chamblasse), Valérie Donzelli (Isabelle), Sébastien Charles (Laurent), Florence Giorgetti (Mme Chamblasse)

Presque rien (2000)

90 minutes
Screenplay: Stéphane Bouquet, Sébastien Lifshitz
Principal actors: Jérémie Elkaïm (Mathieu), Stéphane Rideau (Cédric), Marie Matheron (Annick), Dominique Reymond (the mother), Nils Öhlund (Pierre), Réjane Kerdaffrec (psychiatrist)

La Traversée (2001)

85 minutes
Screenplay: Stéphane Bouquet, Sébastien Lifshitz
Principal actors: Stéphane Bouquet (self), Sébastien Lifshitz (self)

Wild Side (2004)

93 minutes
Screenplay: Stéphane Bouquet, Sébastien Lifshitz
Principal actors: Stéphanie Michelini (Stéphanie), Yasmine Belmadi (Djamel), Edouard Nikitine (Mikhail), Josiane Stoléru (Stéphanie's mother), Corentin Carinos (young Pierre), Benoît Verhaert (Pierre's father), Christophe Sermet (Nicolas)

Les Témoins (2006)

45 minutes
Principal actors: Jonathan, Christophe, Frédéric

Jour et nuit (2008)

8 minutes

Plein sud (2009)

90 minutes
Screenplay: Stéphane Bouquet, Vincent Poymiro, Sébastien Lifshitz
Principal actors: Yannick Renier (Sam), Léa Seydoux (Léa), Théo Frilet (Mathieu), Pierre Perrier (Jérémie), Nicole Garcia (Sam's mother)

Les Invisibles (2012)

115 minutes
Principal actors: Thérèse Clerc (self), Monique Isselé (self), others as themselves

Bambi (2013)

58 minutes
Principal actors: Marie-Pierre Pruvot/Bambi

Les Vies de Thérèse (2016)

55 minutes
Principal actors: Thérèse Clerc (self)

Adolescentes (2019)

135 minutes
Principal actors: Anaïs (self), Emma (self)

Où en êtes-vous, Sébastien Lifshitz? (2019)

6 minutes
Principal actor: Sébastien Lifshitz (voice)

Petite Fille (2020)

90 minutes
Principal actors: Sasha (self), Sasha's mother and father (selves)

Filmography: Céline Sciamma

Naissance des pieuvres (2007)

85 minutes
Screenplay: Céline Sciamma
Principal actors: Pauline Acquart (Marie), Adèle Haenel (Floriane), Louise Blachère (Anne), Warren Jacquin (François)

Pauline (2010)

Part of collection '5 films contre l'homophobie'
8 minutes
Screenplay: Daphné Charbonneau (original idea)
Principal actors: Anaïs Demoustier (Pauline), Adèle Haenel (girlfriend)

Tomboy (2011)

82 minutes
Screenplay: Céline Sciamma
Principal actors: Zoé Haran (Laure/Mickäel), Jeanne Disson (Lisa), Malonn Lévana (Jeanne), Sophie Cattani (the mother), Mathieu Demy (the father)

Bande de filles (2014)

112 minutes
Screenplay: Céline Sciamma
Principal actors: Karidja Touré (Marieme/Vic), Assa Sylla (Lady), Lindsay Karamoh (Adiatou), Mariétou Touré (Fily), Idrissa Diabaté (Ismaël), Djibril Gueye (Abou)

Portrait de la jeune fille en feu (2019)

120 minutes
Screenplay: Céline Sciamma
Principal actors: Noémie Merlant (Marianne), Adèle Haenel (Héloïse), Luàna Bajrami (Sophie), Valeria Golino (the countess)

Index

À l'ami qui ne m'a pas sauvé la vie 43
Abelard and Héloïse 291
Académie Française, dictionary of 296
Adam est...Eve 212
Adolescentes 176, 321
Adonis 303
Adventures of Felix, The see Drôle de Félix
Akerman, Chantal 30, 308–9
Allen, Richard 135
Amateur 174
L'Ami de mon amie 268
L'Amour est à réinventer 44
Amoureux, Les 31
Anglo-American culture 26, 58, 72
Anohni 211
anti-social thesis (queer theory) 6–8, 10
L'Arbre et la forêt 39, 72–6, 315
Archer, Neil 55
Arroyo, José 49, 56
Asibong, Andrew 31, 32
assemblage 9, 11, 12, 270
Audiard, Jacques 252
audience response 20–3
Autobiographie d'une courgette 253

Bambi 28, 176, 238, 240–2, 321
Bande de filles 28, 172, 249, 251, 280–8, 322
banlieue 280–8
Barker, Jennifer 22
Barras, Claude 253
Bataille, Georges 117–18
Baudrillard, Jean 213
becoming 2, 8–13, 15, 18, 19, 21, 23, 44, 133, 160, 224, 225, 250, 268
Being 17 see Quand on a 17 ans
Belle Saison, La 31, 240
Belot, Sophie 250, 265, 266
Bergman, Ingmar 305
Berlin International Film Festival, awards 28
Bersani, Leo 7, 129
beur 4, 25, 53, 178–203, 218
bisexuality 9
Bitter Tears of Petra von Kant, The 106
Bivel, Didier 24
Blanchot, Maurice 85, 96
Blue 286
Bonnet, Marie-Jo 293
Born in 68 see Nés en 68
Bouquet, Stéphane 232–8
Bourdieu, Pierre 97

Boyfriends and Girlfriends 268
Boyle, Clare 64, 65
BPM/120 Battements par minute 32
Bradbury-Rance, Clara 256, 257, 259, 270
Braidotti, Rosi 10, 11
Brokeback Mountain 158
Brun, Catherine 78
Bullot, Fabienne 144

Cairns, Lucille 7
Calderón de la Barca, Pedro 151–3
Campillo, Robin 32
Campion, Jane 305–7
capitalism 18, 115, 116, 138, 139, 142–8, 154, 196, 199, 268
Casablanca 241
Castle, Terry 260, 296
Catullus 47
Cazzeneuve, Fabrice 24
Ce vieux rêve qui bouge 115, 118, 142–8, 317
Céline et Julie vont en bateau 92
César 24, 29, 119, 154, 238
Chambers, Ross 181
Chambre 212 32
Chansons d'amour 32
Chéreau, Patrice 7, 30
Cheval, Olivier 141
Children's Hour, The 27
cisnormativity, defined 2
Claire Denis, la vagabonde 176–7, 319
Clara cet été là 256
Cléo de 5 à 7 92
closet *see* coming-out film
Cocteau, Jean 84, 307–8
Cold Lands see Terres froides, Les

Collard, Cyril 43
colonial stereotypes of passive Arab men 191
Come Undone see Presque rien
coming-out film 24, 39, 57–76, 81–2, 134, 205, 255, 256
Concours, Le 27
Conley, Verena 19
Conolly, Rebecca 308
Corneille, Pierre 59
Corps ouverts, Les 169, 211, 232, 176, 178–95, 232, 319
Corsini, Catherine 31, 240
Côte d'Azur see Crustacés et coquillages
Crossing, The see Traversée, La
Crustacés et coquillages 39, 67–72, 73, 82, 93, 107, 315

Dalton, Benjamin 117, 129, 156
Damiens, Antoine 29
Dans Paris 32
Dasgupta, Sudeep 198
Davis, Nick 15–16, 21, 87
Debussy, Claude 244
Deleuze, Gilles 16
Deleuze, Gilles and Félix Guattari 8, 9, 10, 11, 14–16, 139, 149, 224, 225
Delorme, Stéphane 256, 270
D'Emilio, John 144, 145
Demoiselles de Rochefort, Les 40
Demy, Jacques 40, 45, 99–101, 277, 308
Demy, Mathieu 41, 100, 276, 277
Denis, Claire 176

Désir homosexuel, Le 14, 124
Diderot, Denis 294
Dolan, Xavier 80
Don't Look Down see *Haut perchés*
Douin, Jean-Louis 255
Drôle de Félix 29, 39, 48–56, 65, 107, 166, 314
Du soleil pour les gueux 115, 136–40, 142, 168, 317
Ducastel, Olivier 16, 27
Ducastel, Olivier and Jacques Martineau 21, 28, 29
Duncan, Leslie 228

Eastern Boys 32
Edelman, Lee 8
Edney, Gemma 259
Encore 44, 46
Eribon, Didier 72
Ernaux, Annie 94, 95, 97
Essais 13, 192
Eurydice 98
Eurydice and lesbianism 303–5
Eurydice and Orpheus 305
Eurydice ou l'homme de dos 96
Evans, Caroline and Lorraine Gamman 21
existentialism 106

Family Tree see *L'Arbre et la forêt*
Farocki, Harun 143
Fassbinder, Rainer 106, 121
Faucon, Philippe 256
Faure, Christian 24
Felski, Rita 213
Fémis, La 16, 27, 252
film festivals 28–9
Fisher King 51
Force des choses, La 136, 317

Force of Circumstance see *Force des choses, La*
Foucault, Michel 65, 66, 68, 289, 291
Foulon, Jérôme 212
Fournier, Mat 11
Fracture, La 31
Friedman, Nathan 123
Funchess, Sharon 282
futurity 1–3, 16, 17, 18, 24, 30, 49, 56, 76, 104, 106, 158, 203, 210, 214, 279, 280, 284, 293

Ganymede 303
Gautier, Théophile 147
Gaveau, René 212
Genet, Jean 13, 121
Gerstner, David and Julien Nahmias 32
Gibson, Brian 279
Girlhood see *Bande de filles*
Going South 176 see *Plein sud*
Gonzalez, Yann 33
Gott, Michael and Thibaut Schilt 230, 231
Goût de plaire, Le 40, 314
Graine et le mulet, La 154
Grandena, Florian 57
Grandperret, Patrick 24, 256
Graves, Robert 89
Greven, David 134, 135
Griffiths, Robin 6
Guiraudie, Alain 21, 28, 29

Halberstam, Jack 7, 184, 214
haptic visuality 22–3, 63
Hardwick, Joe 181, 182
Haut perchés 40, 104–7, 167, 316
Héloïse and Abelard 291

Heroes are Immortal see Héros sont immortels, Les
Héros sont immortels, Les 136, 316
heteronormativity, defined 2
heterosexual masculinity, relation to lesbianism/homoerotics 260
Histoire d'Eurydice pendant la remontée 96
Hitchcock, Alfred 133–6, 305
HIV/AIDS 12, 25, 39, 40–8, 49, 80, 97–9, 100, 104, 120, 129
Hocquenghem, Guy 13, 14, 123–4
Holocaust 74–6
L'Homme blessé 7, 30
homonormativity 5, 6, 16, 25, 54, 132, 146, 195, 203
Homosexual Desire see Désir homosexuel, Le
homosociality 267
Honoré, Christophe 30, 32, 46
Huis clos 106

I am a Woman Now 241
I Have to Love Them see Il faut que je l'aime
Ici commence la nuit 118, 122
Il faut que je l'aime 177–8, 319
Iles, Les 33
Ince, Kate 31
L'Inconnu du lac 18, 28, 115, 118, 119–36, 139, 142, 158, 159, 165, 168, 318
L'Inventaire infini 174
Invisibles, Les 28, 29, 174, 176, 238–40, 320
Invisibles, Les (photography) 174

Jagose, Annamarie 5, 260, 261
Jean Vigo Prize 29, 178
Jeanne and the Perfect Guy see Jeanne et le garçon formidable
Jeanne Dielman, 23, quai du commerce, 1080 Bruxelles 309
Jeanne et le garçon formidable 39, 40–8, 70, 82, 93, 100, 277, 314
John, Elton 228
Jonet, M. Catherine 256, 259, 265, 266
Jour et nuit 320
Jours perdus 316
Julie, ou la Nouvelle Héloïse 290
Just the End of the World see Juste la fin du monde
Juste la fin du monde 39, 72, 76–82, 83, 316

Kechiche, Abdellatif 154
King of Escape, The see Roi de l'évasion, Le
Kung-fu Master 46

Lagabrielle, Renaud 48
Lagarce, Jean-Luc 77, 81
Lange, Rémi 32, 67
Lanser, Susan 292, 294, 295
Laronde, Michel 194, 197
Leduc, Violette 271
Lee, Ang 158
lesbian criminality 7
Lesbos, Island of 293
Life is a Dream 151–3
Lifshitz, Sébastien 16, 27, 28, 29
line of flight 11, 139, 155, 283

Little Girl see *Petite Fille*
Lives of Thérèse, The see
    Vies de Thérèse, Les
Love, Heather 305
Lumière brothers 143
Lynch, David 305

Maghrebi-French *see beur*
Ma vie de courgette 253
Ma vraie vie à Rouen 39,
    57–67, 72, 107, 166, 315
Marcuse, Herbert 87, 88, 89,
    93, 102
Margulies, Ivone 309
mariage pour tous 24, 25,
    127, 203
Marie parce que c'est joli 241
Marks, Laura 22, 63, 64
marriage equality see *mariage
    pour tous*
Marshall, Bill 30
Martineau, Jacques 16
Martineau, Jacques and Olivier
    Ducastel, 21, 28, 29
McCaffrey, Enda 133, 158, 160
McGonagle, Joseph 55
McNeill, Isabelle 282, 285,
    286, 287
Marxism 141
masturbator 68, 69
Mauvais genre 174
Meier, Pierre-Alain 213
Mensonge 44
Merriman, Peter 9
*Methodological
    Encyclopedia* 292
metronormativity 116, 240
molar 8–9, 12, 17, 139,
    154, 156
molecular 8–11, 14, 15, 17,
    115, 154, 156

molecular and molar,
    relation 10–11
Mon copain Rachide 277
Montaigne, Michel de 13, 192
Monteverdi, Claudio 98
Morel, Gaël 67
Morgan, Daniel 22
Mouflard, Claire 287
Mulholland Drive 305
Muñoz, José 16–17, 18,
    20, 103
*Muriel fait le désespoir à ses
    parents* 256
Muscles and Cockles see
    Crustacés et coquillages
My Adolescence was Stolen
    see *On m'a volé mon
    adolescence*
My Life as a Courgette see *Ma
    vie de courgette*
My Life on Ice see *Ma vraie vie
    à Rouen*

*N'oublie pas que tu vas
    mourir* 44
Naissance des pieuvres 171,
    249, 250, 251, 253–73,
    275, 280, 285, 286, 287,
    288, 289, 304, 321
  meaning of French title
    (octopus) 270–2
Nés en 68 39, 73, 315
new queer cinema 18–20
No Rest for the Brave see
    *Pas de repos pour
    les braves*
Nolot, Jacques 30
Nos années folles 31
Now the Night Begins 119
Nuits fauves, Les (film) 44
Nuits fauves, Les (novel) 43

Odetta 236
Olympiades, Les 252
Omelette 33, 67
On m'a volé mon adolescence 136, 318
Open Bodies see Corps ouverts, Les
Orphée 99, 307–8
Orpheus and Eurydice 82–104, 290, 305
Où en êtes-vous, Sébastien Lifshitz? 321
Ovid 84, 85, 86, 87, 88, 89, 90, 91, 93, 94, 96, 98, 101, 295, 298, 302, 303, 304
Oyallon-Koloski, Jenny 48
Ozon, François 19, 20, 27, 30, 31–2

PACS 24, 141, 203, 209
parenting, gay 209, 211
Paris 05:59 see Théo et Hugo dans le même bateau
Parking 99, 308
Partir 33
Pas de repos pour les braves 115, 118, 148–53, 317
Pauline 251, 322
Perceval 51
Péron, Didier 190
Persona 305
Petite Fille 176, 242–5, 321
Peuchet, Jacques 292, 293
Philadelphia 44
Photo perdue, photo trouvée 174
photography, Lifshitz 174–6, 223, 236, 244, 245
Piano, The 305–7

plateau 139, 149
Plein sud 176, 226–32, 239, 320
Poliziano, Angelo 85
Portrait d'une jeune fille de la fin des années 60 à Bruxelles 308
Portrait de la jeune fille en feu 28, 173, 250, 251, 288–309, 322
Portrait of a Lady on Fire see Portrait de la jeune fille en feu
Pratt, Murray 50, 51, 53
Preciado, Paul 8, 9, 10, 13, 145
Presque rien 170, 176, 203–10, 211, 216, 226, 232, 319
Prosser, Jay 219, 221, 224, 275
Proust, Marcel 270–1
Provencher, Denis 55
Pudeur ou l'impudeur, La 44
Pullen, Christopher 57
Pygmalion 290, 303

Quand on a 17 ans 30, 240, 252
Queer Palm 28, 29, 31, 33, 119, 238
Querelle 99, 121
Qur'an 186, 187, 189

Ravel, Maurice 244
Real Cool Time see Ce vieux rêve qui bouge
Reed, Lou 211
Reeser, Todd 204, 260
Rees-Roberts, Nick 3, 49, 153, 156, 191, 197, 200, 202, 233
Religieuse, La 294

Rencontres d'après minuit, Les 33
Répétition, La 31
Rester vertical 28, 115, 118, 119, 120, 156–61, 318
Rich, B. Ruby 18–19
Rihanna 285, 286
road movie, queer 48–56, 226–32
Rohmer, Eric 268
Roi de l'évasion, Le 119, 153–6, 157, 159, 169, 318
Rope 133–6
Roseaux sauvages, Les 24, 30, 67, 73
Roth-Bettoni, Didier 28, 30, 46, 66
Rousseau, Jean-Jacques 290

Sappho 293, 295
Sartre, Jean-Paul 106
Schilt, Thibaut 31, 32
Schoonover, Karl, and Rosalind Galt 127, 132, 133
Schultz, Gretchen 260
Sciamma, Céline 21, 27, 29, 31, 252
scopophilia 59, 65, 255, 259
Sedgwick, Eve 68
Seel, Pierre 74–5
Sex of Madame H, The 33
sideways growth 256, 269
Simon, Claire 27
Smith, Frances 284
Son frère 31
Staying Vertical see *Rester vertical*
Stockton, Kathryn Bond 256, 257, 269
Straight Ahead until Morning see *Tout droit jusqu'au matin*
Stranger by the Lake see *L'Inconnu du lac*
Sunshine for the Poor see *Du soleil pour les gueux*
Suréna 58
Swamy, Vinay 54
Sword, Helen 94

Téchiné, André 19, 20, 24, 27, 30–31, 66, 67, 73, 240, 252
Teddy Audience Award 28
television, French, relation to queer 28
Témoins, Les 320
Terres froides, Les 176, 178, 179, 195–203, 232, 239, 319
Thelma 213
Théo et Hugo dans le même bateau 1–2, 4, 6, 17, 19, 25, 28, 40, 82–104, 105, 107, 316
Time has Come see *Voici venu le temps*
time/temporality, queer 183–5, 190, 192, 211–26
Tomboy 29, 172, 249, 251, 273–80, 283, 287, 288, 298, 322
Tout droit jusqu'au matin 136, 317
Transamerica 184
Traub, Valerie 272, 304
Traversée, La 171, 176, 232–8, 320
tribade 291, 296
Tucker, Duncan 184

uchronie 114, 115, 136, 140
Un amour à taire 75
Un amour de femme 256

Un couteau dans le coeur 33
Une autre femme 212
Une nouvelle amie 31
Une robe d'été 31
universalism 26, 55, 56, 66, 126, 194, 242, 276

van Erp, Michiel 241
Van Morrison 237, 238
Vecchiali, Paul 44, 46
Verheyde, Sylvie 24, 256
Vies de Thérèse, Les 28, 239, 321
viewer, queer 20–3
Virgil 85, 91, 96, 98, 158, 160, 298
Vivaldi, Antonio 294, 302
Voici venu le temps 115, 118, 140–2, 318

Wahl, Elizabeth 296, 297
Waldron, Darren 23, 100, 275, 276, 279
Walton, Saige 134
Water Lilies see Naissance des pieuvres
Weber, Serge 114, 123
whiteness 196, 201, 202
Wild Reeds see Roseaux Sauvages, Les
Wild Side 1–2, 4, 6, 8, 10, 12, 15, 17, 18, 20, 25, 28, 170, 176, 179, 211–26, 227, 231, 232, 238, 239, 243, 245, 320
Wilson, Emma 281, 284
'Workers Leaving the Lumière Factory' 143
Wounded Man, The 7

Young, Damon 122–3, 135

EU authorised representative for GPSR:
Easy Access System Europe, Mustamäe tee 50,
10621 Tallinn, Estonia
gpsr.requests@easproject.com

www.ingramcontent.com/pod-product-compliance
Lightning Source LLC
Chambersburg PA
CBHW051557230426
43668CB00013B/1889